GANG COP

VIOLENCE PREVENTION AND POLICY SERIES

This AltaMira series publishes new books in the multidisciplinary study of violence. Books are designed to support scientifically based violence prevention programs and widely applicable violence prevention policy. Key topics are juvenile and/or adult community re-entry programs, community-based addiction and violence programs, prison violence reduction programs with application in community settings, and school culture and climate studies with recommendations for organizational approaches to school-violence reduction. Studies may combine quantitative and qualitative methods, may be multidisciplinary, or may feature European research if it has a multinational application. The series publishes highly accessible books that offer violence prevention policy as the outcome of scientifically based research, designed for college undergraduates and graduates, community agency leaders, school and community decision makers, and senior government policy makers.

SERIES EDITOR

Mark S. Fleisher, Director, The Dr. Semi J. and Ruth W. Begun Center for Violence Research Prevention and Education, Case Western Reserve University, 10900 Euclid Avenue, Cleveland, OH 44106-7164 USA, 216-368-2329 or msf10@po.cwru.edu

EDITORIAL BOARD MEMBERS

Devon D. Brewer, Alcohol and Drug Abuse Institute, Seattle and Departments of Anthropology, Psychology & Sociology, University of Washington

Barbara Cromer, M.D., Professor of Pediatrics; Director, Center for Adolescent Health, School of Medicine, Case Western Reserve University, Cleveland, OH

G. David Curry, Professor of Criminology and Criminal Justice, University of Missouri–St. Louis

Scott H. Decker, Curators Professor of Criminology and Criminal Justice, University of Missouri–St. Louis

Frieder Dunkel, Ernst-Mintz-Arndt-Universitat Greifswald, Germany

Finn-Aage Esbensen, Chair and E. Desmond Lee Professor of Youth Crime & Violence, Department of Criminology and Criminal Justice, University of Missouri–St. Louis

C. Ronald Huff, Dean, School of Social Ecology and Professor, Department of Criminology, Law & Society, University of California, Irvine

James Jacobs, New York University School of Law

Cheryl Lee Maxson, Department of Criminology, Law & Society, University of California, Irvine

James F. Short, Jr., Social & Economic Sciences Research Center, Washington State University

Mark I. Singer, Professor of Social Work, Case Western Reserve University, Cleveland, OH

Frank van Gemert, RegioPlan Groep (Research Institute), Amsterdam, The Netherlands

Michael L. Walker, Executive Director, Partnership for a Safer Cleveland, OH

Stanley Wasserman, Professor of Psychology, Statistics, and Sociology, and Beckman Institute's Human Perception and Performance, University of Illinois

Neil A. Weiner, Center for the Study of Youth Policy, University of Pennsylvania

BOOKS IN THE SERIES

Gang Cop: The Words and Ways of Officer Paco Domingo by Malcolm Klein (2004)

GANG COP

The Words and Ways of Officer Paco Domingo

Malcolm W. Klein

ALTAMIRA
PRESS

A DIVISION OF
ROWMAN & LITTLEFIELD PUBLISHERS, INC.
Walnut Creek • Lanham • New York • Toronto • Oxford

ALTAMIRA PRESS
A division of Rowman & Littlefield Publishers, Inc.
1630 North Main Street, #367
Walnut Creek, CA 94596
www.altamirapress.com

Rowman & Littlefield Publishers, Inc.
A wholly owned subsidiary of The Rowman & Littlefield Publishing Group, Inc.
4501 Forbes Boulevard, Suite 200
Lanham, Maryland 20706

PO Box 317
Oxford
OX2 9RU, UK

British Library Cataloguing in Publication Information Available

Library of Congress Cataloging-in-Publication Data
Klein, Malcolm W.
  Gang Cop: The Words and Ways of Officer Paco Domingo / Malcolm W. Klein
    p. cm.
  ISBN 0-7591-0546-4 (hardcover: alk. paper)—ISBN 0-7591-0547-2 (pbk.: alk. paper)
    1. Gangs—United States. 2. Violence—United States. 3. Juvenile delinquency—United States. 4. Youth and violence—United States. I. Title.
HV6439.U5K584 2004
364.1'06'60973

                                                                2003014353

Printed in the United States of America

♾™ The paper used in this publication meets the minimum requirements of American National Standard for Information Sciences—Permanence of Paper for Printed Library Materials, ANSI/NISO Z39.48-1992.

For cops like Wes McBride and Dan McLeod and Pete Gross and Jim Cook and Larry Kramer and Clyde Kronkhite and Manfred Bauer in Germany

And the one in Sweden who preferred to remain anonymous,

And for the hundreds of others across the country who were willing to share their experiences with me.

And for Margy, who claims the movie rights!

CONTENTS

16   Elite Units, Gang Units, and Paco   174
17   Rampart: The Smoking Gun   182

Epilogue   193

Recommended Readings   195

About the Author   197

PREFACE

In the Epilogue to this book, I have listed a number of books on street gangs that contain a great deal of information about this topic. Indeed, I have used much of the material in these books to frame the issues raised in *Gang Cop*. Unlike those books, *Gang Cop* is neither a textbook nor a research monograph. It is a different, and I think unique, approach to sharing accumulated knowledge about gangs with students and the general public.

In the long run, my principal purpose is to do what textbooks do: share what is known about street gangs. But I have chosen to do this in an unusual way—by using the career of a particular type of individual immersed in the world of gangs. My protagonist, Officer Paco Domingo, has developed views that are at variance with much of what is known about gangs from academic research. Since I am myself an academic researcher, I have combined Paco's story with parts of my own—we are both gang experts of different stripes.

The character of Paco is a composite: he is constructed from real quotes and real incidents and real court testimony I've gathered over many years. These many pieces of Paco are not fictional, even if he is. I have given him a personal background drawn from real people to help tell the story. The story will help the reader understand street gangs through the eyes of the zealous gang cop as well as through the reports of research. Constructing Paco as I have also allows me to relate and use the many contacts I have had with gang cops like him. The contacts are real, the cops are real, and, in this sense, Paco and his story are real.

INTRODUCTION

If we don't change direction soon, we'll end up where we're going.

—Professor Irwin Corey

This book is dedicated to the thousands of gang cops out there who do not fit the picture of Paco Domingo, and especially to those who would feel uncomfortable to find a Paco among them. Says Paco, "I am La Ley"—the law. The brush with which I have painted Paco's picture should not be applied to them. Yet, this disclaimer aside, let us not deny the reality of Paco: he is out there. My final decision to write this book came after Paco's performance as an expert witness in the courtroom proceedings of a murder trial. In those proceedings, he and the prosecutor attempted to establish the defendant's status as a criminal street gang member in order to obtain a harsher sentence. To do that, Paco was led by the prosecutor into testimony that twisted the intent of the law and all but falsified the evidence relevant to gang membership. The defense attorney asked me to review that twisted evidence and Paco's testimony. I did so and prepared the following rebuttal:

MEMORANDUM

To: David Allison, Esq.

From: Malcolm W. Klein

Re: Officer Paco Domingo

Date: February 6, 1998

This is my first report based on the materials sent to me regarding *People v Rubio*. Included in the materials were: crime reports and supplemental reports on past incidents involving OCR members (approx. 70 pages) all dated 1/9/98; crime reports and supplementals on the Callahan homicide, dated between 1/15/97 and 1/23/98 (approx. 18 pages); court transcript dated 1/14/97, including testimony from Officer Domingo, pages 7–51; Cromwell gang unit criteria for identifying gang members and associates; and class paper written by Officer Domingo, dated 2/5/93.

My comments have to do with evidence the OCR (Original Cromwell Rulers) is or was a "street gang," as normally described in professional criminological literature, or a "criminal street gang" as described in penal code section 186.22. The time period covered by such evidence includes 1992 through January of 1997, around the date of the Callahan homicide in Hillston. My credentials for making such a judgment are in your hands.

Before providing details, let me summarize by saying that the available materials do not in any way correspond to one's expectations for typical street gangs, and even less to the penal code description (or intent) with regard to criminal street gangs. I am surprised that an officer of Officer Domingo's experience would attempt to interpret the information provided to label OCR a street gang or as a criminal street gang. His own class paper shows more careful thinking than is to be found in these materials. Consider the following reported OCR incidents.

1. A 1992 car vandalism that strikes one as "kid stuff." A street gang attack would more likely have smashed windows, slashed tires and seats, perhaps even firebombed the car. When the victims confronted the vandals, they meekly agreed to clean up the damage. *No gang would respond this way*—respect and reputation would prohibit this.

2. A series of disturbances in 1995 at an abandoned house at 1933 Valley Way in Cromwell. These seemed rather uniformly to be unsupervised teenage parties with alcohol and some drugs, with graffiti consisting of tags, ganglike cartoons, and other materials not decipherable by the police. There is no pattern of felonies here; in fact, little evidence of arrests by the police. The behavior may indeed be antisocial and boisterous, but it hardly smacks of gang activity per se.

3. Theft of firewood from 1933 Valley Way hardly stands as typical gang activity.

4. The alleged domestic assault two years later by Mr. Lorne on Ms. Washington can in no way be laid to the group, simply because Mr. Lorne was a member of OCR. Nothing in the material reveals the assault to be gang related (i.e., in furtherance of gang goals).

5. The Callahan homicide cannot logically be used as part of a *pattern* of offenses (see 186.22) to establish its gang-related nature. The pattern must exist beforehand. I will refer to this as Officer Domingo "Twist #1" (see below for further twists of facts to fit the prosecution's purpose). Domingo testifies in fact that "for the 5 minutes of fame that OCR achieved by the murder of Mr. Callahan, they were a street gang for the 5 or 10 minutes that that incident occurred." I can't believe that Officer Domingo truly believes in a five-minute gang. Certainly no reading of 186.22 allows for such an anomaly.

Now let's look at other evidence in these materials.

- You have learned and reported to me that no OCR members are in the county's gang rostering system that contains over 100,000 gang member names.
- The Cromwell Police Department had no knowledge of OCR—virtually impossible, if this was a "gang" from 1992 on.
- Witness Lincoln identifies OCR as a "tagging group." Taggers are not gangbangers.
- Witness Tabor cites Mr. Uribo's use of the term "homies," which implies a gang reference. This terminology, originally gang talk, has now become an accepted part of youth culture in this country. Even the clerks and baggers in my west-side upscale supermarket refer to each other as "homey" and "homes."
- Witness Amos refers to 1933 Valley Way as a party home, and OCR as a party group. Domingo Twist #2 consists of labeling the place a "safe house," which he then expands into a discussion of "a gang safe house." Naming it so doesn't make it true; law enforcement officers also use safe houses.
- Domingo Twist #3: He reports overhearing a courtroom hall conversation in which there is a denial of OCR as a gang, but then implies the denial was phony and stated for his ears. Note the logic: an admission would mean OCR is a gang and a denial is used to support OCR as a gang!
- Domingo Twist #4: He refers to names on a back wall at 1933 Valley Way as a "gang roster," without any further foundation. By his logic, a written list, therefore, can't be of a group of friends, or a party group, or a tagger crew.

- Domingo Twist #5: He refers to the attack on Callahan (very possibly a response to a beating several days earlier) as a "payback," another loaded term implying gang. Again, naming it so doesn't make it so.
- Domingo Twist #6: He refers to styles of clothing and graffiti as common gang indicators. In today's youth culture, this is indeed often true, but also often not true. Gang culture has become youth culture; just watch MTV!
- Domingo Twist #7: He testifies that gang members "categorically deny the existence of the gang, that they were ever in a gang. They flat out deny it. They would say it didn't exist." Note the logic, again; admission of gang status shows it's a gang, but so does denial of gang status!

Under cross-examination, Officer Domingo actually agrees on the "party crew" description provided by defense; it's a good description of OCR. He then admits that two of his confidential informants (CI) saw OCR as a party group, not a hard gang. He describes the members as sixteen- and seventeen-year-old high school students from fairly affluent homes in Cromwell. No gang picture here.

- Domingo Twist #8: Questioned on the "primary activity" component of 186.22 as the commission of one or more criminal acts, etc., he falls back on the murder committed by one member to do this: "then it changed the group from a party crew to a criminal street gang." Question: "based on the murder alone?" Answer: "yes." He says prior to the murder that they were a party crew "wanting to become a gang." Question: prior to that they were "just a party crew, correct?" Answer: "that's correct."
- Domingo Twist #9: He testifies that the group disbanded following the murder, and then testifies that this is not unusual for a criminal street gang! On the contrary, that would be highly unusual: violence is a unifying theme for street gangs. When I mentioned this disbanding notion to a graduate student who is a former Bloods member, he guffawed!
- Domingo Twist #10: He testifies that "gangs evolve" (and he's correct), but then immediately contradicts himself with "You either are or you aren't. There's no middle ground" (and here he's obviously incorrect). He says "Wannabe" is a school district term to deny they have gangs, whereas in fact the term Wannabe was originally police terminology that poked fun at potential gang members. It's a term often used by police across the country, yet he reports: "There's no such thing as a

Wannabe." Finally, he destroys his own case by saying, "OCR was in what I would guess—infancy stage would be a good term for them."

In sum, Officer Domingo's logic is poor, he is often inconsistent, evidence that he offers is often twisted to suit his purpose, and most important, he fails completely to show that OCR is anything other than an informal party group. He doesn't even get them successfully into the tagger crew category, to say nothing of street gang or criminal street gang. If this is the basis of the prosecution's attempt to apply 186.22, then this report should surely discourage them should you share elements of it with them. If my testimony is nonetheless required, you can see the form it would take.

I did eventually testify in this case. The prosecutor first tried to question my credentials and then asked how I could claim expertise in light of Domingo's extensive street experiences. He failed miserably. In his chambers, the judge told both attorneys that *People v Rubio* was a straightforward murder case and that there were no gang implications to affect adjudication or sentencing. My friend Paco had gone too far over the edge.

Why am I writing about this police officer? For almost forty years I have been trying to understand street gangs and what we as a society can do about them—for them, to them, around them. I've done this on the streets of gang territories and the homes of gang members; in police stations and probation offices and courtrooms and lockups and social service agencies; in research offices and professional conventions. I've heard many, many cops say things in private or in confidence that they would never admit in public. I've appreciated their candor, in part because it has revealed the discrepancies between some of their views and assumptions of fact on the one hand, and what criminological research has discovered on the other.

In dealing in a practical way with street gangs, the greatest impediment has been, and remains, the absence of shared information about their nature. One can easily understand inadequate information among the general public; most people have no direct contact with gangs. It is particularly understandable among the media, whose attention to drama and the selling of a story dictates what they will entertain as relevant information. Even among my fellow criminologists, I have come to expect something less than up-to-date understanding of street gangs. But among law enforcement officials, and especially among gang cops who are the first point of contact with gangs in many cases, ignorance is not acceptable, nor is the deliberate misrepresentation of gang knowledge. There is simply too much reliable information available about street gangs to allow police—federal, state, or local—to ignore it. If, like the gang cop, one is forced by circumstance to deal with street gangs, then one must know the quarry.

And so this book really has two aims: the first is to describe Paco Domingo, a gang cop, on whose knowledge and skills the public must rely. The second aim is to provide the reader with some exposure to street gang knowledge. Paco is my means for doing this, and Paco, as the reader will learn, has helped to shape my own place in the gang world.

I acknowledge with full appreciation the guidance and constructive critiques of this manuscript in an earlier form received from Scott Decker, Margaret Gatz, Charles Katz, and Cheryl Maxson, all of whom found pleasure in the nontraditional approach I have taken. I have incorporated many of their ideas; those rejected probably reflect my stubbornness more than faults with the suggestions. I am grateful as well to AltaMira's senior editor, Rosalie Robertson, whose skills and supportive spirit have contributed notably to the flow of my narrative and to my morale as an author. I am also pleased to acknowledge the support of the Emeriti Center at the University of Southern California that provided a grant to cover costs of manuscript preparation.

❶

THE RELATIONSHIP DEVELOPS: GANG COP, GANG RESEARCHER

It is my belief we don't know a hellava lot about gangs. I don't know what the hell to do about it as a matter of fact.

—Former Los Angeles Police Chief Daryl Gates, 1980

I write these pages to correct some incorrect images, to bring balance to our views of street gangs, and to debunk the claimed expertise of a small but terribly influential category of gang fighter, that minority of law enforcement officials who pervert the truth about gangs. Officer, then Sergeant, Paco Domingo epitomizes these gang fighters.

I need to digress here briefly just to give you some context. Many years ago, I had taken over a faltering project that was designed to evaluate the effectiveness of a gang intervention program. A team of seven street workers (five males and two females) was working with four large, traditional street gangs, whose total membership approached 800 youths. Their job was to turn these gangs around, or as one of the workers facetiously put it: "Turn these black delinquent street gangs into white pro-social clubs." They used group meetings, individual counseling, court intervention, parents' groups, job training, tutoring, anything at all to "de-isolate" (in the supervisor's term) these youth and integrate them into the community. This was one heck of a challenge, and ours, in turn, was to document how successful they were.

My own background to run such an evaluation was abysmal. With a degree in social psychology, I had never taken a course on crime, on child development or adolescence, nor on social work. My exposures to police activities were limited to helping pull people out of a couple of bloody traffic accidents and intervening in a stabbing of a woman outside my home, plus a few personal victimizations. None of these events was gang related. I was hired because someone thought I was smart and organized and hard-headed, as researchers go; I was also available.

After a few months of intensive street exposure to the gang members and their workers (the kids called them their "sponsors," to the great distaste of the police who said "you shouldn't sponsor gangs"), I was developing some viewpoints. Among these was the need to strengthen the action program—more tutoring, more job training, more outreach to potential gang recruits—so that we'd have something really tangible to evaluate. Another was some increasing skepticism about the role of the police in responding to these kids. A great deal of animosity had developed between the gang workers and the police, and this set the stage for the afternoon in my office that I met Paco Domingo.

I was sitting in my research office—this goes back, you understand, many many years—an office I shared with one of several research assistants on our project. Visitors got to my office down a long hall where the end-view would be of my back in a desk chair as I wrote at my desk or stared out the window to the little parking lot beyond. The hallway was thickly carpeted, although my floor was cracking linoleum. You could come up behind me without my notice if I was at all engaged in thought. And so they did, and stood there until my assistant nonchalantly said "Hi, guys."

I swiveled around to look up at two pretty impressive men. One was tall—maybe six foot two—slender, black, impeccably dressed in a two-piece suit. Damned good looking, I thought to myself. The other was shorter but not short—maybe five-nine or five-ten. He was all chest and shoulders, an upper body clearly outlined in a normal dress shirt that was tight on him. His ethnicity was less clear, maybe Middle Eastern or Mediterranean, darker than me but not by much.

"I'm Sergeant Hector Bascom," said the taller one, showing his badge and offering his outstretched hand in front of a warm, wide smile. "My partner, Officer Francisco Domingo," he continued.

Domingo nodded slightly, eyes fixed on mine, and stuck out his hand. Both handshakes were firm, Bascom's because he wanted it to be and Domingo's because that strong hand was incapable of weakness. This Domingo was particularly striking, I thought. He was a natural for a Hollywood casting call: the muscle standing behind the Mafia capo, or the beach bully with a beer in one hand and the pit bull straining against the wide leather leash in the other. It might be different if he'd smiled during this meeting, but it didn't seem that smiling was one of his ways.

"Dr. Klein"—again, Bascom did the talking—"You're the gentleman we hear is doing the local gang study and talking to the press about getting more resources for the gang members, right?"

I agreed, that was I, and asked if they had something that we could use.

"Yeah," Domingo was now triggered by this. "We'd like you to spend some time with us, see the gangs the way we do—if you're up for it."

Sergeant Bascom's community relations veneer had not rubbed off on Officer Domingo. His response was clearly a challenge. Within five minutes I was in the rear of their patrol car, touring a six-square-mile area that I already knew, our gang project area. It's mixed working class, underclass, lower middle class, single family homes and apartments, many with little lawns and gardens, plenty of small shops, fast-food stands, gas stations, a couple of pool halls, a number of bars and liquor stores, several graffiti-blessed public schools, and ill-kept playgrounds. In short, this was gang territory, or rather a fairly disorganized community that had inadvertently spawned our four large clusters of street gangs.

Cruising with my new escorts, the graffiti that marked rival gang territories was defined by them as an insult to the decent people in the community. The knot of gang members—I knew most of them—"hanging" outside the school at 3:15 was regarded by them as a threat to the worthy students heading home to study and do their house chores. The pool cue being carried by another member I had interviewed just days before was defined by the officers as a weapon. The graffiti I was learning to translate as gang members' internal language they saw as a source of police intelligence as well as ugly vandalism: "Rifa" for we rule, "cons safos" for safety, you can't mess with our signs, "puto" for fag or whore, "5-0" for police, and various numbers and names to specify gang territories.

Well, they had me. The cops' perspective on street gangs was not one to which I had yet exposed myself. That was to change, and I've made up for it over the following years. Officer Domingo—Paco to his colleagues—would be my guide, and often an insistent one. This is, in a real sense, his book as well as mine. When he said in my office, "We'd like you to spend some time with us," neither he nor I could have imagined it would mean decades.

A few months later, I was alerted to an impending gang fight in the parking lot of a taco stand in the area. I couldn't get there, and my other two assistants were already somewhere in the field. So I sent Carolyn, the research assistant who shared my office, to observe the scene. She did, up close and personal. Carolyn maneuvered herself into the midst of a hundred or so excited and nervous young gang members. After only a short interval, several cars—it's called "caravaning"—screamed around the corner, sped noisily in front of the gathered mob, all members of which (including Carolyn) threw themselves on the asphalt lot as shots from the cars rang out. No one was hit, and the leader of the caravaning gang suggested that, when we interviewed him later, the shots were blanks. But Carolyn had her peak experience, and I was proud to say in later years that I never thought of gender as much of an issue in doing gang research, on the street or elsewhere.

Most of my learning experiences were still ahead of me. One of my first lessons was in police department public relations. Paco Domingo, then a juvenile officer, arranged for another ride-along, this time with a patrol sergeant on a Friday night. Since my fellow rider was a newly elected city councilman, it was soon clear that this would be departmental policy exposure, not gang exposure. We answered a number of radio calls, always arriving after the scene had been secured—can't expose city councilmen and young criminologists to the dangers of live crime scenes, can we? Also, it's fairly typical to call in supervisors afterward, to oversee and approve the good work their officers have done, a pattern that many years later would help bastardize the corrupt work of the gang unit of the Rampart station in Los Angeles. At this point, the only one of these evening incidents I can recall was a call to a loud youth party in an upscale part of the city. Responding officers had cornered a couple of partygoers in a garage with several marijuana cigarettes. This was not the dramatic gang incident I had hoped to observe.

By way of contrast, Paco took me to a training class where juvenile officers were being introduced over a period of weeks to various facets of the work not covered in the superficial academy classes in "juvenile procedures." He had a video to show to his fellow cops, lest they think gang work was no big deal. I asked many times, but Paco would never let me have a copy of the tape to show to my university classes. What they would have seen, in a tape made by a gang member to record a bit of his group's history, was a fight between two Hispanic females, roughly fourteen or fifteen years old and members of rival gangs.

The first girl, slightly larger than the other, had started flirting with the boyfriend of the second. Major threats had been tossed back and forth, to the point that both male gangs decided to set up a "fair fight," that is, a one-on-one fight, between the two girls. With little urging, they go at each other—kicking, scratching, pulling hair, poorly landed blows with fists.

Within a few minutes, the shorter girl is getting the worst of it, and another girl leaps from the circle and lands a groin kick on the larger girl, with effect. She is quickly pulled back and the two fighters go at it again and again, the shorter girl faring poorly when, faster than the eye can handle, she lunges forward and the larger girl falls back, blood spurting from her abdomen. Pandemonium breaks loose and the videotape ends. We are told that the victim was taken to the hospital in critical condition, but survived.

Then Paco replays the tape for us and as the critical point comes he puts it into slow motion. Now you can see the shorter girl reach behind her back with the right hand, pull out a long-bladed knife that had somehow been hidden, and even in slow motion push blade first at the belly of the other girl. The blood follows. This is a very difficult viewing experience—no TV drama here; no Hollywood stunt with ketchup. You see a real, live, vicious, and bloody assault, one teenage girl on another. When they first viewed the lunge this audience of police officers, each and everyone, gasped or shouted (I heard one say, "Look out!"). Paco had made his point, and he had made it to me as well. He brought me to that class to remind me: I could never truly enter his world.

His world, the one with the gang members in it, was a world of confrontation. This was not so obvious in the early days when he was still in the Juvenile Division. But over time, and as the gang situation worsened around the country, gang members came more and more to be defined as the enemy, and their territories as battlegrounds to be retaken by the forces of good. Nowhere was this more obvious than in the nationally reported episodes known as Operation Hammer. The Los Angeles Police Department (LAPD), a no-nonsense, proactive organization taking pride in both its technology and its crime-fighting image, decided at one point that enough was enough. It was time to take back the streets, with Operation Hammer. Repeated on a number of occasions, the first episode was the most dramatic.

From all over the city, a thousand police officers were brought together on a Friday night to sweep through the gang areas of South Central Los Angeles. Armed with warrants and instructions on what to look for, they swept up hundreds of people, mostly young, and took them to the Coliseum (twice the site of the Olympic games) to book them and release them at special mobile trailers set up for the occasion. They expected far too many arrestees to be handled in the normal fashion at the police station. There was, by design, heavy media coverage, and the late evening news programs and morning papers gave Hammer priority treatment.

On the following night, the Hammer was pounded again, the only difference being that the entire community knew it was coming and many gang members were excited and prepared to meet the challenge with their visible presence. Over the two nights, 1,453 arrests were made. Of these 1,350 resulted in release without charges. Almost half were not even gang members. There were only 60 felony arrests, and only 32 of these received formal charges. In essence, a great big project to suppress gang activity fizzled badly and inadvertently enraged many thousands of community residents who felt invaded by the LAPD army. But Paco's take on Operation Hammer was unyielding: "They sent the message," he said; "This was LAPD's territory, not the gang members'." Program effectiveness was never a big issue for Paco, only the message, the confrontation, and the assertion of moral right.

I'll talk more about Paco's character as the book progresses, but early on I was far more intrigued than analytic about it. For reasons I didn't understand, but probably had to do with showing me that we could talk together as men, not just as criminologist and cop, he shared an aspect of his family background with me. Again, this was while we were still trying to understand each other.

He said little of his mother's side of the family—they were Mexican—but talked some about his father's side. He did so with pride, and it was important to him. His father's family came from Spain, and more specifically from the region of Catalonia, familiar to many because of its largest city, Barcelona. Catalonia, like the Basque territory to the north, is fiercely provincial. It has its own history and culture, its own language, and its own unique cuisine. For many Catalans, Spanish is their second language. Pride oozes out of the sandy Catalan soil; to many, it approaches an independent state.

Paco has never visited the area, never personally viewed his roots, but he knows it well nonetheless. His father and his grandfather instilled their national pride into young Francisco, and he uses it to separate himself from Latino Americans. He can even describe, secondhand, many features of the town where the generations of Domingos had prospered. Tarragona is a large town, but a town, not a city, about sixty miles south of Barcelona. It is, Paco reports, an old fishing village turned town. Old, here, means very old. He describes a Roman amphitheater, looking out over the Mediterranean. Above it are the ruins of a Roman forum—temple columns and archways, mosaics on some remaining floors, whatever has not been vandalized over two millennia. And the greatest feature, he reports, is the great cathedral with its famous cloisters at the end of the grand plaza. A town with a history, he says, not like the one in New Mexico where he was raised. And Catalonia, he reminds me, produced Miró, Dalí, Gaudí, and Picasso.

The Domingo family, he reports, was always associated with the port. They were fishermen and fish-brokers, owners of their boats, responsible only to themselves, challenged always by the great sea. As he repeats the descriptions of the boats docking each afternoon, unloading their catch and preparing for the cooperative auction, he does it with verve. He's never seen it yet he sees it and romanticizes the seafaring life as the epitome of individual prowess and courage. And I hear him, this proud man who puts so much stock in his heritage, or rather in one-half of his heritage. The other half—his mother's half—fades.

Over time, Paco and I came to respect each other's views, as divergent as they sometimes were, to the extent that we occasionally penetrated each other's professional world. Returning from a professional conference of mine at one point, Paco felt moved to put his reactions on paper, very carefully honed with his best old college prose:

> Two types of scenarios are fairly common. I have enjoyed attending academic conferences from time to time and with some consistency see two common themes repeated. The first is when academicians present a paper or research project, it seems like the reflex response from other academicians is to attack the methodology, the conclusions, the interpretation of the data, or the research design. [There is much truth in Paco's observation here.] The second, more subtle theme, is the complaint that our lawmakers, government agencies, law enforcement agencies, or society in general never make research-based decisions or act upon the recommendations made by academicians (i.e., "Why don't they use the stuff that we produce?") [Again, he's quite right.] My belief is that the second issue is explained by the first. The "users" of academic research are hesitant to implement ideas or recommendations because they know that there is always somebody else with equally strong academic credentials to take potshots at the program.

I quote his statement for several reasons. It is Paco at his most eloquent; my bet is he spent quite some time fashioning it. But it also shows that Paco is no fool; he can be a keen observer of worlds other than his own. And he can take two patterns and interweave them effectively. The rancor that appeared in later years is not seen here, even if the skepticism is. It was only later that he would blurt out, "I never saw a social scientist at a cop's funeral."

But as I said, early on he was less angry, and more doubting. "Social science studies are no practical help to us," he complained, and then critiqued a well-known book on gangs by a Midwestern sociologist, raging "It's garbage because it's based on interviews with gang members." Gang members, he believed, cannot speak the truth and criminologists cannot hear false leads.

Fortunately, by the time Paco's views were solidified, I was somehow immune, or at least an exception. He introduced me on more than one occasion as "a down-to-earth intellectual." I took this as a major concession and compliment and, given the source, I've always treasured it. I've treasured it even more after the time he insisted that I lecture with him at the police academy, and then interrupted me to remind the cadets that I was "just a sociologist" (often confused in police mentality with socialists).

Our divergent viewpoints also proved to be useful in other training settings. I kept a copy of the evaluations written by veteran police officers in a session where both Paco and I presented materials on street gang issues. Here are some of those evaluation responses:

- Two very different perspectives but needed to try to get a grip on the total situation. Klein was a good example of stepping out of your box to see something just a little different. Both were very versed (and set) in their own directions and I think it was nice to have them give their presentations back to back. I gained insight from both.
- Good speaker and presentation. But I don't agree with his theory. But he's a good instructor and gives the other side of view vs. Domingo.
- Klein's knowledge of gangs seemed a little dated. I disagree with his statement "gangs are boring." I think he needs to hide behind a different bush—I could suggest a bush on the corner of Vernon and Morgan Avenues.
- Domingo and Klein both presented two separate viewpoints; both are valid. Keep both of them.
- This fellow has devoted his life to studying gangs. The answer is—fix up your social welfare system and then the problem will go away. Can I have a Ph.D., please?

These affairs with Paco were like "dog and pony shows" on gang realities, but always useful to me, and I hope to him. On one occasion, I discovered some of the side benefits of teaming with Paco. After our lectures to a class, we went for dinner at one of his favorite watering spots, used by many cops because of its proximity to the police academy. Sort of a glitzy place with the standard margaritas and some variations. I rather liked the one with mint. These were followed by mesquite-smoked barbecues of various sorts—and another margarita.

I guess I had one margarita too many, because I drove off without my jacket and, most important, my daily calendar. Without that calendar, I'm totally lost—I panic. When I reached home and realized my stupidity, I called the restaurant but no one could find my jacket. I tried again the next day, with no more success; the jacket had disappeared. Then I called Paco and asked if he could do anything. In very short order, my jacket and its contents magically appeared, to my great relief.

Now, I didn't ask Paco how this happened, what his technique had been with the folks at the restaurant. Cops have both explicit and implicit powers. My guess is that some implicit power was brought to bear on someone at the restaurant, someone who valued the relationship with Paco and his colleagues well beyond the value of a sport jacket that seemed a good fit. Paco retrieved the jacket for me, at what cost to whom I didn't want to know. I had my calendar; I asked no questions.

In fact, there were other occasions, both with Paco and with other officers over the years, when I was aware of possibly questionable activities but chose not to make an issue of them. For instance, in Chicago I was told about a cop who was often called into schools to deal with recalcitrant youth. He was nicknamed "Gloves" because his procedure was to take the offending youngster into the school basement, slip some gloves onto his hands and batter the youth, the gloves protecting the guy's hands and avoiding ugly cuts on the youth. Other Chicago officers later confirmed the existence of Gloves to me. I discussed him with Paco, who also knew about Gloves through the informal police network, but I chose not to ask Paco if he had ever engaged in physical abuse.

There have been widespread reports in such cities as Chicago, Los Angeles, Philadelphia, and Detroit that gang officers and others would occasionally pick up a targeted gang member, transport him to another, rival gang territory, and leave him there (sometimes stripped down to his tattoos). I never asked Paco if he had engaged in such "playful" behavior, although the stories have been told about his department. I don't push. Why? Well, in part I know that inside police knowledge in the hands of outsiders is often seen as a threat. And, of course, if I'm closed out of my contacts for being too confrontational as happened many years later, then my research access is closed as well. But also, in truth I suspect that Paco, under the right circumstances, is fully capable of rival turf drop-offs and of unacceptably rough treatment of gang member suspects. I didn't want to know about things that ethically I might be obliged to reveal. I didn't ask, he didn't offer.

Even if I did ask, I'm not sure he would have offered. He didn't need to justify or explain his own image. Paco has always had a major dose of self-confidence. It creates an almost impenetrable shield around his psyche, around his views of the world. He developed an internal sense—his own sense that what he did was right. Never mind what others thought—the "suits," the "good citizens," the Blacks, the Whites, the Latinos—he stayed on the job in the unit, on the street because what he did was right.

This is not a bad feature for a cop, especially one exposed as he has been to contrary views. In fact, I think he feeds off of his opposition to the world about him. He knows who he is by reference to those he rejects. From time to time, I've been one of those, and it has allowed me to test the soul of Officer Domingo.

I once read to him a statement from a juvenile officer in a training class run by a local university. The officer said:

> All this liberal bullshit. Some of the teachers are okay, but they are the ones with some street time; they know what it's like. Like that professor in Florida. The others sit on their ass, smoking a pipe and pulling on their beard. They worry about the fucking criminals. You know, the death penalty stuff. They get in a big sweat if something happens to one of the assholes; you don't see any sweat when a cop takes a round in the chest. Let some nigger get a bloody nose or a head cold in the county jail, and the liberals come apart. It's a lot of shit.
>
> I've heard all the theories of crime. Let me tell you, crime is caused by assholes. That's the asshole theory. If you want to check that, come on out on the street. See it like it is.[1]

Paco loved every word of it. He agreed with the sentiment about the professors at a time when I was still somehow an exception for him. Paco is a firm believer in the asshole theory, especially in the case of gang members. That's all they are to him, thugs and assholes.

In dissociating me from the rest of "the professors" in our earlier days together, he was implicitly offering me a major bargain: we would accept each other's individual credibility. He wrote me a note once about a newspaper article in which I spoke favorably about a new, experimental police anti-gang program. He said:

> Never in my entire career have I heard you say a kind word about a law enforcement program. Congratulations! I hope this means you have now "seen the light." Remember, it's hard for us . . . to keep our jobs and do good works and fine deeds without a little praise from academia. Just thought I would share this with you. Be assured I'm going to frame it and hang it in my office.[2]

Maybe it was Paco's unaccountable desire to find support in academia that opened the door to me for so many years. Paco got some kind of legitimization from me, and he made it possible for me to move in his world as well.

I remember with great clarity a lecture I gave—tried to give—to a group of officers during the middle of the gang prevention program—the same one that originally brought Paco and Sergeant Bascom to my research office. The program had blown up, with adverse media and political coverage, because the police claimed it had strengthened the gangs and increased gang crime. The program staff retorted that this was nonsense; the gangs involved were already a major problem. You send the firemen to the worst fires, staff replied.

The officers, some fifty of them, had gathered to hear first from the police department spokesman (wild applause, hoots, and hollers). Then they heard from the program director (much snickering, a few boos). I was third and last, coming in as Dr. Neutral, merely to present data on the issues. I was taken aback by their response. By the end of ten minutes, I was the one getting discourteous comments and boos. "How dare I try to be neutral when lives were at stake?" I was asked. This was my first public lecture to a group of cops, and I was really confused, bothered, and more than a little hurt.

Finally, I surprised myself by getting really angry with this boorish audience and yelled out to them, "Goddammit, shut up. You invited me here to get my view of this situation, and you can do me the courtesy of listening to me—uninterrupted. Then you'll have some facts to use to ask me informed questions for a change."

Well, a great silence fell over the room, every cop in there sat up straight, looked at me, and listened to my talk. Occasionally, a hand went up for someone to ask a question and the question was always initiated by "Sir, do you think that. . . ." My outburst, the result of my own sheer frustration, had reversed the whole scene. I had responded in kind to them, authoritarian to authoritarian. I was to be respected. I had balls. And in the back of the room, there was Paco Domingo, grinning broadly and flashing me a thumbs-up signal. Not only had I quelled the riot, I had passed a major test with Paco. I could hold my own with cops, with his people. I had "cojones."

And for all our differences, which grew exponentially toward the end of our two careers, this grudging acceptance by Paco remained. When I finally retired from my university teaching, my university colleagues organized a large party; I was very pleased by the turnout and surprised as almost all invitees actually came to share the day with me. But no greater surprise was possible than when Paco showed up with his new wife whom I had never even known existed. He was visibly uncomfortable there; he knew he would be in a thicket of university people—"those professors"— but he came anyway. I was indeed honored by his attendance. And it brought to mind another time when I wished he had been there.

I was traveling abroad in Athens, just prior to a research meeting. I had been to a recommended cabaret for dinner and a folk music show; lots of wine and ouzo and shouts of *opa!* at the performance.

The return trip to my less-than-elegant little hotel took me through several darkened and uninviting streets. At one point I passed two men walking the other direction on the opposite side of the street. One of them called out to me, "Hey, American"; I turned and stared. He indicated in accented English "I have a very nice young girl for you." I smiled, responded, "Thank you, I'm not interested" and turned back to continue my walk. But he was insistent, calling out her several virtues to me (fifteen years old, virgin, etc.). As I turned to wave him off, I found that he had crossed the street and was moving rapidly toward me. I am tall and slender. He was equally tall and far larger. I was increasingly uneasy. My rejection of the offered virgin seemed to anger him. I insisted again that I was not interested and was expected at my hotel. But he caught up with me, continuing the sale's pitch in a decidedly unfriendly manner. I took heart only in seeing that his companion had remained well behind. The next moment he put his hand on my arm—a heavy hand, indeed. I summoned up my best Gary Cooper attitude and said slowly, distinctly, and firmly, "Take your hand off my arm, now!" He did, to my surprise, and I turned again toward my hotel, now my sanctuary, and strode off. To my great relief, he did not follow but shouted at my back some Greek words whose meaning I can only guess. I don't think "I'm sorry" would have been included.

A minor story probably often repeated by travelers in such settings. I tell it because of my next reaction that, as you can see, has stayed with me throughout the years. As soon as I was free and clear of this feared assault, my mind immediately conjured up Paco, not as my nemesis but as my fantasized bodyguard. I found myself repeating that old refrain, "Where are the police when you need them?" Paco is a man of imposing size and masculine presence. At no time in my days on gang streets with Paco did it ever occur to me that there was any personal danger in that setting, not even during the few times when retaliation drive-by shootings were expected. To be with Paco was to be safe. Aside from the physical prowess he exuded, his self-confidence was worn like clothing. It was a stature that communicated itself to the gang members he interviewed and to the jurors he addressed as an expert witness. And it added weight—false weight to be sure—to the certainty with which he expressed his views. To argue or call into question his comments on gangs always required a willingness to defy some secretly derived truth, available to him and awaiting acceptance from others. He was a hard man to buck, but I sure would have welcomed him, that dark night in Athens.

NOTES

1. Cited by my colleague Robert Carter.

2. The professor label occasionally gets perverted. I know of two occasions, one in Texas and one in California, when police pretended to be professors and researchers to interview gang members about their activities. In the California case, a number of gang members were then arrested for drug dealing. In the Texas instance, the "professors" and "graduate students" learned of a gang's plan to bomb a local police station and an officer's home.

2

PACO: CHARACTER AND VALUES

Today was a historic day for the department. [Why?] We killed our first suspect today. [Are congratulations in order?] Yeah. He deserved to die.

—Paco

Throughout the period before 1980, most communities did not experience street gang problems. Those that did, with a few exceptions, experienced only minor problems. These exceptions—New York, Boston, Philadelphia, Chicago, San Francisco, Los Angeles, El Paso, and San Antonio come readily to mind—set the patterns for official responses to gangs that would be emulated by the growing number of gang-involved cities after 1980.

Gangs prior to that time were generally *juvenile* gangs; groups of adolescents who made too much trouble but matured out around age eighteen to twenty. Because of this, gang problems did not draw forth specialized police officers or gang units. They were handled by patrol, or by the juvenile division of the department. Paco, when I first knew him, was a juvenile officer, but there were some officers like Paco who would be drawn naturally toward gang units as they formed. So the question here is, what do I mean by "some officers like Paco"; who was this guy?

To some extent, he's not hard to describe. He is, by and large, what he appears to be—a straight-shooter, dedicated to crime fighting, dogmatic in his view of a black-and-white world, sexist, self-confident to the point of trusting *his* instincts only, and something of a control freak. In this latter regard he resembles many of his fellow officers who come to feel comfortable in the police world because it offers so much opportunity to *be* in control. Paco carries the need for control to the outer edges of responsibility. As you might expect, these character traits colored his relationship with me, the liberal sociologist. If he didn't appreciate my profession, he nonetheless respected the credentials I brought to bear. I was always "sir" or "Doc," just as he always elicited "sir" from the gang kids he dealt with.

I want to illustrate five important aspects of Paco's character and values, but let me start with an episode that captures much of his attitude. Paco once heard me deliver a series of lectures to a large group of juvenile officers from departments across the country. At the last of these, he had come prepared and gave me a manila envelope. It felt empty, but he instructed me to keep it closed until I got home that evening, and then to open it up and "absorb" its contents. And so I took it home, poured my nightly predinner scotch and soda, sat down and opened the envelope. The following was neatly typed on a single page:

WARNING

Continued Use of SOCIOLOGY
Can Be Hazardous to Your Health
It Can Be Cured If Detected Early.
Learn the Danger Signs.

1. Swelling of the head.
2. Tendency to run off at the mouth about untested theories.
3. Everything appears as though looking through rose-colored glasses.
4. Increased belief that no one is all bad.
5. A feeling that you are right and everyone else is wrong.
6. Bruises on the chest from self-inflicted breast beating.
7. Abnormal Kleenex bill from continuous sobbing.
8. Continual lump in the throat.
9. Loss of contact with reality and delusions of grandeur.
10. Open wound through which the heart can be seen that refuses to heal.

Recommended Cure:

1. Immediate removal from drafty Ivory Tower.
2. A swift kick in the ass.

3. A stiff punch in the nose.
4. Attendance at a cop's funeral.

If sociology was the target that day, many other groups could have been, for Paco lived through opposition and confrontation. I don't want to psychologize very much in describing how he came to this stance. Obviously it starts in New Mexico in a family structure and an ethnic and social class context about which I learned little from Paco, and only then as he volunteered it. I didn't probe. The first aspect of Paco's character in my list of five gives some hint of this background.

Private Life. I learned recently that parts of New Mexico saw two immigrations from Spain. The first was the Conquistadors, who sallied north from their conquests in Mexico in search of precious metals. Cities like modern-day Albuquerque and Santa Fe date back to that era. Although the Spanish domination was short-lived, it left its mark and a proud tradition of power and autonomy.

The second wave from Spain was a more common form of "invasion," but aimed at New Mexico explicitly because of the Conquistador tradition. Paco's forebears were a part of this wave, proud people seeking a familiar context in the new land. Topographically, leaving aside the proximity to the sea, Catalonia and New Mexico look and feel much the same: the climate, the rocky hills, and the dry plains. Thus Paco grew up in the Southwest, traditionally a mix of Anglo, Mexican, and some Native American cultures, but in a subculture that traced its roots to Spain and was more Hispanic than Latino. His eventual response to Chicano and Latin American gang members was colored by this infusion of the Spanish heritage.

Quite by chance, I interviewed a juvenile officer in Paco's old hometown about the possible gang situations there. He reported that the area where Paco grew up was an affluent, primarily white section of town. "Our Hispanics are really white, except for their skin color. We get outsiders claiming pieces of the area, but it's affluent and primarily white; it really doesn't yield fertile ground [for gangs]."

Growing up in New Mexico, young Paco was Francisco to his mother, his name said with a soft, lilting accent—Fran-cees-co. He describes her as warm, quiet, supportive, and loving, strictly a homemaker. To his father, he was Frank—a short, strong name, a man's name at any age. His father was proud, masculine, a strong physical disciplinarian, a man raising another man. In school, too, both names were used, Francisco by the teachers and Frank by the kids. "Paco," he says, came later in the Marines when he was assumed to be Mexican American and there were hosts of Pacos and Chicos and Chuys and Memos. Paco, as a name, came later to be reserved only for good friends of whom he had few. Most were fellow officers; one was a criminologist.

He had few interests outside of work. Although too muscle-bound to be an effective golfer, he nonetheless liked to get on the links and see how far he could drive the ball; putting was a balancing source of frustration. I asked him once about why there are so few Hispanic golfers, and which ones he admired. Paco's character predicted his response: Lee Trevino and Chi Chi Rodriguez were characters, not real men. Seve Ballesteros, of Spain, was the easy choice. He also gave grudging mention to Nancy Lopez who could drive the ball further than any other woman he had heard of.

Paco's other physical sport was bodybuilding. Starting in the Marines and continued at the police academy, weight lifting became a regular practice, almost a duty. "It gives me an edge; they're bodybuilding in the joint, so why shouldn't we?" My own university's weight room also became an occasional setting for the routine, and it was there that I joined him in conversation on occasion (I did *not* work out—not my style). He concentrated on maintaining upper body strength, bench-pressing up to 350 pounds, and then maintaining his status with forward and behind-the-head weights at 225 pounds.

It was that massive upper body that I noted when we first met, that I wanted by my side that night in Athens. And I'm sure it caught the attention of both gang members on the street and jurors in the box as Paco walked slowly forward to the witness stand to bury those same gang members with his descriptions of their commitment to evil. If I were a gang kid being confronted by Paco on the street or in the interrogation room, I'd call him "sir" just to be on the safe side.

Another aspect of Paco's private life was just that, the privateness of it. He seldom spoke of his family. I learned of an earlier divorce that he blamed in part on his police career and his unwillingness to share it with her. He hung around only with a select group of police buddies, and like most officers he chose to live far from the inner city that was his work setting. His home, which I never saw, was some twenty miles out in a quiet, middle-class suburb that was more rural than suburban. Lots of city cops lived out on the fringes like this. Housing was cheaper, crime levels were lower and strictly petty-ante stuff, and it was quiet. There were no restrictions on barbecues and beer parties.

But when it was time to kick back for days, or a week, Paco and many other officers headed further out, to "the river." If you've been in the Southwest, you'll know the setting. I drove through it recently to get some sense of what these guys were after.

They usually go without wives, occasionally with girlfriends some of whom are also officers. They go in RVs or rent small cabins or mobile homes. It's good enough for a few days on the loose; a living area with a TV, a fold-out couch, table and chairs, a dinette, a small bedroom with a queen bed, and a refrigerator big enough for frozen foods, soft drinks, and plenty of beer. As described in one newspaper, the place is "party-hearty."

They fish, they hunt birds, they booze and barbecue and most of all they bond with each other.

So I went to the river to get some feeling for its attraction. The approach to the river is through sand dunes with rounded rock outcroppings, scattered yucca, and scrawny chaparral. A broad band of green lies on both sides of the river, foretold by signs for RV camping and boat rentals. Then you drive through a strip of every conceivable kind of fast-food restaurant, low-rent motels, garages, and bait and sport shops.

This is "good ole boy" country, where all the road signs are aerated with bullet holes, the pickup truck is the dominant vehicle, and the tourists' sedans and SUVs continue through the one-street town and across the river with no inclination whatsoever to stop.

Along the river, occasionally shaded by willows and cottonwoods, there are small marinas and RV hookups. The river that looks blue in the reflected sky turns out to be a dull brown as one approaches it, especially when churned up by the occasional jet skier; no water-skiing is in evidence. If you gaze out from the river, beyond the RVs and campers and trailers, what you see are dry, barren mountains, low on the horizon to the east and west. There's a river canyon nearby, good for lazy fishing. Not far away is a wildlife refuge, where the waterfowl don't always recognize the boundaries and thereby become the victims of the informal shooting range of Paco and his buddies. Coots, ducks, herons, and others are at risk here. It is a place made by man, not for man. And yet this is where they come, Paco and his buddies, good ole boys kicking back free of restrictions, sharing crime-fighter war stories, making occasional forays into the water or the chaparral for fish and game. If you want to escape the daily crap of inner-city America, this place can do the trick.

So where does this lifestyle leave Paco as a gang officer? The overall answer, I think, is that it reinforces his emotional and value distance from his gangs. He defines himself as different. He has little empathy for them. He is particularly hard on Latino gangs, even more so than on the equally prevalent black and occasional Asian and white gangs. His department, of course, has always assigned him to areas where Latino gangs predominate, so he's constantly thrown up against them.

What little Spanish was spoken in his family has been enough to handle the "Spanglish" of the street gangs, that colorful mixture of English and Spanish that gang members often adopt to reinforce their own sense of group culture. He handles it well enough to maintain his control of street situations and interrogations in the station.

The flip side of the distancing, however, is that Paco sometimes fails to distinguish effectively between types of gang members, between core and peripheral member, or between those with greater and lesser propensities for violence. It is easier to stereotype them all as violence oriented, as thugs, as irresponsible thieves with little respect for the rights of others. In Paco's view, the fault for this always lies in the families that fail to instill in their youths the moral values and self-discipline he derived from his family.

"This whole generation," he said, "is lost. It's too late for them." The trouble with this, of course, is that over several decades of exposure to gangs and gang cops, I've heard the same thing said about each successive generation.

Street Life. Quite naturally, these personal values of Paco are expressed in his approach to his work. At heart, he's a street cop, and an uncompromising one. Nor is he unique in this; he fits a pattern that emerges from a good deal of research on policing. Paco is not alone. In a 1995 work, criminologist Robert Worden[1] described five police officer types as follows:

a. Professionals: firm, but fair in their handling of suspects.
b. Tough Cop: employers of "curbstone justice," whose common sense and experience overrides legal restrictions to achieve informal maintenance of order.
c. Clean-Beat Crime Fighters: they like to be tough, but believe in due process. They are easily frustrated by ideal images in practice and thus begin to bend the law.
d. Problem Solvers: they recognize contextual causes of problems. They are service oriented, seeking informal but not coercive control.
e. Avoiders: because their goals appear unattainable and due process gets in the way, they become minimal performers of duty; they just put in their time.

To me, Paco is clearly a combination of types b and c. In the earlier years, his balance of values favored the clean crime-fighter approach, but over time, as gangs became more prominent and he moved from the juvenile division into the gang unit, he became more like Worden's "tough cop."

I doubt Paco would ever go to the extreme of that type, as seen in the LAPD Rampart scandal discussed in a later chapter. The principal character in that scandal, gang cop Rafael Perez, said he had been a "by-the-book cop" until he joined the gang unit in the Rampart Division of the LAPD. But once he joined, Perez admitted, he learned "the Rampart way," which meant doing what needs to be done to get the desired results. For Perez and his colleagues, this included false arrests, planting dope and guns on gang members that they wanted removed from the street, illegally turning the members over to the immigration officers to get them out of the country, and perjuring themselves in court with little fear of contradiction. This was the path Paco was on as well, from Crime Fighter to Tough Cop, but to the best of my knowledge, Paco never engaged in the extreme illegalities of Officer Perez and his colleagues.

For example, Paco once described to me an experience that took place some weeks after his graduation from the academy. He and his training officer (T.O.)—an older, experienced, streetwise patrol supervisor—were chasing a felony suspect on foot to the roof of a tall building. When Paco caught up with them, he found his T.O. hanging the suspect over the roof edge, swinging him by his feet to and fro over the pavement seven stories below. It was either admit guilt or drop headfirst. The T.O. got his confession; he also got fired, and Paco told him that if it came to court testimony, he, Paco, would report what he had seen. Informing on a fellow officer is a widely accepted no-no in police ranks. Doing so to one's training officer, in particular, could turn a rookie into a job applicant elsewhere. Coming out of the academy, Paco started out as more of a Problem Solver than a Tough Cop.

Later, when Paco joined the juvenile division, he found that direct crime fighting was emasculated by duties in intelligence and community relations and education. But in the gang unit, intelligence functions were directly relevant to street control and crime investigation. Presentations to the community could not be ignored as much as the officers would have preferred, but they were made more palatable by using crime-fighter rhetoric and massive exaggerations of the gang problem.

Along with the crime fighter and tough cop styles, for police officers there is always the demand for control, described earlier. I don't know how many times, either when cruising with gang cops or hanging around with gang kids, I've witnessed the no-probable-cause confrontation. A typical scene: The police car pulls up to a clique of gang members on the corner. The cops signal everyone to stop where they are (control #1), then call them by their individual moniker or overall gang name to show off their street knowledge (control #2). The police then demand to know why they are on the corner and what's been happening recently (control #3), and finally order them to disperse (control #4).

There are lots of these no-probable-cause rousts on the street. Sometimes the control mechanism includes handcuffs applied whether needed or not, orders such as "place your hands on your heads," "get down on your knees," "face away from me—don't look at me, y'a hear," and "on your belly—lie down" (known as "proning" the suspect). Sometimes there are good reasons for this treatment—reports of shots fired, observation of a drug deal, an informant's warning, for example—but most often it's just control, control, control. These are nose-to-nose confrontations, when the targeted gang member is slow to respond, or resistant, or seems to have "an attitude." "I'm not happy about what's goin' on on this street," said Paco, as if it were *his* street. "If I see you anywhere around here in the next sixty days, I'll bust your ass!"

The techniques are applied to small groups of individuals on the street or in a yard, to individuals already known as gang members, to anyone in the area of a reported incident, or to a carload of known or suspected gang members. And in the most counterproductive case, they are applied to gang lookalikes or "wannabes," via the accepted police lore: "If he looks like a duck, walks like a duck, talks like a duck, then chances are he's a duck!" (If you play the part of a gang member, we'll treat you like one.) For the cops, they have just proved who's in control; for the gang members, they've just been shown why they must bond together to face the police enemy. Gang cohesiveness has been reinforced, not reduced.

For Paco and "tough cop" types like him, such confrontations confirm their own self-image, so it's not just a matter of gang surveillance and control; it's also a reaffirmation of the call to duty. Paco's car, his base of operations, is a valuable tool in this process. It's his "shop," as he calls it, a portable control center run by him for his purposes. In it, he is accountable only to himself, and he can roust those gang members pretty much at will. He can pound the hammer on a street group just as his department used Operation Hammer to send the control message to an entire community.

Consistent with his tough cop status, in the last few years Paco has had permission to carry a military assault weapon in the trunk of his car. He's never used it, but symbolically it redresses the balance against the increasingly lethal armament now available to street gangs. Paco is something of a gun aficionado. He has his own small collection of hunting weapons and several others he won't discuss; he believes strongly in the NRA philosophy of gun ownership, in contrast to his department's official position. The gun means control. The odd thing, in Paco's case, is that I've seldom known anyone in so little need of a weapon to achieve control. He does it by attitude and posture alone, with instant success.

There is an additional facet to this picture, implicit in what I've said but important to stress. This is Paco's moralism. Despite a growing tendency over the years to stray from pure legality and pure truth, Paco is a truly moralistic being and he speaks with pride about his straight moral values. This rigid self-image helps sustain him in his job of battling against the bad guys.

His colleagues call Paco and those like him "cowboys." The John Wayne image of the moralistic loner is appealing, yet seen by many officers as not quite appropriate to the team effort that good policing requires. But Paco retorts that to "hook 'em and book 'em" is what the job is all about. When he exaggerates the gang mentality in his court testimony (as I will describe later), he is only trying to guarantee that the gang members stay hooked. And for those who think policing is a matter of careful intelligence and processing of investigative materials, he counters with street terminology. Those officers have "squint jobs"; they live at their desks, while he's in his "shop" in the street. For Paco, a "good bust" justifies his time because another knucklehead, another asshole, has fallen.

To better understand Paco, I occasionally related silly cop stories to him to get his reaction. This first one only puzzled him rather than amused him. The incident is taken from a report from the Office of Citizen Complaints in San Francisco:

> Two officers were properly admitted into complainant's residence to investigate a robbery. Shortly thereafter, complainant arrived with her puppy; also present were two other adults, a mentally and physically disabled child, and an infant.
>
> Confusion ensued in the wake of two events; the disabled child touched the officer's leg and the puppy began yelping. The officer pulled his gun and threatened to shoot the puppy. The officer later reported that he believed complainant had elicited an attack response from the puppy. Although the complainant was arrested for aggravated assault against a police officer with a deadly weapon—namely the puppy—the officers left the puppy at the scene.
>
> Three days after the incident, a video recording was made of the puppy encountering two other strangers in the residence. A San Franciso County Animal Care and Control Specialist analyzed the video and reported that the puppy is not vicious, nor is it trained or able to respond to commands to attack. The criminal charges against complainant were dismissed.

But I did see Paco chuckle at another control situation. It happened when I was cruising on a Friday night with five officers in a police van. It had been a very dull night: two juveniles picked up in the subway with a six-pack of beer; a sleeping female drug addict with a bag full of silverware stolen from a nearby apartment; a drunken bar brawl that was over by the time we arrived; two extended coffee breaks; and a conversation with a SWAT team that had an outdated tear-gas gun in an unarmored Volkswagen van.

Excitement had been hard to come by. But just in time before the end of the watch, a radio call came in about a marauding group of Skinheads in the Old Town section. "Go, go!" was our response. We turned around, drove rapidly through town to Old Town and quickly found the suspect group walking down the hill directly toward us. As the van came to a stop and I was told to remain inside, the sliding door was slammed open and my officers poured out, ready to do battle. They were met, however, by about a dozen young Skinheads who were doing nothing different from the rest of the tourists on their evening walks. The Skins greeted the officers with smiles, saying "good evening" and the like, providing absolutely no occasion for police intervention. The officers, their adrenaline flowing and itching to assert control, could do nothing but exchange pleasantries and urge the group on its way.

As we reentered the van, the frustration and disappointment was thick. The night's capper was a flop. Then, as we started along the road, an obviously drunken older man was spotted urinating against a signpost. Unfortunately for him, the sign at the top said "Police." This was taken as an insult, so my frustrated cops finally had a target. They grabbed the drunk, threw him immediately into the van (and across my lap), and off we went to the station with our evening's trophy—public intoxication and defacing of public property.

This time Paco found the humor and understood my amused reaction to the incident. It could happen in any police force in any country; it was understandable, and it did deserve the chuckle we shared. But not so the puppy story, which Paco felt had a more serious implication: you have to be ready for all forms of attack.

Response to Authority. As I've pointed out, Paco is a loner. The street and his car were his comrades; they structured his life. Every arrest was a satisfaction; every conviction was a victory. Thus, over the years, Paco has had many satisfactions and a number of victories. They've been enough to send him back to the streets time and again.

Over those same years, Paco had had ample opportunity to advance in the department, to move up the ranks. Yet the highest he ever went was sergeant in the gang unit, twice actually. The first time he was busted back down to Officer Domingo for insubordination. The second time, some years later, he kept his tongue and maintained a pseudo-official status as supervisor in the unit.

Asked why he never took the lieutenant's exam, he responded as others like him had responded—he was afraid he'd pass. Paco has never respected the lieutenants and the captains; they left the streets. Although when he found "a cop's cop" among them, such a man commanded his respect. But there weren't many such people in his sight over the years. Working for promotion was a character flaw to a street cop like Paco. I once complimented him for some plans for reducing gang activity: "It's really nice to see someone in the department really thinking through ideas." His response was, "Oh yeah, at the line level we do." "Suits" work for the organization; cops fight crime.

He offered examples a couple of times. In one, he described the use of a motorized battering ram to punch a hole in the wall of a crack house and capture the dealers before they had a chance to flush and destroy their dope. The house had been under surveillance by the narcotics squad, and the information was passed on to a special departmental task force headed by a command officer. As it was the first use of the battering ram mounted in front of an armored personnel carrier, the chief went along for the ride and there was major press coverage as well.

The ram pounded the wall, leaving a hole large enough for a man to walk through. Indeed, the next morning's paper showed a picture of a task force member standing in the gaping hole. The paper also reported the sad fact that this was the wrong house. Inside, the task force members found a terrified woman and her young child. The crack house was down the street. The "suits" had taken over, embarrassing the department and the officers who, in Paco's view, should have been allowed to bust the dealers in their own fashion—in the right house.

Paco's other favorite example has some poignancy to it. An officer was shot and killed in the line of duty. The services were scheduled a few days later and, as is always the case on such occasions, drew absolutely everyone on the force who wasn't needed for minimal duty assignments. Long lines of patrol cars and "motors" (motorcycle officers) wound through the city to the chapel and then to the burial site. But the chief, in Washington, D. C., for meetings, did not fly back for the services; he didn't show at his own cop's funeral. For Paco, that totally destroyed any credibility that the chief might ever have had. All for one and one for all, unless you're a "suit," so Paco never became one.

PACO: CHARACTER AND VALUES25

The Gang as the Enemy. As a gang cop, Paco couldn't exist alone, in a vacuum. He and his gang members were functionally tied to each other. Given his background, the nature of the gang members helped frame his perspective. His family, church, and Spanish traditions prepared him. Being labeled Chicano, "Taco," and "corn-lover" because of his presumed Latino background set him up for his gang assignments—the Mexican American gangs simply reinforced his Hispanic self-image, to their discomfort. Black, Asian, and white gangs, too, were the enemy, but he was more willing to explain their situation on occasion as justifiable reactions to their own settings. The Latino gangs received no such understanding; they were a disgrace.

Much is made of ethnic differences in gang makeup, both in police circles and in academic research. In fact, however, such differences are far less striking than the similarities. Paco's greater distaste for one over others is a function of what *he* brought to the table. The same basic street gang structures I will describe in a later chapter are to be found in Asian, black, and Hispanic (or Latino) gangs. The kinds of youth who become embroiled in gang life are much the same, despite race or ethnicity. The behaviors they exhibit, both criminal and noncriminal, reveal similar patterns. The marginalization and alienation from society unites gang members beyond race, or immigration status, or geographic region. The need for identity, status, group respect, and protection from real or imagined enemies is shared across ethnicity, nationalities, and races. Yes, there are cultural differences, but they pale once the group dynamics of the street gang take hold. Paco has trouble grasping this fundamental fact; so do many of his colleagues in law enforcement, and their mouthpieces in the media. So, sadly, do some of my criminological colleagues.

An interesting sidelight was Paco's reaction to what he called the "wimpy" groups, the little copycat gangs that spring up in many communities. He couldn't respect them; their violence was minor or tentative, their character was all symbol, no substance. *Placas* (graffiti) and gang-style clothing don't make a gang. When Paco talked like this, I wondered whether secretly, emotionally, he would prefer that these copycat groups become full-fledged street gangs—a cop's gang—with automatic weapons and drive-by shootings. A gang isn't a gang if it doesn't engage in macho behaviors. It takes macho behaviors to engage the respect-as-enemy of the macho cop.

Personal Style. Several other aspects of Paco's character have seemed to me quite consistent: his views on partners, especially female cops, his approach to sex, and his concern with officer safety. The three are obviously a bit intertwined.

As I've noted earlier, Paco preferred to work alone, something he was able to do more easily when wearing a sergeant's stripes. No matter where stationed or assigned, he was a floater, seeking out his targets for interview or merely to let them know he was there. With one or two others, he liked to engage in a "roust," known more nicely as selective enforcement, hitting the corners and stoops where gang members gathered in order to move them along. Occasionally, he was part of a strike force or task force of interagency coordinated, multisite searches or sweeps. But he was a poor partner. John Wayne seldom had a partner. Partners require empathy and constrain individual autonomy. One result of this loner mentality, tolerated if not condoned by his superiors because of his successes, was that Paco was much admired and respected by his fellow officers, but he was not liked much.

When it came to women as partners, Paco all but refused to consider it. In the early years, this was no problem. Female officers were not plentiful and were seldom assigned to patrol duties. Paco worked with them in the juvenile division, of course—they seemed appropriate there—but gang units, fortunately from his point of view, seldom drew female officers.

Like many of his fellow male officers, Paco was a genuine sexist. He commented once about a woman who worked the homicide squad: "Ginger is about the only female officer I can respect." We often had research assistants assigned to collect data from police files, many times within the gang unit itself. If they were female undergraduate or graduate students, they were subjected to considerable good-old-boy treatment.

During one project, we took full advantage of this situation by hiring a female officer on leave to pursue a master's degree in public administration. She was to help us with training in penal code and other official nomenclature while extracting data from police files, but we soon found she also helped us establish immediate rapport with the station officers. The reason was simple: she was a knockout, especially the body that she encased closely in attractive clothing. She was a blond who drove a white Corvette (it's true, I swear it) to the station on each day of data collection. We got all the cooperation we wanted. If officers could drool, these guys would, and Paco was often in attendance.

Then, when her academic leave was over, she returned to duty, assigned to patrol. That's when she was reminded of the other side of the female officer coin. On her very first watch, she was sent to an apartment where a man had been reported to have committed suicide with a shot to the head. This was to be her baptism under fire.

Normally, one doesn't send a lone officer, to say nothing of a newly assigned female, to such a scene. She walked in unprepared for the sight before her. Just imagine what a close-in shot from a .45-caliber weapon will do to a man's head. She was confronted with gross splatters of blood and brain matter all over the wall, dripping down to the floor, and fecal matter soiling the man's clothing. Understandably, she lost her lunch on top of it all.

And when she had gotten the backup that should rightly have preceded her, she returned to the station, very much shaken, to be met by a dozen male officers who couldn't wait to see her reaction. Paco hadn't sent her out, but he was among those gleefully awaiting her return: boys will be boys.

I don't think Paco's views and practices are very different from those of many fellow officers. Women on the force were resisted for decades, in some cases accommodated only as the result of civil suits and federal mandates. But the sexual issue gets complicated, and I was privy to only a few glances of it. Paco once commented that: "You're not a man if you haven't been with a prostitute." This kind of old-world attitude surprised me a bit; maybe it was a hand-me-down from his Spanish male tradition. I would have expected something more like the time-honored "If you have to pay for it, you're in trouble," but cops get special opportunities with prostitutes that are not so readily available to others.

My eyes were opened more widely in our early years when I was present at a few after-hours police parties. On several occasions, these took place in connection with professional retreats held in the local mountains to develop better coordination between social agencies, police, probation, and the courts. This was in the early '70s, when Paco was still a juvenile officer.

What I remember most clearly about those occasions was that coordination ceased after dinner or the last evening session. That's when the cops went off to their assigned dormitory and brought out the booze. If you want to hear and see really hard partying, go to a late-night cops' party. After one of these in Paco's department, four of the officers left at close to 3:00 A.M. and proceeded to caravan around the neighborhood. After shouting and firing their weapons wildly as they drove drunkenly through the streets, they ended up arrested, suspended, and fired, experiencing jail from the other side of the bars. Paco was not with them.

I've never known a group to go at partying so fiercely as do the police. The women were no exception. In those days, at least, if a female officer was to be accepted into the comradeship of her peers, she had to equal or outdo them in all areas possible. Raunchy language, sexual advances, drinking, and control were such areas. The balance across them, I'm sure, was

not easy. I'm not a late-party man myself, and as uncomfortable in such settings as Paco was in some of mine, so my exposure was brief and superficial. What I saw and heard was impressive, though; yet another part of
Paco's world I would not easily penetrate.

On one other occasion, I was invited to an old-time juvenile officer's retirement party at a local restaurant. It was the same scene all over again,
but this time I deliberately sat to the side to watch the women interact. I
saw no raw sex, no groping, and no material for salacious writing. But
what I did see were female officers acting altogether like their male counterparts. They drank as hard; if anything, they told more dirty stories,
more "war stories" about crimes encountered or investigated; they traded
sexual innuendoes with equal creativity and gusto. They were "making it"
in a macho man's world, and I was both amazed and saddened by it. Those
were the days before female officers began to file complaints and civil
suits over harassment and unequal treatment.

I mentioned earlier that these issues are intertwined with that of officer
safety. Female officers are often seen as liabilities as partners, especially on
patrol. Paco is strong as a bull. He's a marksman who returns to the academy shooting range more often than required. He doesn't get the highest
rating, but he's not interested in badges and ribbons. He's good enough to
meet his self-confidence needs. But officers' safety relies on more than
themselves. It is generally the very first priority in every police department.
It's dependent on positioning, alertness, backup, and sometimes technology
(the helicopter, the Kevlar vest, communication equipment). But for most
officers, and Paco paramount among them, if you are "partnered up," then
the technology is not the issue, the partner is. "It's just me and my partner
out there" is the statement heard over and over again, like a mantra.
Women are smaller, slower, weaker, less likely to command immediate respect according to the Pacos. Paco'd rather work alone than with a woman:
he feels safer that way. When he was raised to respect women, it wasn't to
respect them as men.

NOTE

1. Robert E. Worden, "Police Officers' Belief Systems: A Framework for Analysis." *American Journal of Police* 14 (1995): 49–82.

3

PACO CONSIDERS THE EUROPEAN COP

Those are ESSO men—you know, Every Saturday and Sunday Off.

—Paco

Late in his career, when Paco had become widely known in police circles as a gang expert, he accepted invitations to lecture in other jurisdictions. These included a few overseas occasions as well, Japan and South Africa being the ones I heard about. What I could discern from his short reports was that he undertook these trips to proselytize, not to learn.

As an academic researcher, my own trips abroad resulted in more extensive descriptions. I often shared these with Paco, but in time I realized that his reactions to my reports only ended up confirming again the basic character and values that guided him. My earlier trips were in the early '70s, when Paco was still in juvenile and I was doing research on police handling of juveniles and the diversion of juvenile offenders to community treatment. A second set of trips was in the late '80s and early '90s, when Paco had reached his tough cop mentality as a gang cop and I was initiating cross-national studies of street gang patterns.

Both sets of trips were in Europe, where policing is generally less hard core than in the United States, where juvenile offenders are more commonly viewed as social welfare problems rather than criminal problems, and where local police are more likely to cooperate with social agencies than they are in America. But scratch a European cop and underneath you're more than likely to find a cop, not a social worker. Many among those I cruised with had been to the States and envied the stronger character of American police. What I noted on these trips, when reported back to Paco, provides yet another way to see the world through Paco's eyes.

ON POLICING

The city of Arnhem in Holland lies in the low hills of the eastern edge, near the border with Germany. Toward the end of World War II, it had been the site of a famous engagement between Allied and German forces, retold in Cornelius Ryan's book, *A Bridge Too Far*. At the time of my visit, it had a force of 400 police officers, including a combined juvenile and sexual offense division commanded by a thirteen-year female veteran with a law degree. She had read both American and Dutch theories on delinquency prevention, and reported that 80 percent of arrested juveniles are counseled and re-leased back to the community, a rate that would be considered terribly high in any U.S. city of similar size. Paco simply scoffed at this practice. He got more incredulous when I reported that they used a number of bicycle patrol units, community referrals, and victim assistance, and had just hired a social worker for liaison work. They were also about to hire a street corner worker to make contact with three known delinquent groups (gangs in our concep-tion) who specialized in burglary and motorbike theft. I then listed for Paco the incidents that occurred during my watch with a patrol unit:

1. Cruising the red-light district.
2. A vehicle stop of some Germans in a Volkswagen to see if they were seeking drugs.
3. A vehicle stop of a large American car, presumed to be a pimp car.
4. Cruising a disco area.
5. Backup at a minor traffic accident.
6. Pick up of a homeless female mental patient for transport to the sta-tion. Coffee break.
7. Call to pick up a carbooster and his loot (two radios and clothing); transport to the station. Coffee break.
8. Two stops of wrong-way drivers.
9. Stop of a motorbike with a helmetless passenger; issue a citation.

Paco's response is noted at the top of this chapter: "ESSO men—you know, **E**very **S**aturday and **S**unday **O**ff."

Just imagine his derision of some of the juvenile practices I reported from Stockholm:

1. For children under fifteen years of age, their parents must agree to the police disposition of their cases; over fifteen, the youth must agree. In cases where agreement is reached but then parents or youth change their mind (about a treatment facility, for instance), the case is either dropped or must be reinvestigated.
2. At a judicial hearing, the case is presented by a social worker. A defense lawyer is at the hearing but not the prosecutor. Incarceration cannot be forced, except in the case of a narcotics user.
3. In a "rebate" system, new offenses charged against juveniles already in a treatment program or awaiting entry are folded into the current case. Even the Stockholm police were very unhappy about this practice.
4. While 50 percent of juvenile arrestees are released to social authorities that then apply their own discretion, there is additional discretion at the prosecution stage. For example, depending on how the prosecutor gets along with the local social authorities, between 20 and 50 percent of juvenile burglars are released at that stage.
5. Following some unfortunate police abuse cases, each holding tank has a "Citizen Witness." This is a politically appointed volunteer who observes the processing of suspects as a neighborhood representative. He or she even signs the arrest and booking report. Once obviously resented, these observers now seem easily accepted by the officers.

Paco, of course, had no sympathy with such gentle procedures and restrictions. The threat of police work as social work, whether in fact or only in perception, always limited his enthusiasm for juvenile work and almost certainly colored the attractiveness of gang work in the years to come.

But he did have sympathy for the plight of some of the Stockholm patrol officers with their frustrations. They were not allowed (as was true in Arnhem as well) to carry out undercover narcotics "buys," nor fence sting operations, nor any other practice, so common in the United States, that smacked at all of entrapment. Their standard issue side arm at the time (since replaced) was a Walther PP, a small-caliber handgun with bullets not much larger than a .22-long. I handled the loaded weapon (no American department would allow such a thing), and indeed found it to be very small, light, and unimpressive. They referred to it as their "girl's gun." A recent shooting of a felon in Mälmo (in southern Sweden) reportedly required

nine hits, the last one finally piercing the aorta. One officer claimed it took
five shots to take out a hit-and-run cat.

Their SWAT team van, a van with glass windows and no armoring, was
equipped with only tear gas, flack vests, and a small fireman's axe for forced
entries. With these, the team pointed out, they were supposed to deal with
barricaded suspects, riots, and terrorist attacks. The van in which I cruised
was similarly civilian issue, as I learned when we went on a full-siren run to
a reported barroom brawl and found that the van slowed down on each hill
we encountered.

One of the reasons these Stockholm officers fed me all their complaints
was that they were in a battle with national police authorities and the par-
liament to give them more modern, technologically advanced, crime-fighter
equipment. Many of them had visited U.S. departments and wanted the armament, the leather jackets, the souped-up cars, and the legislative supports they learned about in the States. The fact that they needed less because their crime problem was so much less than ours was not an argument
they accepted. Nor was it one Paco accepted.

At later stages of the European research, I reported some preliminary
findings on responses to the emerging gang problems in Europe. Paco—
who by then was a gang cop—had similar reactions to the absence of an all-
out attack regardless of the seriousness of the problem. I brought him five
examples, as follows:

1. *Zurich*: International drug gangs brought hashish and heroin into
   Switzerland. The Zurich response included its famous "Needle Park"
   by the river, where addicts could hang out and shoot up without official intervention. Zurich police expressed ambivalence about this approach; there was no ambivalence in Paco's reaction, or to the police
   tolerance for the collections of young gang members whom they were
   satisfied simply to deride as "toy gangsters."
2. *Frankfurt:* There were numerous gangs identified by the police here,
   both native German and immigrant in makeup, but no gang unit existed to deal with them. Rather, juvenile officers maintained extensive
   intelligence files on the groups and left action against them in the
   hands of regular patrol officers who did not have ready access to the
   intelligence files.
3. *Berlin:* I was there prior to reunification and could report only on the
   situation in West Berlin. It was not to Paco's liking. Although there
   were a number of both specialty and traditional gangs in the city—I
   will describe these in a later chapter—the Berlin police merely as-

signed a few officers to keep tabs on them, really a very primitive form of gang intelligence. There was no gang control operation in the department despite many run-ins with Skinheads and some vicious Turkish gangs, so vicious that a formal gang intervention social agency instructed its street workers to avoid all core members of the gangs. Perhaps they remembered the stories, apocryphal or not, of the Turkish troops with the United Nations' forces in the Korean War who responded to the Chinese trumpet blaring charges with their own shrieking counterattacks with long, curved scimitars circling over their heads. In Berlin, the Skinheads were learning to regret their initial attacks on Turkish and Kurdish immigrants, but it was still a gang war without official intervention.

4. *London and Manchester:* Here, Paco found more to praise. In these British cities, there were drug gangs—"Yardies" from the Caribbean and Chinese and Asians (the British term for Indians and Pakistanis)—who were drawing attention from the narcotics divisions of the local constabularies. Manchester, in addition, had some very American-like street gangs in its housing projects ("estates"), although they, too, were thought to be heavily involved in the drug trade. Since at that point Paco had come to believe, quite erroneously as it turned out, that the U.S. drug trade had been heavily infiltrated by street gangs, he was happy to contemplate narcotics officers involved in gang matters.

On the other hand, neither city had formed a gang unit, and Paco knew from experience that narcotics officers had their own agendas and were necessarily lax in building knowledge about street gangs. In fact, official Britain (the Home Office and other parts of the government) was in active denial of any street gangs in England. For Paco, denial makes no sense. You can't organize a response against something that doesn't exist. In an interview survey of over 300 police departments in the United States in the early '90s, over 40 percent had originally denied their gang problem until literally forced by gang incidents to recant. The Home Office was thus repeating a common error, missing one of Paco's cardinal rules: know and recognize your enemy.

5. *Stockholm:* This city, much to its consternation, has had street gang problems since the late 1980s. The news media have been more forthright about this than have the local authorities. Two examples warmed Paco's cynical heart. The first was a volunteer social agency that developed a modified street work program. I was introduced to

the program, and then saw it in action in the underground section of an area called Sergelstorg in the heart of downtown. In the company of a police officer who knew many of the gang members by sight, we arrived at Sergelstorg at about 11:00 P.M. A very noticeable collection of gang members was lounging on one side of a large mall area (one didn't need a cop to identify them). On the other side, ignoring the group and eventually abandoning the area later that night, were the street work volunteers I had met earlier. They wanted nothing to do with the group; Paco would have walked right up and started taking names!

But the description Paco *really* liked was of the wall in the central police station that was covered over by a sheet. The officer who had been with me in Sergelstorg—a female officer I told Paco—made sure no one else was in the room, and then removed the sheet. There on the wall, arranged in groups of varying sizes, were photographs of scores of Stockholm's street gang members identified by her. There were lines connecting individuals to each other in the groups and some connecting individuals between groups. Each connecting line represented an arrest of two or more cosuspects. She had drawn on the wall, and covered it so no one would know, a clique structure of Stockholm's gang world (or groups of arrestees for those in gang denial).

Paco thought this was a silly exercise, being based on youth arrested together rather than on street observation and interrogation. That's where *real* gang information comes from. And then he felt fully vindicated when I explained to him that this clique structure system had been learned by the officer in a class at the university, taught by a sociologist!

Paco's responses to these overseas descriptions of juvenile policing and weaknesses in gang control practices could easily be elicited by visits to selected U.S. jurisdictions. I think he would be equally condescending regardless of the setting. For Paco, any practice that minimizes the seriousness of the gang issue, or puts constraints on law enforcement's (and his) ability to exercise control over gang members is a practice that encourages gang formation and the predations of those people he defines as mere hoodlums. And because of this, Paco and those who share his values are faced with perhaps their greatest challenge: the recent national love affair with community policing. I want to turn to that issue next.

4

STREET GANGS
AND COMMUNITY POLICING

You wanta put the police on the sidelines.

—High ranking police official at a 1990s conference
about community policing

In the parlance of policy analysts, community policing has become a "hot button" item. It is "state of the art" at best, a fad at worst. For Paco and other police specialists, it is a threat to their styles, maybe even to their existence. The threat comes in two forms. First, community policing reduces Paco's autonomy and power, taking some discretion out of his hands and giving it to community residents. "You can't use community policing with gangs," he complained to me; "Give them an inch, they'll take a yard."

The second threat is equally of concern to Paco and other specialists. In its ideal form, community policing favors the generalist officer, the jack-of-all-trades, especially at the patrol level. The corollary is the diminishing and in some cases the dismantling of special police groups such as the gang unit. It strikes directly at the elitism that tends to accrue to such units, be they gang or narcotics or SWAT or terrorism or other designations.

To understand this, one needs to look at the spirit in which community policing was developed and at some variations on its theme. Modern policing has come to be defined in terms that are strange to Paco: affirmative action, diversity, management by objectives, MBAs, community policing. A traditional cop asks whatever happened to good old crime fighting?

Community policing, explain its adherents, is less a program than a philosophy, less a set of activities than a strategy. At its heart is the notion of a partnership between police and community, a realization that crime reduction and prevention are best achieved through this partnership. The police are a part of the community, as are the firefighters, the hospitals, and the social workers. They serve not by forays from the outside, but by involvement from within.

Critical to this philosophy is a strategy about resources and decision-making. In its ideal formulation, what I have elsewhere referred to as the "strong version" of community policing, the decisions about how police resources should be targeted and deployed are made jointly by the police and community residents. Usually, this is facilitated by a residents' committee in some form, working closely with the local police who service the area.

Let us consider an example of a community in transition. An older, established white area is slowly being changed due to decreased housing values and "white flight" to the suburbs. Moving in are a combination of younger minority professionals with young children—they could be Hispanic, Asian, or Black, it doesn't matter—and working-class families with inadequate job skills and the need for cheap housing. Single-family homes are becoming duplexes, or are being replaced by cheaper apartment complexes. Ethnic restaurants are followed by ethnic groceries, as well as by men's clubs, bars, and liquor stores. Within a few years, social problems escalate to the point that they feed community deterioration and change.

But this is a community-policing city, and there is sufficient social structure that the heterogeneous residential and business inhabitants have developed a community council to work with the police on dealing with social problems. These problems include, but go beyond, criminal activity. The council has identified a set of problems to be dealt with, including the following: increased signs of prostitution; drug sales in and around school grounds; deteriorating homes, streets, and alleys overlooked by the sanitation department; a halfway house for the mentally ill from which residents seem to be wandering and scaring young children; an increase in home burglaries; plans for a freeway extension through the area; rumors about adolescent fighting between different racial groups; and wall graffiti and other indications of street gang activity in the area.

This is not an unusual scenario in and around many U.S. communities. Some of the problems are not included within the traditional scope of police concerns. Others have become the almost exclusive concern of special police units such as the juvenile division, the narcotics squad, or the gang unit. The philosophy of community policing says all the problems listed above can become the concern of the partnership between residents and police, including enlisting other partners—the housing authority, the sanitation department, the school board, and so on.

Community policing, in the strong version, reduces the pursuit of bad guys, requires getting to know the community better, and responds to minor issues like zoning regulations. "Kicking ass" doesn't fit well; spending time with residents does. Special training for officers is required. Appreciation of different sets of community values is needed. More police patrol presence is needed, in cars and on foot (or bicycles), with officers prepared to deal with a wide host of issues. Specialists like Paco take on less importance, especially as budget constraints require that the increase in beat officers be at the cost of specialized units.

Sometimes Paco would lapse into gang jargon to impress local residents with his special street knowledge; to "jack" (rob), "smoke" (shoot dead), to "dis" (show disrespect), to "run a train" (gang rape or serial sex by several males), to be "sexed in" (initiation of a female by forced sex), to be sent on a "mission" (commit a particular crime, sometimes as an initiation—not exactly analogous to the Mormon practice!).

I've heard him talk of "Darwin Awards," facetious praise for the killing off of the least fit to survive in the gang world. On such occasions, he would refer to gang members as knuckleheads, punks, assholes, and poo-butts, trying to "catch drama with the cops." Paco used his terminology to "dis" the gangs, forgetting that they were, for better or for worse, an indigenous part of the very community he was supposed to respect.

But—and this is so important to community policing—local residents must be empowered to participate in the informal social control of their own communities. The community council, in this strong version, helps set the priorities for the use of police resources. In the changing community described above, the cops may want to crack down on the prostitutes, the drug pushers at the schools, and the growing street gang presence. But the residents, while agreeing about the prostitutes, want to move first on the sanitation problem, the halfway house, and the racial strife. In the strong version of community policing and with the invariable problem of limited resources, the community council argues that prostitution should be the first order of business—the narcotics and gang problem must not drain off significant police resources because they are merely reflections of community deterioration.

In this setting, Paco and those of like thinking, along with many traditionally oriented police officers, become very upset. They don't want to waste their time with community councils. As one of his bosses complained, "We can talk all day about the need for involved communities and involved witnesses and people who will take direct action whether it's individual or community based, but . . . that damn sure isn't happening."

Community organization is a tough, complicated process that often fails. The police certainly are not trained to develop or sustain it. Further, the community residents, for the most part, are quite ignorant about the situations the police deal with, even those of a less serious criminal nature. To prove the point, Paco took two young female community residents out on a Friday night ride-along. After getting the usual signed waiver of liability and giving exaggerated instructions on what to do in case of emergencies such as shots being fired, he and his partner that night said their first assignment was to check out a local bar. They drove to the bar, entered, and ordered beers for the two girls. Then, in response to a phony phone call to the station, the officers left the girls at the bar to respond to a hot call in the neighborhood. The "call" took about an hour, leaving the girls on their own, in a strange bar in a strange section of town.

They had been in bars before, of course, but this one was different. They became the center of attention; they were approached—oddly they thought—several times; they were given free refills by strangers. They were becoming very nervous when their police escorts finally returned and ushered them back to the car. Paco tried but couldn't keep himself from snickering, at which point his partner pointed to the red-faced young ladies and broke out laughing. They finally admitted their ruse: they had deliberately left the girls on their own in the city's most notorious gay bar. The girls—both students in my criminology class—were furious and demanded to be taken back to the station.

Instead, Paco promised to make it up to them by hitting a place the vice squad had identified as a small-time, illegal gambling setup. Intrigued, the students agreed so off they went. On arriving at the spot, an innocuous apartment building, the officers, with the students behind them, busted through the door unannounced and surprised six men sitting around a long poker table. As the men jumped to head for the rear door, Paco's partner jumped up on the table, his hand on the holster inside his jacket, and shouted, "Freeze!" They did.

Then, on Paco's instruction, they returned to their seats and for the next half hour or so played various versions of poker, instructing the young ladies in the rules and gambits of the game while the officers looked on. No arrests were made, no warnings were issued, and no apologies given. The girls, with a night full of new and for them exotic experiences, returned to the station and home. They reported this all in the next class to the great amusement and awe of their fellow students. Paco's report to me was succinct: he bet those girls would never again think that the community could handle police problems. Even gay bars and gambling are the purview of the police, not some community council.

Paco and most police departments engaged in community policing have a strong preference for what I have termed the "weak version" of community policing. In this version, there are community councils, and there is some nontraditional emphasis on the lesser criminal and social problems that plague the community. And the police do listen to community complaints and they do increase car and foot patrols, as *they* deem necessary. However, priorities about problems and decisions about the use of police resources are made by the police. These often reflect community-expressed values but they need not. Policing is still police business. Specialized units are retained as much as possible. If there's a problem, call 911.

In my own home community, I received a phone call from the chairperson of the police community advisory council (as it was called), asking me to be a member. I asked him who the other members were and how they were chosen. He explained that most were members of the local school committee and were recruited by the police lieutenant in charge of our local community policing effort. I then asked how he had been selected as chairperson, and he responded that the lieutenant had asked him to serve. I reported this selection process to the department commander in charge of community policing in my city, a man who reported directly to the chief. He was pleased with my report, saying, "You have to pick the Advisory Board members very carefully. It's not a matter of democracy—if you leave it up to a vote you could get a bunch of activists on the boards." And Paco agreed fully. Not happy with the need for any formal community input, he suggested: "We should appoint our own Advisory Council first—beat 'em to the punch—then you could just say, 'We already have an Advisory Board.' Some of their people could give us trouble."

There are further consequences to this "weak" version, with the police at the helm. One of my colleagues, doing research on the process of community policing and with the promise of full cooperation from the department, asked for the names of the Advisory Council members in the university area so he could interview them. He was refused by the district commander's office because (a) the names were confidential (one wonders from whom!) and (b) "they are the eyes and ears of the police, who shouldn't be harassed for other purposes." Somehow, in this setting, the weak version had been further distorted to the point that "secret" council members have simply become police informants.

In the same city, another incident came to light. In community policing, 911 emergency calls are supposed to *decrease* because there is greater access of residents to their local police. But a liaison officer to the Advisory

Council urged his members to *increase* the volume of 911 calls because re-sources are allocated to an area in part by the number of 911 calls received. Again, the council is to serve the police, not vice versa. "Yeah," said Paco on hearing of this, "the department's all politics now. Once you get to the $60,000 level, or 80 or 100, it's just circling around the chief's office. At the street level, you know, we're on our own." One of his partners, in the same conversation about the involvement of community residents, exhibited a to-tal lack of comprehension about it: "I grew up in that area. We were poor, living on *papas* [potatoes] and frijoles, so I know their lingo, their mentality. They can't put anything over on me."

Oddly enough, or at least so it seemed to me, Paco tied the traditional con-cern with officer safety into his distaste for community policing. "Number one," he noted, "is always 'officer down.' If one of your guys is in trouble, you gotta go—everyone goes. That's gotta be the number one priority." And com-munity policing just seems in his mind to muddy the waters of what used to be this and other clear priorities: "You used to know what was rewarded—good arrests, cracking heads, clearing out the prostitutes or the homosexuals. But now, with community policing it's not clear who wants what. The citizens want you to get rid of graffiti or something. You're supposed to leave the 911 calls for the patrol guys, unless it's an officer down thing."

Fortunately for Paco and other resisters, there is another "new" police approach to dealing with community priorities that sits far better with them. Often confused with community policing but *clearly* different in phi-losophy, this approach is most commonly known as Problem-Oriented Policing (or POP). It combines a concern for elements of community ser-vice with modern, computer-aided crime analysis. In brief, POP often in-volves identifying "hot spots" where criminal activity is elevated or increas-ing, and targeting those areas for special attention (undercover operations, selective enforcement, increased patrols, special task forces, etc.). Hot spots can be identified by accumulating crime reports, or by officers' re-ports, or by citizen complaints.

Quite often, the accumulation of small problems is seen as a precursor to larger ones. An area showing increasing social problems, or the emergence of minor criminals such as purse-snatchers, squeegee pests, or public drunks, is pinpointed under POP and a crackdown ensues. In New York City, the police department called this community policing and a "zero tolerance" approach. Well, if you'll reread the earlier description, you'll see this is a perversion of the term. It's not community policing, it's policing the community: same words, very different meaning. But it appeals to Paco. When he talks about community policing, he may only mean zero tolerance, and by arresting his gang members for even the slightest violations, he's policing the community.

5

DEFINING STREET GANGS

We have a saying in the gang unit—GMB: guns, money, bitches.

—Paco

I mentioned earlier that Paco was admired by many of his fellow officers, but that he was not well liked. One of them—one of my favorites, a gang cop, sergeant, advisor—gave me a tape recording of a lecture Paco had given at a national training workshop for gang officers. On the tape, one hears Paco making quiet fun of an academic definition of street gangs (my definition, in fact, from an earlier book that I wrote), and then offering his own: "I'll tell you what a gang is; it's a group of thugs. They're hoodlums, they're crooks and criminals."

This was not one of Paco's most articulate pronouncements. It yielded an unfortunate message for his trainees, for officers chosen to work in gang details across the nation. In the previous four chapters, I've used various approaches to "defining" Paco—who and what he was and has become. But I need to define street gangs as well, to clarify what they are. They are *not* what many people take them to be, and not what Paco often takes them to be.

With his thugs, hoodlums, crooks, and criminals definition, what has Paco missed? At first, his approach sounds much too narrow, yet oddly enough it is much too broad. If street gangs were defined only in criminal terms, they would include terrorist groups, motorcycle gangs, organized crime cartels, and prison gangs. A highly placed police official in Scandinavia confided to me once that "we use a gang definition that's really broad, so we can apply it to as many groups as possible." The National Youth Gang Center in the United States made the same error, leaving the definition so open that it included many small informal groups that occasionally indulge in antisocial acts but hardly deserve the label of street gang. In Illinois, Dr. Greg Scott of the Illinois attorney general's office noted that in jurisdictions not reporting gangs, 42 percent nonetheless reported having such informal youth groups—"troublesome youth groups"—that might well be caught up in this simplistic thugs definition. But each of these other groups is different enough to require its own characterization, and so different from street gangs that they only obscure the character of Paco's and my target groups. So, again, what has Paco missed? The list is long, but certainly includes the following points.

First: Most gang crime is minor. The thugs definition misses this fact. Eighty percent or more of it involves graffiti and other vandalism, petty theft, minor fighting, burglary, joyriding and auto theft, lots of alcohol use and somewhat less drug use, some usually small-scale drug sales, and so on.

Let's take the example of individual fighting. Paco was testifying in a court case about intergang violence, and the following dialogue was recorded.

Prosecutor: Going back to our discussion of one-on-one fights, when those fights are witnessed, how does the concept of backing up and loyalty affect the behavior of those individuals watching this one-on-one fight?

Paco: My experience is that the other gang members will join in the fight.

Prosecutor: Have you ever seen an instance in your career as an investigator where a one-on-one fight was witnessed by members of the gang involved—gangs involved in the fight where it remained a one-on-one fight?

Paco: I don't recall one, no.

This conclusion, that all fights become group fights, is simply not true. I believe Paco knew this when he testified, but a conviction in that case would be more likely if he testifed that all fights are large gang affairs. In my own experience, every fight I saw was a one-on-one. Of course, there were true gang fights or fights in which one victim was ganged up on by several others. But one-on-ones are common, despite Paco's sworn testimony to the contrary. Major crimes—rapes, robbery, aggravated assault, drive-by shootings, homicide, and attempted homicide—constitute a small portion of all gang crime. Crime is crime, of course, but the thugs definition emphasizes the worst of it only. It is, therefore, highly misleading about the true nature of gang crime.

Paco provided a nice example of misreading crime levels, because he was convinced, in the 1980s, that the gangs were in control of the drug trade, especially in the sale of crack cocaine. Gangs could be attacked just like drug cartels, he felt, by the use of conspiracy laws as applied to the cartels. When I argued against this, stressing the informal nature of most drug sales by gang members, his response was "it takes one guy to sell it, right, and another to provide it to that guy, right? Well that's two guys conspiring to sell drugs, so gangs are conspiracies and we can hit 'em with conspiracy laws." What this does, of course, is to twist the language and the definition to suit one's purpose, not to provide an accurate picture of gang behavior.

Second: Most gang activity is noncriminal. You wouldn't know this from listening to Paco. "Their world revolves around money. Their way of obtaining money is by the sale of crack cocaine. Along with it comes women, sex, everything else." Gang members sleep like the rest of us (perhaps longer in the morning), eat like us, play like us, and mess around with the opposite sex like us. Many of them go to school or work, although not so steadily as most of us. And far more than most of us, gang members simply do nothing. They hang around, walk around, sit around, loaf, tell exaggerated stories of gang exploits, and otherwise waste the day, often in each other's company. It is, in truth, a fairly boring life punctuated by occasional spells or incidents of excitement—much like a street cop's life, in fact. They are a bother to us, but for the most part they fail to live up to the statement of Paco's former chief, that they are "a corrosive acid eating away at the structure of our society."

Third: Street gangs are social groups. The thugs definition totally ignores one of the most obvious and important aspects of street gangs, namely that they are groups. As such, they have properties that affect their members' behavior both positively and negatively. On the positive side, they provide their members with an identity and status otherwise often lacking in youth drawn to gangs. Part of effective gang prevention involves offering alternative sources of identity and status, a social work approach of no interest to Paco.

Most street gangs have only moderate levels of cohesiveness. We can reduce the level of cohesiveness and thereby reduce the gang-precipitated antisocial behaviors. Alternately, we can increase the level of cohesiveness and thereby increase criminal involvement. Paco over-estimates gang cohesiveness, and then reinforces it by the overt sup-pressive activities in which he exults. The best sources of gang cohe-siveness are intergang rivalries and well-meaning attempts to break up the gang. Paco helps create the monster he engages by providing the opposition off which gang cohesiveness feeds. When the Greek war-rior cut off one of the Hydra's heads, two others grew in its place. The street gang shows that same regenerative capacity. Hercules eventually defeated the Hydra. Defeating street gangs by picking off some lead-ers is far more than a Herculean task.

Paco's stereotype of the gang, the hoodlums, also leads him to per-ceive it as organized into leaders and followers. Some of these lead-ers he calls "shot callers," those older members (O.G.s, for Original Gangsters) who presumably tell others who to target for assaults and drive-bys. Paco's notion is that if you knock off the leaders (via arrest and conviction) you can effectively damage or even destroy the gang. The lesson of the Hydra is again instructive. New heads grow to re-place the old. Further, most gangs don't have such clearly defined leaders. Leadership varies by function—fighting, partying, sports ac-tivities, and so on—and it varies over time. It also tends to be age specific; older "leaders" have less influence on younger members than the age-peers of those members. Gang leadership, in other words, is a complex phenomenon, hardly captured at all in Paco's stereotypic image.

Fourth: Street life almost becomes a part of a gang culture. It is seen by members as more than an activity: it is a *right*. The thugs definition ig-nores the "street" in street gang. Criminal behavior is only one aspect, and sometimes an outcome of the loose, hanging behavior of gangs. "Hanging and banging" is a common phrase connecting gangbanging and street life. Thus harassment of gang members on the street strikes them as being not only mean-spirited (which it often is) but also as illegal, thus contributing further to their disrespect for the law and its officers. Cops and gang members both view the street as their rightful space. For the gang members, it may seem like their only remaining available space, as home and school are often sources of conflict and rejection.

There are many youthful groups that can get into trouble with the law. That doesn't make them street gangs. The street gang is different, special. Sometimes cops and prosecutors try to make a gang out of something else. I testified in the case cited earlier where Paco claimed a group was a gang because they had painted graffiti on the back wall of their hangout and had partied loudly there on numerous occasions. There were no criminal charges recorded against them, and there was no recording of the "gang's" existence in police files. But Paco wanted the extra gang charge in order to increase the court's sentence. Following my countertestimony, the judge laughed at the prosecutor and threw out the gang charge.

In another instance reported in the news, prosecutors invented the term "bully gang" for the same purpose; to increase the punishment against four boys involved in a stabbing. This was a suburban clique that had adopted 1950s-style haircuts and clothing. They, like the previous partying group, evidenced no meaningful street life and little prior criminal involvement. Once again, the gang charge was dismissed. All street gangs are groups; most youth groups are not street gangs.

Fifth: An aspect ignored by the thugs definition is the neighborhood or community context of street gangs. Paco is a cop only, and has no taste for doing social work or community organization. That's in part why community policing goes against his grain. But in the long run, gangs don't die because of anti-gang intervention, but when public leaders successfully reshape the communities that spawn them. It is the community that most deserves everyone's attention, but it won't get that attention by following Paco's lead and only attending to the criminal behavior of current gang members. Future gang members will only replace the current ones if the community continues as a spawning ground. Paco and others who seek to intervene play the role of the legendary Greek, Sisyphus, who was condemned to push the rock up the hill only to have it roll back to the bottom each time. He should have reshaped the hill, just as we must reshape the context that produces the gangs.

All right, so Paco's thugs definition is inadequate. Where does this leave us? We already heard him on the tape ridiculing my academic definition. He could have selected several other academic definitions equally well. Criminologists have tried for decades to come up with an adequate definition of street gangs. Many of these have contained common elements and yet each has shown that we cannot easily come to agreement. After all, gangs are informal groups generally lacking the usual trappings of formal organizations—dues, membership lists, clear membership criteria, organizational charts, constitutions and bylaws, and so on. Thus, we are trying to define an ambiguous, diverse, and often changing phenomenon. Perhaps it can't be done, and we have to settle for a looser characterization: street gangs are not this and that, but they do generally share a, b, c, and d characteristics.

This was the approach I took in my 1995 book, *The American Street Gang*. I excluded terrorist groups, prison gangs, motorcycle gangs, Skinheads (I've since altered my position on Skinheads), and most adolescent groups whose members occasionally get into trouble. Then I characterized the street gang as *primarily* male, *usually* ethnic and racial minorities, with a strong street life, *primarily* youthful, engaged *to varying degrees* in criminal activity, and *probably* committed to an antisocial group identity, being *usually* versatile in their criminal offending, and lasting anywhere from *months to years*. Well, the dimensions are here, but quite obviously there's room for much variation. So maybe this is as close as we can come.

This failure to typify gangs and gangs' members frustrated one of my graduate students who wanted to know what it would really be like to study them. He wanted the "drama" of gang life, so I related to him two of my more memorable incidents, which considerably reduced his desire to become involved. The first was the day I was introduced to a gang known as the Latins (a pseudonym). Following my endorsement by their gang worker and my attendance at their weekly meeting, I was mysteriously left alone on a basketball court with one member—early twenties, large, notably tattooed, and very Paco-like in his posture. He spent twenty minutes interrogating me about my purpose in the area, what I "really" wanted, and why I thought I had a right to be there with his compadres.

I answered as best I could—academic research, learning about such groups so they could be helped, and so on—and it turns out, I passed muster. He went back to the group and reported that I was O.K. What I learned later from the gang worker was that I was being checked out to see if I was a "narc" (undercover narcotics officer), or a man who "liked young boys." Had I failed this test, I might well have become a gang victim, said the worker.

The second piece of drama is reported in *The American Street Gang*, in an episode involving two very different types of gang members. I quote here from the book:

a setting in which a fringe member, a lonely and unhappy kid, was seeking more direct involvement in his gang. A core member, violent (there were many proofs of this) and committed to the group, openly resisted the fringe member's advances to the group. He initiated a truly vicious fight. An adult attempted to intervene to prevent serious damage but became caught between the two gang members who, trying for a death grip on each other, instead had a mutual death grip on the hapless adult. It was after about five, white-knuckled minutes of stalemate that the younger boy finally lost his grip. The adult was able to extricate himself from the vise, bruised, almost with the breath squeezed out of him, and knowing forever after that who joins and who does not join would be decided by the gang not its observer.

My first editor of that book did not want me to admit it, and so I didn't, but I was that hapless adult. As you can readily see, the incident left a lasting impression on me of the different personalities to be found among gang members, even among gang fighters.

On one occasion, Paco was asked in court to define gangs. "The most widely accepted definition of what a gang is," he responded, "is two or more people gathered together for antisocial or criminal behavior." When I heard this, I thought of two famous brothers in China who were finally apprehended by the national police after engaging in a spree of criminal episodes. According to Paco's response, the two brothers became a street gang. But Paco's response wasn't just a shot in the dark. It was an informal version of an "official" gang definition, carved into stone for future generations by its incorporation into state legislation.

Originated in California by lobbying prosecutors and since copied in a number of other states, the Street Terrorism Enforcement and Prevention Act (STEP) was designed to sidestep constitutional vagueness issues by defining gangs as *criminal* groups, in some states as "quasi corporations." Its purpose was to provide enhanced sentences (i.e., longer time in prison) for individuals convicted of serious offenses while they were members of street gangs. It is such legislation that brings Paco and other gang cops to court even in cases where they may not be the arresting or investigating officer. Their function is to testify as expert witnesses to the gang affiliation of the defendants and thus get them off the street for additional years after their conviction. Many states now have similar acts. For example, the Illinois version is called the Illinois Streetgang Terrorism Omnibus Prevention Act (ISTOP). Common to all STEP-type acts is the stipulation that gang offenses are defined in terms of the furtherance of the group's interests (e.g., drive-bys, graffiti, witness intimidation, and so on). Illinois also includes that the offenses have been "ordered, ratified, authorized, insisted upon, or otherwise sanctioned by gang leadership."[1]

The STEP Act, and variations on it, defined a "criminal street gang" as *three* or more persons (Paco was off by only one) who knowingly associate with each other with a primary purpose of committing serious criminal offenses. These offenses are usually specified in the legislation and are gang-stereotypical, such as assault, robbery, murder, drug sales, shooting into an inhabited dwelling, drive-by shootings, and attacks on police officers.

I would point out several problems with this definition that is not descriptive of gangs, but rather a convenience for establishing longer sentences. First, its name is purely political; the "terrorism" is a gross overstatement, and the "prevention" is nowhere to be found in the legislation. Second, the phrase "three or more" is ludicrous; street gangs don't come in threes. Third, it suggests that the commission of major crimes is a primary purpose of gangs, whereas, in fact, it is normally a by-product of gang formation. Fourth, in limiting the definition to named serious and stereotypical gang crimes, it completely overlooks the vast majority of offenses that gang members commit.

I suppose if the STEP Act definition was only used in court hearings, the damage would be limited. But Paco's reliance on it typifies what is in fact taking place. All across the country, justice officials, the media, and politicians are adopting this narrow violence-flavored definition as the true character of street gangs. I've already heard some criminologists using it, which to me means that we are using a conviction-oriented convenience to define a social phenomenon. The result will be to distort understandings of the phenomenon, the street gang. This builds false knowledge, with terribly misleading implications for gang control.

Another problem with the STEP Act definition is that while it is useful to the prosecution for its purposes and to cops like Paco who wish to further those purposes, there is nothing in the act to require definitional consistency. Dr. Scott's Illinois report cited earlier notes that his survey of 778 Illinois chiefs and sheriffs showed a very strong preference for the narrow ISTOP definition. Yet, in reporting the number of gang crimes in their jurisdictions, they used the broadest of definitions—any crime in which a gang member is involved. So, a narrow specific definition is used to ensure conviction, but a far broader definition is used to quantify the prevalence of gang crime. The same responsible officials use different definitions for different purposes. No wonder the situation is confused.

And no wonder definitional inconsistency serves the purposes of the police, and especially gang cops like Paco. In Arizona, there are seven criteria for determining who is a gang member. Meeting any one of these is enough to label a youth a "gang associate," and only two of the seven can serve to apply the label "gang member." Professor Charles Katz has summarized several research reports that show police acting more punitively and with excessive force against gang members than against others. Easy labeling of youth as associates and members can clearly exacerbate these excesses.

I stress the point because of these distortions. The STEP Act, and Paco's narrow perspective, must not be allowed to become our accepted image of street gangs. Academics do not have sufficient voice, the *gravitas*, to offer a more acceptable alternative in the policy arena. But once the STEP Act is allowed to define the terms, everything else fails because it provides violence, serious crime, criminal association, and conspiracy all in one easy-to-swallow package. And being written into law, it is given uncommon legitimacy.

Having said this, I should make it clear that there is understandable reason that academic and law enforcement definitions and characterizations of gangs should differ. Paco's view, for instance, is built in large part from his experiences, and these are overloaded with core gang members, those most involved in criminal pursuits and heavy-duty offending. His settings are street stops, arrests, interrogation rooms, and courtrooms. The criminologists' perspective comes from nonconfrontational street observations, private times and home times, and interview and questionnaire responses as well as police and court files. The criminologist sees a far broader spectrum of gang members, gang behaviors, and gang contexts. On the other hand, most criminologists do not share Paco's exposure to stops, arrests, and interrogation.

In a sense, Paco sees his "gangster" (his term, not mine) as a young crook, where I see a troublesome youth. Paco's view of gang territory is one of potential street domination. Even when still a juvenile officer, Paco once warned me that the neighborhood in which I was about to carry out my research wasn't worth the bother: "Every kid in there is a gang member," he assured me. When my research team had completed our data collection, we found that there were slightly over 100 gang members in that area we called Ladino Hills: 100 out of a couple of thousand gang-age youth.

After all this, I have not yet offered any "definitive definition" of street gangs. And I won't; it may not be possible. But a recent development has at least yielded another interesting alternative. I mentioned in Chapter 3 some of my forays into Europe and Paco's response to them. In the late 1990s, I became very involved with a large number of European as well as a few American scholars in observing a developing street gang problem in Europe. Relatively free of street gangs until the 1980s, a number of European cities were seeing the emergence of "gang-like groups," as some local researchers called them. At several small conferences, an attempt was made to see what the American gang experience might have to offer in places like London, Manchester, Stockholm, Copenhagen, the Hague, Paris, Brussels, Berlin, Frankfurt, and a group of cities in central Russia.

Central to our concerns was how to define "street gang," because many Europeans, having only a Paco-like stereotype of American gangs, denied that Europe really had a gang problem. The difficulties in surmounting this issue proved to be complex and quite touchy, but at the end of the fourth meeting specific research projects were developed to compare gangs across Europe and between Europe and the United States. The "consensus" definition of street gang came in two parts, agreed on as a reasonable jumping-off point.

In the first part, street gangs were defined as "any durable, street-oriented youth group whose own identity includes involvement in illegal activities." In the words of Jack Nicholson's movie character, maybe this is "as good as it gets."

The second part of the approach in the Eurogang Program (as it is now called) is that while most youth groups do not deserve to be called street gangs, any group should be considered a street gang if it fits into any one of the five categories recently described in the United States. These five types of street gangs—Traditional, Neo-traditional, Compressed, Collective, and Specialty gangs—will be described in the next chapter. Any group, the notion goes, is a gang if it looks like one of these five. Significantly, Paco's definition encompasses only one of these, the Traditional gang, or an unusual combination of the Traditional and Specialty gangs. He has missed the complexity of street gang structures.

In place of information about street gang structures and gang member characteristics (see Chapters 6 and 10), police across the nation develop "intelligence files" designed to help them in their gang assessments. Access to these files shows how extensive the information may be. The accompanying table, compiled by an agency of the U.S. Department of Justice in *Urban Street Gang Enforcement* (1997), shows what can be included.

This compilation is, of course, an ideal. Most international and U.S. gang intelligence files lack most of this information. The information brought to

Data Elements Commonly Included in Gang Information Systems
Taken from Page 36, *Urban Street Gang Enforcement,*
Bureau of Justice Assistance, 1997.

Gang File	Gang Member File	Moniker File
Gang name and moniker	Person's name and moniker	Person's name
Ethnic composition	Gang name and subset	Street name (moniker
Number, names, and	Residence address and	which may be the
monikers of members	other locations frequented	same for several
(and whether hardcore)	Phone and page numbers	people)
Turf boundaries	Social Security Number	Date of birth
Hangouts and hideouts	Race and ethnicity	Gang affiliation
Associated hazards (for	Physical description with	
example: dogs,	photograph	**Vehicle File**
weapons, lookouts,	Identifying marks (for	Owner's name
booby traps, explosives,	example: tattoos and	License plate number
and toxic materials)	scars, with photos	(state and year)
Symbols	Place and date of birth	Make of vehicle
Graffiti samples and	Membership status (for	Model of vehicle
photographs	example: hardcore, etc.)	Color
	History of violent behavior	Interior and exterior
Color	School background	oddities
Alliances and affiliates	Associates and their	
Rivalries	addresses and phone	
Assets and locations	numbers	
thereof	Criminal history (for	
Drug customers and	example: arrests,	
suppliers	dispositions, jail or	
Distinctive identifiers (for	prison time served,	
example: clothing,	associated ID numbers)	
hairstyles, tattoos, and	Current criminal status	
jewelry)	(for example: bail,	
Hand signs, rituals, and	probation, parole,	
rules	release conditions, and	
Communication methods	warrants outstanding)	
	Fingerprints	
	Field contact information	
	Family data (involvement	
	of family members in	
	gang activity)	
	Other comments	

bear in court cases in which gang members are charged with even the most serious crimes relies not on such files, but on the personal knowledge and beliefs of the gang cops who testify. And most of them cannot produce the extensive data listed above.

NOTE

1. This quote is taken from Dr. Scott's report, *Illinois Law Enforcement Responses to Street Gangs*, August 15, 2000.

6

STREET GANG STRUCTURES

They have the discipline of Organized Crime.

—Paco

When public officials and academics try to describe the organizational properties of street gangs, they often err either by understating them or by overstating them. I've heard Paco do both, depending on his needs and his audience. In reality, the structure of gangs provides clues about how to deal with them. For clarity, we need to distinguish as best we can how these groups differ from the ordinary, run-of-the-mill troublesome youth groups found in many schools and communities. We also need to distinguish them from organized crime groups and cartels, from prison gangs, even from terrorist gangs. Paco helps us do this, inadvertently, by virtue of his stereotype of street gangs.

Paco is used to "big city" gangs, gangs that have in some cases existed for decades in cities like Los Angeles and Chicago. He sees these groups as large, with maybe 100 or more members and sometimes coalitions that number in the thousands. They have subgroups based on similar age or shared locations. They are primarily male—Paco cares little about female gang members in any case—and primarily black or Hispanic, occasionally Asian, and rarely white. He sees them as having strong leaders—O.G.s ("Original Gangsters") or "shot callers"—who wield major influence over other members. He senses that there is an organized core of highly criminal members, that they share strong codes of loyalty and a strong commitment to protecting their turf. Since the 1980s, he has come to view them as highly involved in organized drug sales and rather uniformly willing to resort to serious violence to accomplish their goals.

And in much of this, he is simply wrong. I'll describe later the variety of street gang structures that have been identified by recent research, both here and abroad. Suffice to say at this point that Paco's stereotype of the large, long-enduring gang with strong territorial claims and a number of seriously criminal members does indeed exist—it's generally called a Traditional gang—but comprises at best only about 10 percent of all American gangs. Most gangs are *not* of this kind.

Further, and equally important, most gangs have a code of loyalty more in rhetoric than in fact; often weak and transitory leadership; a wide range of crime seriousness, most of which is nonviolent in form; at least a moderate involvement in drug sales (but plenty of alcohol and drug *use*); only moderate levels of cohesiveness; and, surprising to many, a gender mix that often approaches 25 percent or more females.

Paco's stereotype, of course, is many people's stereotype. It has been fostered by police, federal law agencies like the FBI and DEA, and the print and broadcast media over many decades. Research consistently reveals the falseness of this image, but who reads original research?

Police generally, and Paco particularly, tend to characterize street gangs by race and ethnicity, by crime patterns, and by the leader–follower mentality that oversimplifies the complex interpersonal relationships within gangs. And by stressing these three issues mostly, Paco and his cohorts simply miss much of what a gang is all about. Here's Paco, addressing these questions as an expert witness in three criminal court cases as he responds to the prosecutors' set-up queries:

- In today's society, there is a phenomenon of different gangs. We have Hispanic gangs, black gangs, Asian gangs, Southeast Asian gangs, Pacific Islander gangs, and Filipino gangs, motorcycle gangs, prison gangs, and also white gangs.
- Within a set [one term for a large gang member cluster of subgroups] you have three ranks: O.G.s, Original Gangsters; then you have Gs, Gangsters; then you have the B.G.s, Baby Gangsters. And O.G.s are the shot callers, the ones that decide what is going to happen. Under each one of these O.G.s you have a clique; you maybe have ten–fifteen members that specifically work for him, that he kind of controls.

- Gs are the worker bees, the ones that go out and put out work for the set, for the 'hood. B.G.s want to become an O.G., so these are the guys who are going to assist in drive-by shootings, or steal guns used in drive-by shootings, or transport narcotics, or sell narcotics.

Well, this is certainly an appealing and dramatic depiction, certain to impress a jury with the seriousness of the gang threat as organized criminality. And for the jury, it certainly justifies Paco's follow-up testimony about the proper police role with gangs:

> We have one goal. That is to suppress gang activity. We go out and we control the gang members where we find them; if they're on a street corner, in a car, in an apartment building, wherever we can locate them. Most gang members readily admit to gang membership. They're proud of it. It's their life—"yes, I'm a gang member."

So what is Paco missing? Among other things, he's missing the fact that most street gangs are smaller than his stereotyped gangs are—smaller, less structured, and less cohesive. He's missing the nontraditional gangs I'll describe later in this chapter, the ones that are most plentiful around the country. He's missing the white gangs, including the Skinheads. He's missing the major differences between large, Traditional gangs and smaller Specialty gangs, and, at the same time, confusing drug trafficking gangs with his large, territorial gangs. He's overlooking the frequently transient leadership in street gangs, and confusing hard-core criminals with youth influential among their gang peers at each age level. He's overlooking the majority of gang members who are not at the core of their structure, not heavily committed to gang rivalries and paybacks, and not central to the violent offending that so engages Paco.

Most gang members never get to fire a gun, as is true of most police officers as well, and are far less involved in murder and mayhem than they are in vandalism, petty theft, drug and alcohol use, and curfew violations. Paco clearly overlooks the girls in the gang, although the boys don't. He has trouble distinguishing between the less-involved members of the gang and the far larger number of youths who have grown up in the same neighborhoods, have known gang members well from the school and the street, yet have not committed themselves to gang life. Paco may call them "gang associates" to avoid defining who is and who isn't gang-involved, and may thus paint these neighborhoods with far too wide a brush.

And—with such phrases as "once a gangster, always a gangster" or "the only way out is feet first"—Paco ignores the fact that the vast majority of street gang members outlive their membership. In gangs other than his stereotyped Traditional gang, average membership tenure has been shown to be around one year. Most gang members don't die early, don't end up doing twenty-five to life in the state prison, and don't end up as drug addicts. They get jobs, they get married or otherwise entangled in family responsibilities, and they often go back to school. On average, they do less well in these arenas than do their non-gang peers, but still they "make it" in our society. I've known politicians, teachers, professional athletes, probation and parole officers, and even cops who matured out of gang life and moved on. I could name a few gang researchers as well, and plenty of people who now sincerely devote their careers to gang prevention and intervention programs. To Paco, most of them are suspect.

In contrast to these gang elements that Paco misses or overlooks, he's clearly one up on most people—including many of his police colleagues— about how street gangs often start up. He understands the common research finding that most gangs don't uniquely form specifically to establish themselves as criminal organizations. He noted in court one day: "I've seen the gang start as a group of seven or eight guys who are students at the high school; I've seen it go from just a group of guys that were hangin' around together to a group of hard-core criminals that are out shooting people, stealing, carrying on."

And indeed, gang research from the 1920s until now continues to document various sources of street gang development, with no single pattern dominating. Under certain circumstances—especially where rivalries develop—youthful play groups, singing groups, and break-dancing groups have become street gangs. Tagger crews on occasion have become "tagbangers" and, thereafter, street gangs.

Gangs develop in housing projects where peer groups tend to be more isolated and unsupervised. Sadly, they can result from busing gang members from one school area into another. They have emerged on military bases both because some military recruits join to escape their previous gang life and because the adolescent children of families living on the bases can form ganglike structures.

Ironically, court placements of young delinquents, gang or non-gang, bring real and potential members together in detention centers, placement centers, juvenile institutions, and prisons. In many correctional facilities, forming and joining inside-the-walls gangs may seem the best protection against other groups. Notorious prison gangs such as the Mexican Mafia, La Nuestra Familia, the Aryan Brotherhood, and the Black Guerilla Family not only recruit within the walls. They can also exercise influence over street gangs on the outside, especially in developing and controlling drug markets, which themselves are sources of street gang formation.

Paco has seen all this, or heard it on the gang grapevine. He's more concerned, of course, about the influences stemming from the prisons and other correctional facilities, so that he often forgets the more benign sources of gang membership. He tends to lose sight of gang joining as a response to needs for status, identity, fellowship, and presumed protection; what remains pivotal for him is the crime connections, since this after all is what he is charged with controlling. He's a cop, not a child psychologist.

And what of female gang members, that substantial category all but ignored by Paco? Up to 25 percent of gang members may be female. They need Paco's attention, along with that of social service workers more generally. They, too, can have strong group loyalties; they, too, commit levels of crime far surpassing that of non-gang girls. Their pattern of crime is very similar to that of the males, although at lower levels of frequency. And all too often, they become early mothers out of wedlock.

In many cases, females are members of dual-gender gangs, although usually playing secondary roles. They are there, whether Paco pays attention to them or not. In some cases, especially in what I will later describe as Traditional and Neo-traditional gangs, they form female subgroups attached to the larger male structure. In rare if newsworthy cases, they form totally separate, independent female gangs. Good books have been written about these gender issues in street gangs (see the Fleisher and Miller books listed in the Epilogue). Paco should read them.

We need to look a little more closely, as well, at the notion of formal gang organization. As soon as the word "gang" appears in the news, it brings with it a host of connotations that go beyond the meaning of the term "street gang." Gang can also mean terrorist gang, or prison gang, or criminal gang as in organized crime. In each of these instances, the word gang implies a level of structure and organization, a capacity for criminal conspiracy that is simply beyond the capacity of most street gangs. Especially over the last decade or so, Paco has been losing sight of this distinction. He does so because it is easier to lump all gangs together, and because court convictions and longer sentences are enhanced by the projection of street gangs as organized, or as stated in some state legislation, "quasi-corporate organizations."

I don't think anyone would confuse a terrorist gang with a street gang, although there is the famous case of Chicago's El Ruk'n street gang agreeing to supply arms to Libya when that nation was a training base for international terrorism. As for prison gangs, there are states—Illinois, Texas, and California come most immediately to mind—where organized prison gangs have included some street gang membership, and have attempted in some instances to influence the activities of street gangs on the outside. But these connections have been greatly overblown by examples taken from the Black Gangster Disciples in Illinois and the Mexican Mafia in southern California.

The strong leadership and street codes of loyalty in these notorious prison gangs do not translate well to the loose relationships one finds in most street gangs. Similarly, the vertical authority patterns and the adoption of specific roles are unlikely in the loose and shifting organizational soup of the street gang. The prison gang's rules of behavior may be easily enforced inside the "joint," but outside the relationships are too shaky and occasional to allow for their ready enforcement. The prison gang, especially within any one institution, is a single organization; the street gang is more a set of friendship networks, where even who is or who is not a member can be unclear.

Similarly, organized crime groups such as drug cartels can't remain in business without strong leadership, codes of loyalty, severe sanctions for failure to abide by these codes, and a "business" sense that permits the accumulation and investing of criminal proceeds. The street gang needs little of this to maintain itself. But to confuse organized crime groups or prison gangs with street gangs leads to easy overgeneralizations. Listen to some of these from Paco's court testimony:

Paco: Members are involved in homicides, attempted homicides, drive-by shootings, witness intimidation, burglaries, armed robberies, vandalism, petty theft—kind of runs the whole gamut.

Question: Do you have an opinion as to whether this offense was committed for the benefit of, at the direction of, or in association with a criminal street gang?

Answer: I don't particularly care if somebody is a member or not. We operate under the penal code that says "in association with." There's no differentiation in the law for membership versus association.

Question: If I had friends who were members or associates of a gang and I happened to go out and have a beer with them once a week, would that make me an associate, in your mind?

Answer: If you have a pattern of ongoing associations, according to the law, it does.

Question: So to be an associate, you merely have to be seen with another gang associate on three occasions, is that correct?

Answer: That's when we classify them as gang associates; that's correct.

Question: How do you get out of a gang?

Answer: You either get killed—that's one way—or another way is you get jumped out[1] of a gang. Another way is you move far, far away and you never come back.

Now in reality, most street gang members don't get killed. Many, but probably most don't opt for being jumped out. And most don't move "far, far away"—most residential movement is to other locations in the same minority neighborhoods of the same city. But normal moves—going back to school, getting a job, and getting married or otherwise attached—are not dramatic events that signal desistance from gang activity, so Paco misses them or dismisses them as superficial. "Once a gangster, always a gangster" he likes to say (so that, using figures of current gang prevalence in the United States, we might guess that there must by now be up to ten million gang members in our communities—ridiculous, isn't it?).

Professor Scott Decker of the University of Missouri–St. Louis conducted some interesting research in San Diego, St. Louis, and Chicago. Using the most organized street gangs in each of those cities, he asked about pivotal criteria of formal organizations. He included leadership, regular meetings, and written rules for normal organizations. For criminal organizations, he included crime specialization, organization of drug sales, use of profits for the gang itself, the funneling of funds into legitimate businesses, relationships with neighborhood businesses, relationships with gangs in other cities, relations with prison gangs, and connections with organized crime following street gang participation.

In the case of the Black Gangster Disciples in Chicago, Decker found many of the characteristics of formal groups and of organized crime groups. But he found little of this for their counterparts, the Latin Kings in Chicago, and virtually none for the San Diego and St. Louis gangs, *even though these had been nominated as their most organized street gangs by the local police.*

I've literally spent years, even decades, trying to demonstrate to law enforcement, to the media, and to political leaders that most street gangs are only loosely structured, with transient leadership and membership, easily transcended codes of loyalty, and informal rather than formal roles for the members. I'm doing the same thing now in Europe, where the Paco-like stereotype leads numerous officials to decide they don't have a gang problem because they don't see counterparts to the Black Gangster Disciples, the Crips, or the Bloods as presented in the media. It's difficult to get people to discard the stereotypes and to accept the results of several decades of gang research—my own and many, many others.

Paco knows this at heart, but his job encourages him to ignore the facts: street gangs are *informal* groups. Most have no membership rosters, written rules and constitutions, oaths of office, and formal positions. The gang is as much a *perceived* unit as a "real" one—we use *judgment* in defining and describing it. To mold its structure in our minds to fit our needs is to engage in the reification of a fantasy.

Gang legislation in various states (really, anti-gang legislation) reifies what Paco and his prosecutors want in order to convict the gang members and get them off the street for as long as possible. Such legislation says a gang can consist of as few as three people, that one of the principal purposes is to commit the most serious crimes, that it is organized for criminal purposes, and that it is thus subject to conspiracy convictions.

Well, take your choice: listen to the researchers, or listen to the prosecutors. Paco caters to the prosecutors. He has listened to me and my little lectures for years but denies the legitimacy of social science or criminological data, because such data don't fit with his filtered experiences and don't seem to help him hammer his gangsters.

There are hard-core leaders: I've known a number of them. But there are also non-hard-core leaders, more of them. There are leaders unknown to the police because they don't get arrested. My favorite was a very criminal and very influential eighteen-year-old, finishing high school, who was unknown as a gang leader to the police because he only had one charge against him, a sex charge brought by the parents of his girlfriend. The girl died in childbirth and this young man went to court in a custody battle with the girl's parents to care for the baby. He won—the gangster won, and the police never did learn of his pivotal role in the gang. Ironically, this young man's name was also Francisco, and his gang moniker was "Paco." To the best of my knowledge, that Paco never met my Paco.

Gang leadership is transient; the roles and who is seen as influential change over time, and this varies greatly by age. Yes, there are in some street gangs individuals who might be called "shot callers." But they can't call the shots for everyone, only for those so committed to gang mentality or so desirous of higher gang status that they'll respond to the shot callers. Most "associates" or "affiliates" or "peripherals" or "fringe" members or "wannabes"—whichever term Paco wants to reify—are not so malleable that they'll go out and kill in response to a shot caller. Life isn't that simple.

I will try to illustrate how messy this business can get, the business of trying for clear, prosecutable definitions of gang membership. Here's testimony in a California gang trial, where Paco was brought in to apply the anti-gang STEP Act, his own agency's definitional criteria, and his own experience. This testimony is particularly interesting because the defense attorney doing the questioning is less naive about gang matters than are most I've observed.

Question (Defense attorney): What is the difference between an associate and a member of a gang?

Answer (Paco): I don't know what a member of a gang is.

Q: 186.22 of the Penal Code refers to gang members, does it not?

A: Can I refer to that?

Q: Sure. You stated on direct examination that you are familiar with this Penal Code section. Correct?

A: Yes, sir.

Q: And just for the record, this Penal Code section is the definitive code section that deals with gang prosecutions, correct?

A: Yes, sir.

Q: Okay. Why don't you take a look at Penal Code section 186.22 and see if it mentions member of a street gang.

A: Yes, sir. It does.

Q: And what does it say about a member?

A: "Any person who actively participated in a criminal street gang with knowledge that its members engaged in or have . . ."

Q: So then Penal Code section 186.22 refers specifically to members of a street gang, correct?

A: In that sentence, yes, it does.

Q: Can you, as an expert, define to me what a member of a street gang is as opposed to an associate?

A: I don't know what a member is.

Q: Does that particular code section define association?

A: No. It defines what a criminal street gang is and what a criminal street gang means, what the predicate offenses are, and what—my statement is that it does not define membership. Membership is not a requirement under that code section.

Q: Could you just listen to my questions very carefully and answer my questions? My question was . . .

Prosecutor: I'll object.

The court: Excuse me. Actually, all counsel approach the bench. Off the record, please.

(Whereupon an unreported discussion was held off the record.)

The court: Back on the record. You may continue.

Q: Does the Penal Code define "association"?

A: No.

Q: Does the Penal Code define "affiliation"?

A: No.

Q: Does the Penal Code define "member" as . . .

A: No.

Q: . . . it relates to the gangs?

A: No.

Q: Do you have your own definition for association?

A: As it pertains to a criminal street gang under the Penal Code and what this scheme of the Penal Code says and 186.22.

Q: What is your definition of association?

A: The person has to have some type of an indicator that they are involved in criminal street gang activities. It can be the substantive offense that you are—that they were arrested for. There can be other factors that are taken into consideration.

Q: What are those other factors?

A: Gang-related tattoos; admits membership; requirements about their gang affiliation, regular ongoing association with other individuals that have some of those aforementioned factors, to name a few.

Q: Any others?

A: There's several more.

Q: What are they?

A: Gang-related photographs, gang specific clothing, request special housing, identified by a reliable source as gang involved, identified by a confidential informant as gang involved, correspondence with gang members on a regular basis. I don't have the rest of the list with me.

Q: Is there a specific written list?

A: There's a—there is a process that we use.

Prosecutor: Objection. Vague.

The court: Overruled. The answer stays in.

Q: Is there a specific written list?

A: There's a process that we use to determine if someone is gang involved.

Second attorney: Objection. Nonresponsive.

Prosecutor: I'll object to the question. It's vague.

The court: To the first objection. The objection is overruled. Also, the second objection is overruled.

Q: Is there a specific written list of gang-related factors?

A: Yes. We use a criteria list that outlines what a gang involvement—what we would evaluate for gang involvement.

Q: You mentioned gang-specific clothing. What specific clothing are identified as being gang related?

A: Depends on the gang. You'd have to narrow that down for me.

Q: Any gang in this county.

A: Would you like me to go through every criminal street gang in the county and describe what is specific to them?

Q: Do you have a written list that outlines each one of those?

A: No.

Q: Could you give me the list as to the gang in this case?

A: For gang-specific clothing?

Q: Yes.

A: Considering this gang, blue bandanas are a traditional way of, for lack of a better term, as describing membership. That's something that's been a tradition with these gangs for many, many years.

Gang-specific clothing has a tendency to change with gang—with clothing styles. Gang-specific clothing can include things like specific belt buckles that have Os on them, and we deal with five or six individuals who all have O belt buckles on. Baseball caps that have the name of the gang written on them. Clothing that has the gang—name of the gang written on it.

I have seen gang-specific clothing on things as simple as blue shoestrings in shoes that originally came with black shoestrings. There's a variety of ways that people claim their affiliation through clothing. I see people do it with the way they button their shirts. Where one shirt—the top button is buttoned, the second one is not buttoned, and the next three are. It's not just my observation. You can talk to gang officers around the state, and they'll tell you the same thing.

Q: I asked you specifically as to this gang.

A: That is what I am referring to.

Q: Okay. Is there a difference between affiliation and association?

A: Not necessarily, no. Affiliation, association—are affiliated with something, associated with it.

Q: So when you use the word affiliated, you mean exactly the same thing as associating for purposes of gangs. Is that correct?

A: You can pretty much use those two terms interchangeably.

Q: What's the difference between being affiliated and/or associated and being a member of a gang?

A: I think it's . . .

Prosecutor: I object, your honor. I think it's beyond the scope of direct. I don't believe there's been testimony that anybody is quote, end quote, a member of a gang.

The court: Sustained.

Q: Was my client a member of the gang?

A: I don't know if he was a member. I don't classify people as members. He had an ongoing association with the gang.

Q: Was, in your opinion, he a member of the gang?

A: As I already said, I don't know if he was a member. He had an ongoing association with it.

Q: You testified that you are a member of the gang task force. Right?

A: Yes.

Q: And you testified that you have had a relationship with my client that began sometime in late July and continued on in August and September and October, and during your association with him you discussed various gang activities with him. Is that correct?

A: Yes.

Q: Based upon your position as an expert witness here on gangs and your contact with my client, was he a member?

Prosecutor: Objection. Asked and answered.

The court: Sustained.

CROSS-EXAMINATION

Q (Defense attorney): Good afternoon, sir. I provided you with a copy of Penal Code section 186.22. And if you recall on cross-examination, you were asked whether or not there were any definitions in that code section referencing association or affiliation.

Have you had an opportunity to review that Penal Code to see . . .

A (Paco): Not . . .

Q: . . . if there are definitions in there?

A: Not really, No.

Q: If you might take a moment and review that and provide to the court whether or not there is in fact a legal definition for association and/or affiliation.

A: I'm looking for association, is that right?

Q: Association and/or affiliation.

A: I don't believe I see it in here.

Q: Okay. So then if there's no legal definition of association or affiliation in Penal Code section 186.22, where does that definition originate from, if you know?

Prosecutor: Objection; vague.

The court: Overruled. You may answer.

The witness: I'm not sure I understand your question.

Q: Who makes up that definition in this county?

A: I'm not sure I understand your question, sir.

Q: Let me ask you this: who makes the decision in this county to label someone a gang associate?

A: Who makes the decision?

Q: Right.

A: Other officers and myself.

(Note: Now ordinarily, Paco doesn't get into this sort of quagmire. As an experienced gang officer and a court-approved gang expert, his definitions and descriptions are accepted without much challenge. The presence of an expert witness on gangs for the defense side is rare. Less rare, and sometimes quite nervy, is the attempt to undermine his testimony by attacking his credibility, as a *generic* gang expert.)

Q: And could you inform the court what level standards and training certificate you hold currently?

A: I currently hold a basic post.

Q: A basic post?

A: Yes. That is the lowest certificate.

Q: Can you tell us any specific books that you have read that are of assistance in the field of gangs?

A: Yes, sir, I've read . . .

Prosecutor: I'm going to object to the line of questioning under section 866(B).

The court: Overruled. You may answer.

The witness: I've read a book called *Running Scared, Mi Vida Loca. Gang Days in L.A.*

Q: Running Scared. Was that just the title, *Running Scared*?

A: Running Scared, Mi Vida Loca, Gang Days in L.A. And I believe the author is Luis Rodriguez. And it was written—he was—I'm sorry. He's a former gang associate of Lomas Street gangs in the Los Angeles area.

Q: Have you read any other books that deal with gangs?

A: Yes, sir, I have. I've read a book called *Do or Die*. The author's name is Leon Bing, and it deals primarily with Crips and Bloods in the Los Angeles area.

Q: Any other books?

A: I read one called *Krews*, spelled K-R-E-W-S. Deals with street gangs in the New York area. I do not recall the name of the author.

Q: Have you read anything about gangs written by Frederic Thrasher?

A: No.

Q: How about Professor James Short?

A: No.

Q: Lewis Yablonsky?

A: No.

Q: Professor Irving Spergel?

A: No.

Q: Professor Malcolm Klein?

A: No.

Q: How many seminars have you taught?

A: I don't know, number-wise.

Q: You don't know?

A: No, I don't. We do presentations and displays. We talk to the citizen's academy, talk to other officers, we go to other P.D.s. As far as an exact number of presentations, like things like that I've done, no, I have no idea how many.

Q: So you go to them. Let me ask you this: How many seminars have you ever taught at where these people came to you?

Prosecutor: Objection; relevance.

The court: Overruled. You may answer.

The witness: I don't know. I can't come up with a number.

Q: Have you ever attended the FBI Gang Training Academy?

A: No, sir, I haven't.

Q: Do you have a Ph.D. in anything?

A: No, I don't.

Q: Master's degree in anything?

A: No, sir.

For my own part, I don't expect Paco, or most gang cops, to be conversant with the criminological literature on gangs. Their expertise is of a different kind. But I sure do sit up straight when I run across one who has read some of this material. And they, too, are out there. I wish there were more of them. I hope some of them will read this book and seriously consider the different pictures that emerge from the street and the campus. In turn, I have, myself, been greatly informed by my time with Paco and with literally hundreds of other officers.

It was in part because of this that my research colleagues and I turned to experienced gang cops across the country to see if we could get a better grip on the nature of gang structures. We started with a select group of sixty gang officers who gave us responses to a number of structural questions about the gangs they knew best. From this we derived a tentative typology that seemed to make sense, that tied police experience to academic impressions. We then interviewed several hundred additional gang officers to check out and refine this typology. We continued by having the National Youth Gang Center try the typology on several *thousand* police jurisdictions all over the country, while a colleague in the Illinois attorney general's office did the same in hundreds of police departments throughout that state. What follows is a brief summary of the findings, a new typology of street gangs that has been confirmed in several ways.

Five contrasting street gang structures have been identified The first, called the *Traditional* gang, is similar to Paco's stereotype of gangs generally: large, territorial, long enduring, with a wide age range, subgroups or sets based on age or residence, and a versatile ("cafeteria-style") crime pattern. Paco's vision of the typical gang is confirmed, but its typicality is another matter.

The second structure, the *Neo-traditional* gang, is very much like the Traditional gang but newer—usually in existence for ten years or less, smaller, with a narrower age range of its members. It seems to be a transitional form: if it remains in existence for another five to ten years, it will grow larger, extend its age range, and become a Traditional gang.

The third structure, little recognized in earlier decades of research but now the predominant form, is the *Compressed* gang. It is labeled "Compressed" because of its smaller size (fewer than fifty members usually) and the restricted age range of its members. Typical Compressed gangs are adolescent or very early adult groupings, without well-defined subgroups. They generally endure for less than ten years, as members mature but are not easily replaced by new generations of recruits (in contrast to Traditional and Neo-traditional gangs.

The fourth structure is the least common; an amorphous group labeled the Collective gang. This, too, is a transitional group, more loosely structured than the other types. It has some amorphous community ties but is not strongly territorial. It shows low cohesiveness yet a large membership—perhaps more than a hundred. It is this loose, ill-formed structure that makes it transitional: it is either likely to be forced into a more traditional form by pressure from other gangs or law enforcement or to retract into one of the smaller forms or dissolve altogether.[2]

The fifth structure, frequently but incorrectly fused in Paco's mind with the Traditional gang, is called the *Specialty* gang. The name comes from the fact that these groups do not manifest the wide versatility of crime patterns common to the other forms. They specialize, often in drug distribution but in some cases in burglary, or auto theft, or in extremist pursuits for example. The Specialty group generally labeled a "drug gang" is where Paco gets off base, in part because of the 1980s belief that Traditional gangs became the major distributors of crack cocaine (they did not, although there were some notable exceptions). Skinheads can also generally be classified under the Specialty gang structure, less a problem here than in Europe.

Specialty gangs garner a lot of publicity, as do the Traditional gangs, and so the media and the general public understandably conclude that they are one and the same. But the Specialty gang, because it has such a narrower, more dedicated focus, is quite different. It usually lasts fewer than ten years, is small (on *average*, around twenty-five members), and is the most tightly structured of all five forms. It has to be tightly structured to stay in business. It is often postadolescent but with a narrow age range. It often starts as a break off subgroup from a larger gang—thus some of Paco's confusion. It also may start up very deliberately to suit its particular criminal purpose, unlike most other gang types where crime is the by-product of joining together for identity, status, and a sense of belonging and protection.

Our own national survey of gang officers revealed Compressed gangs to be the most common; they were reported in 75 percent of all jurisdictions we surveyed, while Traditional and Specialty gangs were each reported in only half as many locations. Further, in cities reporting that they had a predominance of any one type, 60 percent reported the predominant form to be Compressed, and only 10 percent reported either Traditional or Specialty forms as predominant. Paco, and many other law enforcement spokespersons, have simply missed this pattern of gang structures.

Does this gang structure picture hold up in other research? It does. In a survey of all police jurisdictions in Illinois, that state's attorney general's office found that 74 percent of all gangs fit within the five structures. A national survey of jurisdictions across the nation was conducted by the National Youth Gang Center (NYGC). The NYGC also found a 74 percent fit within the five structures.

Why can't 25 percent of police-reported gangs fit into the five-category typology? I can offer two reasons. First, as I have stressed before, street gangs are *informal* groups and as such vary among themselves and over time. To expect them to fit rigidly into any scheme may be asking for just too much regularity. Second, our own original research that developed the typology asked police experts to describe their gangs that didn't fit into any of the five types. We then analyzed those nonfitting descriptions and found that most of them, in fact, *did* fit. The officers perceived some of their gangs to be unique, when in fact they were not so unique at all.

This same kind of follow-up questioning was not built into the Illinois or NYGC surveys. Had it been, they, too, could probably have reduced their 26 percent nonfitting gangs very substantially. It's a guess, of course, but a good one I think.

Closer questioning in the Illinois study revealed that only 11 percent of all cities could not effectively use the gang typology. Further, it showed that many gangs were labeled Traditional because they shared the Chicago gang names such as the Black Gangster Disciples, but that they were actually Compressed structures. The confusion was caused by the gang name, not its structure: Paco in Illinois. Finally, the Illinois researchers also asked whether stereotypical factors of the Traditional gang could be applied to most Illinois street gangs, and the answer was no—most local police officials did not respond in Paco-like fashion.

I can add one other pattern to these U.S. data. In the newly formed (post-1980) gangs in Europe, Traditional gangs have emerged on only rare occasions—in Berlin, Glasgow, and Kazan, Russia, to date. Compressed gangs are far more common, and there is a larger problem with Skinhead types of Specialty gangs. The typology seems to work in Europe, albeit with different patterns of prevalence.

What the structures do not accomplish explicitly is to clarify Paco's (and other people's) confusions over *levels* of gang membership—member, hard core, associate or affiliate, fringe, wannabe, and so on. I can offer at least some light here. It is worth remembering that gang membership is a continuum, ranging from those highly committed to the group under all circumstances to those only occasionally hanging around with members of the group. This is a true gradient, and we try to break it up by suggesting hard categories like hard-core members, or shot callers, O.G.s as well as associates, peripherals, and wannabes. Gang membership isn't static enough to make these categories terribly useful. Member commitment and involvement varies over time, it varies by context, and it varies by who does the categorizing.

I remember clearly the morning I received the call. A member of the Latins gang we were studying had been killed by a rival gang, shotgunned standing at the head of the outside stairs when the locked door wouldn't allow his escape. I knew this boy, Manuel, knew he was a well-respected core Latin member. We turned out the troops—the three workers and two researchers hit the street, as did Paco and several patrol cars. I took my place at the taco stand, a few blocks down from the high school on the main drag through Latin territory. If the Latins were to mount a payback, they'd come by the stand. So would the rival gang, if they were going to cruise the area.

I'm pleased to say that no further action took place, but I learned a thing or two while shelling out food money at the stand. First, most Latins members that day and for several days more disappeared—stayed home, kept their heads down, and clearly signaled that they were not so "hard core" after all. Second, the ones who gathered at the taco stand—a dozen or so— were scared as hell, unnerved by every suggestion of a squealing tire, a car horn, or the sight of an oncoming car slowing down as it approached. I, too, was ready to go prone at a moment's notice, but then I was never raised to be an O.G. and never, over the preceding year, had I been so popular with these kids as I was that day and night. They hung around me as if glued; I was safety, the shield against the drive-by. Mind you, those gathered together out in the open like this were only a dozen, a dozen out of over a hundred Latins members. The others were making themselves scarce, even though they were often highly visible in other contexts. Membership—and levels of membership—tend to be fluid, depending on the context. Commitment to the gang is not stable over context, nor over time.

I've found through my involvement in a number of court cases over the last ten years—like the one yielding Paco's testimony in this chapter—that these categorical distinctions between hard core and associate, and all their variations don't clarify much. They are artificial, too-easy ways of ordering a rather nonordered gang world.

But let me suggest how the membership gradient applies to some of the gang structures. For instance, Traditional and Neo-traditional gangs certainly contain the whole gamut of member commitment from the most hard-core to the least involved fringe members. But this occurs at *each* age level, in the age-related subgroups that comprise a large part of the overall gang. When Paco talked about O.G.s, Gs, and B.G.s within a clique or subgroup, he was trying to capture some of this. But he also believes that the overall structure of one or several hundred members, above and beyond the cliques, has a small number of O.G.s or shot callers who hold dominion over all others. This "super-gangster" is, in fact, so rare as to be of little value to our understanding of a gang's internal structure. But we can clearly distinguish a wide gradient of involvement in these Traditional and Neo-traditional gangs. And it bears repeating that who is and who is not highly committed can vary greatly from one observer to another. Remember my description of the gang member Paco, known to me by observation and by the report of other members as central to the group, yet unknown to Paco Domingo and the patrol officers in the area.

Contrast this situation with Specialty gangs. Let's take the drug gang as an instance. Here, to maintain a successful business, the group is smaller, tighter, and focused, with well-understood roles such as street dealers, lookouts, middlemen, maybe enforcers, and those hard-core older leaders who bank the proceeds and deal with the high level sources of the drugs. Here there can be few truly fringe members; there's an organized set of rules, each necessarily filled to accomplish the drug business. The reader can get a good feeling for this from reading Felix Padilla's book, *The Gang as an American Enterprise*, about a Puerto Rican drug gang in Chicago.

Collective gangs offer another contrast, because the membership in these is most ambiguous, most shifting, most inconstant. Mark Fleisher's description of his Fremont Hustlers in Kansas City provides a lovely depiction of this pattern, where (in his case) leadership or hard-core membership varied by function (drug source, social skills, house as hangout) and by time. Fluidity, not hierarchical structure, is typical in such a group.

Does gang structure make any practical difference? You bet it does. When Paco generalizes across gangs, failing to see the patterns that don't support his stereotypes, he obviates any appreciation of separate approaches to gang prevention and control. And when, paradoxically, he said in court, "you got to remember, each gang is unique," he just as clearly denied meaningful patterns.

We know several things from research that evaluates gang control programs, and from responses to gang programs. Research suggests clearly that different structures, to some extent, require different approaches. Let me offer three examples: Traditional, Neo-traditional, and Specialty gangs.

Most of the gang program evaluations have involved Traditional gangs. A quick summary of their results is that these programs have either had no effect, or have in fact made the problem worse, increasing gang cohesiveness and levels of gang crime. By singling out these gangs for special attention, the programs inadvertently provide the members *and potential recruits* with exactly what they want; identity, status, and a group in which to take pride. Gang size increases, members bond more tightly to each other, and offending levels increase. Paco knows about this, but he doesn't care, because his ideology drives his perceptions and masks available information.

In the case of Neo-traditional gangs, which the survey by the NYGC finds the most common by a narrow margin over Compressed gangs, the transition to the Traditional form will be facilitated for the same reasons. Nothing feeds gang cohesion among its members more than some form of common enemy—rival gangs or open attacks by police and others. The crackdowns by law enforcement, the harassment by Paco, will not deter the committed or the excitable gang member. Rather, the challenge of the attack will feed the gang member mentality, moving it toward the Traditional structure of more committed members.

By contrast, however, the Specialty gang should be Paco's meat. Harassment, special anti-gang injunctions, and a host of other crackdown procedures won't do much to reinforce an already well-structured gang. But this gang is in business, and it's hard to carry on gang business in the face of enhanced enforcement. Police visibility defeats drug selling; gang injunctions force the group to diffuse, to move to new but probably less lucrative market areas; the secret acts of Skinheads are hampered by publicity and ridicule.

Paco's advice? Crack down hard on *all* gangs.

My advice to Paco? Concentrate on the Specialty gangs; don't throw boomerangs at Traditional and Neo-traditional gangs. These latter groups are entrenched in their communities. Only heavy and sustained community development will alter the need for these long-standing gangs.

As for the Compressed gangs, maybe *no* action is best. They seem to be primarily adolescent groupings, and adolescents do mature eventually. It makes sense to avoid enhancing their identity and status, given the structure of these gangs. Rather, deal with *individual* members when an arrest is justified, and avoid stressing the individual's gang membership. Ignore his or her status—the *act* should get punished, not the membership. And given the adolescent status, perhaps some intervention with parents and teachers makes sense, though not for Paco, of course. This smacks of social work, and he's a crime fighter.

NOTES

1. Meaning to be beaten up by a group of fellow gang members.
2. A detailed description of a mixed-gender Collective gang, the Fremont Hustlers, is provided by Mark Fleisher's book, *Dead End Kids*, published in 1998 by the University of Wisconsin Press.

⑦

CHANGES IN STREET GANG CULTURE

In the old zoot suit days, a gang fight meant bare fists, a bicycle chain and maybe a knife. But now these people come in heavily armed. When a fight is over, there's a body or two on the street.

—*U.S. News and World Report*, September 17, 1973

The quote above was only barely true in 1973, but it was a harbinger of hard facts to come. I've suggested already that Paco changed over time, becoming more punitive in his approach to gang members and more extreme in his stereotype of the gangs. Such changes were not only the result of Paco's inherent character, they were also reactions to the changing gang scene over several decades. In the next chapter I'll look at this in terms of Paco's career in the department, but it is only fair to him in this chapter to document some of the changes in the gang world that helped propel his personal changes.

In my first field project with street gangs in the mid-1960s, the research team identified 800 gang members, male and female, over a three-year period. I came to know many of these youngsters through personal observations in public settings and in "club" meetings. I had conversations with many scores of them and, in truth, developed a personal fondness for many of them. I also learned to be wary of a number of them whose capacity for insincerity and manipulation was sometimes matched by their willingness to engage in violence—a level of violence beyond my capacity to tolerate. And yet, over those three years, among over 2,000 arrests and a myriad of violent incidents, only one homicide, a stabbing in a large crowd of youths, was reported by our gang workers or by the police.

Eight hundred gang members, three years, but only one killing. In today's media-hyped gang climate, that sounds truly anomalous. Yet, as Paco pointed out, "they fought with fists and clubs—there were no guns—and if someone got killed it was shocking, a tragic thing."

My second, smaller field project in the late 1960s, lasted just a year and a half. This was some six years after the first was initiated, and yielded a higher violence level. Among our 100 gang members, we logged 111 assaults, threats, and raids between our gang and others. Two of these resulted in deaths (one ours, one theirs). But within another two years of project completion, we learned of half a dozen more deaths, both from violence and from drug overdoses. I knew a number of these victims (and a couple of the perpetrators as well). The two projects were in different areas, involving different ethnic groups, but I couldn't escape the feeling that things were getting worse.

And certainly in one respect, they were worse. By the early 1970s, firearms were becoming more common, more accessible, and more lethal. Said Paco even then: "Today the weapon of choice among gangs is no longer a tire iron, or a baseball bat, or a bicycle chain or a zip gun. Gang members today are using high capacity assault weapons." I was seldom personally involved in situations where weapons were openly flashed, but several of these illustrate the change over time.

- Early on, in the company of a street worker assigned to a local gang, I watched a group of four of his gang members leaving a public playground swinging several weapons. One was a large, heavy chain, and another, a heavy club with a long spike sticking through the end of it. Both could be lethal, but the worker refused to react to their presence with "his boys" because he didn't want to lose rapport with them. Paradoxically, the same gang worker became director of a very punitive anti-gang corrections unit designed to return all released gang members to correctional institutions.

- Somewhat later, at a club meeting, a high-status gang member showed a large machete strapped in a sling inside his long coat. The worker saw it and did nothing. The worker's supervisor, a man I learned to admire greatly for his strength of character in dealing forthrightly with gang members, was also on the scene. He, too, saw the machete, walked quietly over to its owner and within thirty seconds and with no fuss he was carrying the weapon out to his car. He lost no rapport, but I'm sure gained further respect from the members present.

- Several years after this, I engaged an older gang member in conversation about the gun he said he was carrying. Perhaps in emulation of that earlier supervisor, I tried to persuade the owner to let me have the gun (I knew that as a child he had actually shot his own father). I was unsuccessful, perhaps because other members of the group were nearby and there was face to be saved. A week later, the same lad approached me with a smile on his face to say "Hey, Doc, you know that gun you wanted me to get rid of? Well, I did." I was very pleased of course—pleased with myself for my successful if delayed intervention. Maybe I saved someone's life, I thought, and a prison career for my gang member. But the bubble burst when he said, "Yeah, I traded it in on a Luger!"

I saw a .45 caliber gun up close once. It was pointed at me from five feet away by a nervous security guard who feared I was interfering with an arrest of a petty thief. To this day, I swear that gun was huge and I was truly unnerved; I didn't move a muscle until it was swung back toward the equally frightened thief, a homeless man who had tried to pilfer a bottle of wine from my local supermarket. I don't like guns, not in anyone's hands, be they cop or gang member.

Paco does like guns. He likes them for himself, for his partners, for shooting game and other targets when he vacations on the river. But he doesn't like them in the hands of his gang members. The proliferation of serious, lethal firearms among gangs over the past two decades has made his life more dangerous. It has sent him to court far more often to testify in assault and murder cases, and has decimated any residual humane feelings he might once have had for the socially oppressed gang member. If Paco has become relentless in his pursuit of violence, give some of the credit to the increase in gang violence itself: more assaults, more homicides, more lethal weapons readily available for use.

Give some credit, as well, to the enormous proliferation of street gangs across the nation. In 1960, there were about fifty places known to have gang problems. Most of these were in and closely connected to New York, Boston, Philadelphia, Chicago, El Paso, San Francisco, and Los Angeles. The number of known gang cities doubled by 1970, and doubled again by 1980, but then all hell broke loose. In a rapidly accelerating curve, the fifteen years from 1980 to 1995 saw a dramatic explosion of gang-involved cities, towns, and rural areas. The NYGC, using surveys supported by funds from the U.S. Department of Justice, located almost 5,000 law enforcement jurisdictions reporting gang activity in the mid- to late 1990s. Five thousand is a horrendous number. Many towns with fewer than 10,000 in population are involved. Almost all cities above 100,000 are involved. The media, politicians, police, and courts all over the nation have become alert to street gangs, even though most of the gangs are of the smaller, less criminal Compressed and Specialty type.

Paco has thus become one in a large number of gang cops across the country. I have personally interviewed over 250 of them, and our research surveys have added many hundreds more. Most are not hardened like Paco, but he's hardly alone out there. Police have come to see street gangs not as the peculiar abominations in the big cities of the 1960s, but as a widespread threat to law and order all around them. No wonder Paco feels he's fighting a losing battle: for over twenty years he has been.

This is not to say, of course, that Paco has seen or had to fight gangs in 5,000 jurisdictions, nor the 30,000 gangs or 800,000 gang members estimated to exist in the 1990s by the NYGC. But anywhere he goes he does see the signs of gang life. The culture of the gang has spread throughout the nation, diffusing even more widely in American youth culture. The graffiti he sees, the baggy pants and converted sports caps, the tattoos and earrings, the "gangsta rap" music he hears all remind him everywhere he goes that his problem is now a common one. The police have a saying about criminal suspects: if it walks like a duck, talks like a duck, and acts like a duck, than it probably *is* a duck. For Paco, if a youngster walks, talks, and acts like a gang member, he probably is one. And thanks to the media-based diffusion of gang culture, any kid in America can walk the walk and talk the talk. Paco sees them and hears them and knows in his gut that they will act the part as well; they cannot be tolerated.

Nor is this cultural diffusion of gang styles limited to Hispanic and black groups. There is some evidence of a reversion to some of the white gangs of the 1930s to 1950s, probably due to the emergence of street gangs in suburban communities. A gang cop in one such community in the Midwest told me of "some reports of white gangs, sometimes reflecting rivalries in the home countries—for instance Albanians versus Yugoslavians (we call 'em 'Wiggers'—'white niggers')." I'm pleased to report I never heard such direct racist remarks from Paco.

Along with the spread of gang culture comes the increase in challenges from gang member to gang member, gang to gang. Gang members used to join to *gain* respect. More and more in recent years Paco hears them *demanding* respect. To *dis* someone, to disrespect him is, as Paco hears it, the ultimate challenge, the final call to attack and retaliation among gang members. In a recent court case, for example, an inebriated white partygoer merely kicked the fender of a passing Asian gang member's car. Within an hour he lay dead, beaten and shot by a dozen vengeful Asian gang members.

Paco has become very sensitive to this payback norm, and then predictably overstates it. An attorney in court refers to threatening phone calls and a drive-by, and asks Paco about the likely response.

Paco: Given the totality of all those circumstances involved, there's going to be payback.

Q: That's *any* gang member thinks that way?

A: Exactly. Correct. The turf is an area the gang claims; the area that they will defend, they will guard. *Anybody* that intrudes upon that turf from a rival gang, some kind of violent confrontation *will* occur. An individual that commits a violent act, such as a drive-by shooting, would be considered in the gang culture as being someone of greater stature. They would be someone the gang would look up to.

The italics in this quote are mine, added to point to the overstatements in which Paco has come lately to indulge. No qualifications are offered; *all* gang members *always* do this in *all* cases is the message to the jury, or to any audience calling on Paco's expertise. And the newspapers will quote him: Gospel truth. Did he say that the 18th Street gang had 20,000 members? Then that ridiculous number must be true and that figure is printed in the papers, repeated on the TV news, and becomes part of official truth. Don't dis Paco.

Another change over the years that has affected Paco's stance is in the ages of gang members. Research does not demonstrate that younger kids have regularly become involved in gangs, but there's no debate about the other end. Paco and researchers alike can no longer talk only about "youth gangs" or "delinquent gangs," groups whose effects on the rest of us might be considered slight and likely to ease as maturation settled in. Street gangs, especially of the Traditional and Specialty types, have increasingly involved older members, people in their twenties and thirties.

Why should such an age expansion have taken place? One reason, certainly, was the increasing joblessness among minority youth beginning in the early 1980s. The pattern was highly visible in the changing job markets, the movement of large industries and employers out of the central city, and the consequent loss of opportunity. With nothing to ease them out of gangs, more of the older members retained their gang affiliation and activity. The "bangers" became "hangers."

Second, new or expanded criminal enterprises, the drug markets in particular, called for other participants, those less subject to teenage uncertainties. Check out the ages of arrested members of drug gangs, and you'll find they are typically between the early twenties and mid-forties. Adolescent gang members can't be trusted very far with vials of crack cocaine, with large financial proceeds, or with loyalty to the enterprise when under police interrogation.

Finally, Paco suggests, and I think he's correct, that the respect accorded to the O.G.s, is enough to keep some of them "hanging and banging" around the younger members. Remember that most youth join gangs for the identity and status they were not otherwise getting. Hanging on into older age continues to satisfy such needs.

What does this mean for Paco? A greater challenge. Older gang members are more mature, trickier, more likely to be doing serious harm in the community, more likely to use violent methods, more likely to bring prison gang experience with them, and so on. They epitomize the enemy more clearly.

Does the O.G. want to "retire?" Another myth that Paco feeds with his overstatements is that once you're a gang member, there's no getting out. I know from research that most gang members—not all—get out informally, by swearing off and just not hanging around anymore. Jobs and girlfriends, wives, children help a good bit. But to Paco, leaving the gang is more difficult: "If the gang member has upon his body some kind of sign or symbol that represents the gang, the sign or symbol has to come off and they don't take you down to the local hospital and laser it off. They cut it off, burn it off, or some violent act like that."

> *Attorney:* To quit the gang and get out of the lifestyle, what options does one have?
>
> *Paco:* He could attempt to petition them and try the march-out method, which would probably mean he would die. He could try to move out of the area and run, which would probably mean he would die. Probably his only method to get out safely would be to cooperate with law enforcement and hope for a witness protection program.

This latter quote is more than mere exaggeration. It is clearly self-serving as Paco was testifying against a fringe gang member accused of having performed a contract "hit" on an older, vicious gang member who had become an informant for local police and the U.S. Drug Enforcement Agency (DEA). This time, Paco tries to invoke sympathy for a truly bad actor in order to get the maximum penalty for the accused. He failed. The weak evidence for this motive led to a plea bargain of only five years in prison.

The drug selling connection to street gangs starting in the early 1980s with the crack cocaine explosion is another change seriously affecting Paco. While it is certainly true that some number of street gang members, especially among black gangs, became visibly and widely involved in street sales of crack, and thereafter other drugs, it is *not* the case that they became centrally involved in the mid- and upper-levels of drug distribution. The research nationally on this is quite clear. But Paco, many large urban police departments, and far-removed federal agencies such as the FBI and the DEA came to believe that street gangs had become the principal drug marketers of America. Further, they endorsed wholesale an undocumented belief that gangs automatically brought increased violence to the drug markets. It was a convenient myth, bringing two evils together in a pattern of great appeal to the public and the media.

Many things resulted from this presumed confluence of evils, drugs, and gangs. The FBI got into the street gang investigation business, and the DEA applied its drug control and RICO (Racket Involved Conspiracy Organizations) mechanisms to local gangs. Police gang units and narcotics units attempted to mount joint operations and politicians and legislators wrote new laws targeting street gangs as criminal organizations. Paco, like many others, had ever more reason to approach street gangs as unrepentant monsters selling dope for profit and destroying additional lives beyond those taken by firearms. Total suppression of gangs was justified, and no amount of contrary research findings about the weak gang/drug nexus could penetrate this mentality. But trust me: if we had gotten rid of the drugs, the gangs still would be there, and if we had gotten rid of the gangs, the drugs would still be there.

Finally, and in a similar vein, the formation of formal prison gangs reinforced Paco's view of the seriousness of the problem. Prison gangs formed separately in the 1970s and 1980s among black, Hispanic, and white convicts to serve as protection against each other. In some instances, prison control was seriously affected by these gangs, and assaults and murders became all too common occurrences.

Eventually, street gang members sent to prison often felt that for their own protection they must join prison gangs like the Mexican Mafia ("La EME"), the Black Guerilla Family, or the Aryan Brotherhood. Often they were recruited, willingly or otherwise. There was not a strong connection between prison gangs and street gangs out on the street, but there was nonetheless much talk of such a connection, especially around rackets such as the drug market. Some of these were affected by, even run by, the prison gang members inside the joint.

The confusion of prison gangs with street gangs became quite common, and Paco was sucked into this, just as he was into the gang and crack mythology. And since prison gangs were characterized as tightly organized, vicious, "do or die" operations, for Paco the connection became yet another proof of the importance of his job as a street gang cop. Once again, in the court testimony below, I have emphasized certain phrases to illustrate his overstating the evidence.

Q: Now, ultimately did the Mexican Mafia grow to where they actually controlled the day-to-day activity of the street gangs?

A: Yes, Ma'am. Only about 400 members and most of them are locked up in our more secure facilities, so very few of them operate outside the prison, but they control *all* Hispanic gangs in the areas that they operate out of. For instance, Los Angeles has about 90,000 Hispanic gang members, so the few Mexican Mafia members who operate there *control that huge army.*

Q: What happens when a gang member is placed on the green light list? (The green light list is of "hit" targets chosen by the prison gang.)

A: Well, first of all *every*— if they are on the street—*gang member* of the surrounding gangs who is a loyal [member] will attack at *every* opportunity. Then if a person is in custody, *any* loyal [member] who is in custody and has access to the person of that gang *will* attempt to assault him.

There is, of course, more than a modicum of truth to such depictions. Prison gangs can and do order hits. Sometimes these are carried out. Dozens of people have died as a result. But this is not *the* pattern; it occurs in some areas, among some gangs, at some times. But the Pacos of the police world (and other worlds) have bought the pattern as an overall reality. When they do, no wonder, again, that they offer extreme solutions. Paco didn't start with such views, but the changing nature of the gang world took him over, and in truth he was ready, by the nature of his character, to be taken over. And so Paco Domingo, my quiet juvenile officer, became my less-than-admirable gang cop. That path is described in the next chapter.

8

CHANGES IN PACO'S CAREER

Criminology Student: "I'm really impressed with these juvenile officers: they seem smart, and they really care about kids."

Police Researcher: "Yes, that's often true, but if you scratch a juvenile officer, underneath you'll find a cop."

Long before he became a gang cop, and before his years in the juvenile division, Paco took his turn in patrol. He was in patrol when he and Sgt. Bascom came to see me in my office, as described in Chapter 1. In those early days, I asked to go cruising with him again on several occasions. This is when I began to warm up to him: within that gruff exterior there was a cop's humor that I came to appreciate in him and in other cops as well.

When you go out on a ride-along in Paco's department, you first have to sign a formal waiver, taking responsibility for anything that might happen to you. You wanna play cop, you don't blame them for what happens. It's a formality, of course. Your escorts do their very best to make sure you remain safe. The waiver also reminds you that patrol business is serious business. One of my male students reported going on a ride-along where the first call was to the scene of a bank robbery in progress. As he told the story, just as the patrol car pulled into the bank's parking lot, the driver yelled at the student in the back seat, "duck down, now!" As he did so, a shotgun blast splattered the rear window behind him. No injuries, but a full plate of fear. It's the kind of story that stays with you when you go out.

My first venture with Paco was as dull as possible, the midnight shift (4:00 to 12:00 P.M.) with only a few minor calls on either side of free food at a hamburger take-out joint. At one point, we passed a small industrial plant with high fencing topped by rusting barbed wire. Paco stopped by the fence and signaled me for silence: "There should be a guard dog there, and I don't hear it." He turned on his spotlight and lit up areas beyond the fence, finally locating the dog on the top step of a doorway, sound asleep.

The spotlight did not wake the dog, a large Doberman. Paco honked the horn, and still no reaction. Then he took an electric megaphone from the back seat, set it out the window, and barked furiously at the dog—"woof, woof, woof you mother-fucker." The dog stirred, raised its head, made a low growl, and settled down again. It was enough; we drove on into the night, seeking further adventure but finding none. I tore up my waiver.

Some months later we went out again, this time with Sgt. Bascom as driver. The area was strictly industrial, no residences or retail businesses. The streets were totally empty by midnight, and we simply cruised aimlessly, it seemed to me, until about 3:00 A.M. Then we spotted a large van on the opposite side of the street. There seemed to be no reason for it to be there, so Bascom passed the van, did a U-turn, and pulled up behind it. Bascom got out and approached the driver's side. Paco and I approached the passenger's side, but Paco signaled me to stay well behind him. I couldn't see what Bascom was doing, but Paco approached the van door, cautiously stepped up on a narrow running board, and peered in. I was close enough to hear what followed, as Paco asked, "What are ya doing here? It's three o'clock, nothing's open, this isn't a parking lot. You gonna answer me? Don't just make faces at me, man. I asked you what you're doing here at three o'clock."

There seemed to be no response. Paco signaled that I could come forward. I did, climbed up, and peered in. As I turned back to Paco, I saw the biggest grin on his face I'd ever seen, or ever would again. He had been having a conversation with a large German shepherd. The van was otherwise empty.

Most patrol beats are pretty dull. Anything that breaks the pattern of monotony is welcomed, whether it's a silly animal incident or a hot call. Patrol for Paco was not all it was cracked up to be. He wanted more action. He had seen some in Vietnam. After finishing high school and having little idea where he should go, Paco opted for the Marines. There's no surprise in that; many police come to their profession after a stint in the armed services, and the Marines is thought to be a great training ground. Paco was a Marine. So was Rafael Perez, the LAPD gang cop who precipitated the largest police scandal in decades.

For Paco, the Marines meant order and structure, uniform codes of behavior and serious goals, a cohesive organization and camaraderie. In fact, it sounds eerily like his stereotype of the Traditional gang. One former Marine cop meets another; "Hooh-ah," they both call out, cementing the old ties. Paco went further; he joined the military police and although he didn't know it at the time, received his first exposure to his ultimate antagonists. Both in Vietnam and during his assignments to bases in the Southwest and the West, he came across gang members who, understandably, had trouble adjusting to the rigors of Marine life. They were the scumbags of the corps, and he learned early to disrespect their ways.

From the Marines to a college program in criminal justice was an easy transition for Paco and many others. It was at the training academy that patrol was offered as *real* police work, and Paco bought the story for a while. He was offered no lessons on street gangs—they were a tangential problem in his early days on the force. He was given only eight hours of class time on juvenile matters. Almost all of this was on special juvenile procedures, not on the nature of delinquents or delinquency. It seemed as if an assignment to juvenile would be an assignment to paperwork and social work; not his style.

But a significant series of events changed all this. After two years in patrol, a brief stint at the jail reintroduced Paco to street gangs—mostly kids in their late teens who surprised him with their veneer of toughness and all-for-one-and-one-for-all moral code. The Marine in him could understand this, even if it was in the wrong hands. He was then reassigned to the juvenile division, not long after we first met in the mid-1960s. In many police departments, "juvie" is the pits; it's the counterpart to outpatient departments in major surgical centers. Juvenile is low status, "diaper dicks," "Kiddie Korps." But not so in this department; Paco took the assignment because he was told that juvie was a fast route up to detective, to "real" investigative work.

And indeed it was. His first captain took a high-level state job. His first lieutenant went on to be a watch commander and eventually chief of a suburban police department. Bascom spent two years in juvenile, and was promoted out as lieutenant in the detective division, then captain—one of the first black command officers in the department. He ended up as a high-ranking official in the civil rights division of the U.S. Department of Justice. Officers who shone in juvenile could go on to robbery-homicide, the narcotics division, and other choice assignments. Paco felt briefly ambitious, so juvie had an obvious appeal. He had not yet learned what was at the core of his own character, that he was to be, at heart, a street cop.

Paco's first spot was as one of two juvenile officers at a local station house. His "partner" was a twenty-year veteran who knew all the ropes, all the procedures, but had retired in place. They never patrolled outside together, because the kids were brought to the station. Paco's partner was good with kids, firm with parents, and believed in prevention. He was typical of quite a few veteran juvenile officers who would stay on to pension time and knew they were not moving up in the department. Paco learned much from him at first, but despaired of the man's loss of zeal for police work.

The station was old, although a new modern one was being built. All brick—dirty brick—on the outside; inside, it was cramped by temporary walls and lines of desks. Kids came in and were placed in holding tanks—barred cells—until Paco or his partner could get the appropriate paperwork under way and interview them at a desk, in full hearing of a dozen or more detectives crammed into the same room. If the parent was there he, or usually she, was accommodated by drawing up another chair. Confidentiality was not and could not be offered in such a setting.

It was a lousy place to deal with a family, but then so was the whole neighborhood. The station was next door to two bail bondsmen's storefronts, close to a fire station with its sirens, down just a block from an overcrowded, fenced-in elementary school built almost seventy years earlier. The homes were duplexes, apartments, and homes with chicken-coop-sized houses or converted garages in the backyard. Auto shops, gas stations, storefront churches, and liquor stores broke the monotony of the residences. It wasn't a slum, but it wasn't where you'd want to raise your child. The old station house was a visible reminder of this. Even the station was the occasional target for the ever-present graffiti.

But then the department decided to centralize its juvenile division. Leaving each older station with a veteran officer, like Paco's older partner, it moved all other juvenile officers into a remodeled four-story building close to downtown. Named for its street, the Columbia Road building was hidden behind some car dealerships, wholesale furniture stores, and nondescript commercial buildings. No one came to Columbia Road except cops, kids, and parents. Nearby, however, was a cavernous German restaurant with evening *gemutlichkeit* musical entertainment and terrific food. It became one of my favorite haunts for lunch and dinner when visiting Paco and his buddies at Columbia Road.

If you didn't know, you wouldn't readily recognize Columbia Road as a police facility. It didn't bristle with antennas on the roof like other stations. The parking lot had a few black and whites (patrol cars), but mostly unmarked juvie cars and private autos. I remember one clear identifier in

1964, however; almost every car in the lot, including Paco's, sported "Goldwater for President" bumper stickers. Cops are a conservative lot.

The interior was spacious. On the third floor were enough holding tanks to handle the needs of the whole city for temporary detention until kids were transported to the secure facilities at the Juvenile Court Detention Center. On the second floor were most of the offices for juvenile officers and detectives. There was also the newly established gang office, to which I'll return in a moment. There was a small weight room for those like Paco who wanted to keep their muscles tuned up. Downstairs there was the "cop shop" (squad room), several meeting rooms, some interrogation rooms with one-way glass and hidden mikes. The juvenile commander's office was cavernous and doubled as a meeting room. I divided most of my time between the commander's office and the juvie desks upstairs.

I would have spent more time in the gang office, but at that early stage in gang unit development, it was a farce. There were three so-called gang intelligence officers. They were not field officers, but merely gathered information from arrest reports that were filed at Columbia Road and occasionally interviewed juvenile gang members when the detectives were through with them. I was shown their intelligence files on the gangs involved in my project. Where we had rosters of well over 100 members active in each group, they had 10 or 15. Their mug shots were up to three years old, making many of them all but unrecognizable. They had *no* information on the girls' groups, although we were observing seven female auxiliary gangs with up to 200 total members. They knew little about the gang structures, size, or criminal involvement. Our gang workers were way, way ahead of these guys. I hasten to add that two decades later, gang intelligence in large departments like Paco's had vastly improved and continues to do so now.

The gang unit's approach was epitomized by their proudest accomplishment. A large, citywide map was affixed to one wall of the office. On it were located all the gang-related incidents for several years, those brought to their attention by the juvenile officers, other patrol or detective units, and the various city newspapers (none of whom, of course, had a common definition of what constituted a "gang-related" incident). On their map were scores of pushpins, one for each incident at its reported location. There were black pins for black gangs, brown pins for Hispanic gangs, and yellow pins for a few Asian gangs. There were no white pins.

Paco showed me this room, but he was not part of the unit. I've never asked him, but I'd bet he would look back on this "gang intelligence" with the same disdain as I had at the time. This was not his kind of police work.

But while at Columbia Road, Paco did find ways to exercise his talents more directly, finding targets for his energies. He learned to hate parents and caretakers who seriously abused their young children. On a number of occasions, to prove to me that he was doing serious, important police work, he opened up case files and put them in front of me. They contained photos, some in gruesome color, of tiny children, even babies, with the open wounds and scars of physical abuse: battered and sliced penises, cigarette burns on vaginas, arms, and legs; and backs discolored with large bruises and sharp, pinpoint lacerations. I stopped looking after awhile; I had two young daughters and didn't want my images of them to meld with the images I was being shown. But Paco had made his point. He was doing real police work, finding the evidence and taking to court the "perps," the perpetrators of real violence against innocent victims.

He also dabbled with drug education in the schools—precursors to the politically oversold DARE (Drug Awareness and Resistance Education) program—and came to believe in prevention only in the sense of prevention at an early age. Get to the kids, get to their parents, using teachers as informants, before the path to crime could be established. Youth sports programs, especially boxing and martial arts, took some of his time. When juvenile reform laws spread across the country in the mid- and late 1970s, this was helpful too. It took responsibility away from the police for minor offenders such as runaways, incorrigible kids, truants, kids engaging in early drinking and sex. It left juvie and Paco with a chance to concentrate on more serious issues such as sexual abuse, pedophiles, young drug sellers, possible kidnappings, and—increasingly—street gangs. Each of these let Paco play detective, got him out on the street, and enabled him to start fulfilling his need to develop the tough cop role.

In the process, he moved up to *Sergeant* Domingo, a status he both enjoyed and feared. He enjoyed it because he could now call the shots, train the troops, and set some priorities. He feared it because it cost him some street time, required more paperwork, made him more responsible for the actions of others, and—most of all—took him closer to the "suits," the lieutenants and the commander at Columbia Road. He didn't much like this; they were no longer real cops, having become organization men.

But before long, he was busted back down to Officer Domingo for ignoring chains of command and hotdogging on his own. Paco had developed what I call "the practitioner's conceit": the feeling that if you're doing the job, you must be doing it right. You were trained for it, you were experienced in it, and you got what you were sure were good results, therefore you were on top of things. This conceit is not peculiar to police; it is shared by many social workers, lawyers, certain judges, many teachers (including university faculty), physicians, and so on. I always recall the quote from a juvenile counselor, "I can't believe that fifteen minutes with me won't help any kid." Keep in mind that what Paco saw as his strengths in Columbia Road, others saw as problems: responsibility principally to himself, the need to be in control and not be controlled by others, disdain for teamwork, lack of concern for organizational needs and realities, and chafing at the bit of supervision.

At this point, when he was busted back down—not to his total dissatisfaction—Paco looked for other paths. Juvenile was no longer doing anything for his career or his frame of mind. He saw it as the home for female officers and old-timers. He had some obvious choices: training, organized crime, internal affairs, the narcotics squad, vice, anything that didn't require him to give up his autonomy but challenged him as a true crime-fighter. Investigations, he learned at Columbia Road, took too much patience and provided too little action. He'd never be a good detective. As a sergeant, he could have taken the lieutenant's exam, so I asked him why he didn't. He saw no point in that; he'd be a "suit," and too far from the street. Paco was in fact learning who Paco was.

And then there was the gang unit. These were being formed in the late 1970s, and needed experienced street cops, not the kind he saw putting pins in maps at Columbia Road. He asked around, talked more with me, and heard things he liked:

- Street gangs were pulling in older members.
- Guns and violence were increasing in gangs.
- Gangs thought the street belonged to *them*.
- Most juvenile homicides were gang related.
- Prison gangs were beginning to form, and in some cases to connect with street gangs.
- In gang work, you could (if you wanted) be out of uniform, you could work irregular hours, and supervision was loose. The suits didn't know gang work, just wanted it handled and cleaned up.

Did I mention Paco's academic career? After the Marines, he went to school at a state college and majored, of course, in criminal justice. I never got the sense that much of the training rubbed off. It was too intellectualized, not practical enough for him. He remembered one professor in particular. She had done a study in a large southwestern city that concluded that the gang situation there was not what had been claimed, that a "moral pan..c" had been created by the police department for their own purposes. This had infuriated Paco at the time; police create a problem in order to fight it? Crazy! Gangs created themselves, and professors should stay out of the way of legitimate police business. The threat was real, not "created." That memory helped tip the balance. Paco applied for the gang unit.

It turned out he still had to pay his dues. Before Paco could hit the streets, a "suit" learned of his academic training and his tenure in the juvenile division that included some early prevention activities. He was assigned to learn how to identify kids who are most likely to join street gangs. Early identification, said the "suit," will let us do early prevention. Sounds easy, but it isn't. And Paco failed, as fail he must at that point. What led kids to join gangs was only partially understood.

Kids joined for status, for identity, for something to belong to, for excitement, for protection. Some joined to increase their delinquent activities. All this was known, and academics and police could agree on much of it, albeit putting different emphasis on the delinquent activity component.

Paco and researchers also knew that gangs emerge in poorer areas of the city, mostly among marginalized and minority populations, where employment is lower, schools are worse, adult criminals are more active, families are less intact yet larger, and so on. But this, too, was not enough because administrators asked Paco *which* kids are most at risk? In all but the very worst gang areas, most gang-aged youth do *not* join or commit themselves to gangs. Best estimates, in most gang areas, are that somewhere between 5 and 20 percent of kids will become gang members. How do they differ from the other 80 to 95 percent of kids *in those same neighborhoods?* This emphasis is important: gang and non-gang youth share poverty, poor schools, broken families, and all the rest. So why do some join, and others not? That was the answer Paco sought, and it wasn't available. But it was a good question, and he puzzled over it for many years.

Were he given that same assignment today, Paco could do better. We could point him to some research in different cities that yield similar results. Start with this discouraging fact: there are well over a hundred factors ("variables" in the criminologists' argot) that predict which kids are likely to become the more delinquent. There are factors about the individual, the family, the schools, the peers, and the neighborhood that produce fairly good predictions—*fairly* good, but not yet *very* good predictions.

But when you apply these same factors to both gang and non-gang youth *from the same neighborhood*, most of them fail to predict which kids will be gang and which will be non-gang. The best bet, of course, is to predict that *none* of them will join gangs. You'd be right in somewhere between 80 and 95 percent of these predictions. That's a helluva good batting average. But if we want to mount *gang-specific* programs, we want to go at the other end; so how can we predict the 5 to 20 percent who will join?

Simple answer number one: we can only do it imperfectly, with lots of errors. Answer number two: we can do better than chance. Researchers have been finding some important factors that make gang membership more likely in a gang-involved community. To summarize research in Rochester, Denver, Seattle, Long Beach, and San Diego, these are at least the following:

1. Earlier involvement in delinquent activities
2. Earlier self-concept as a delinquent
3. Absence of helpful adults outside the family
4. Exposure to a set of stressful critical events, such as parental break-up, death in the family, broken love-matches, etc.
5. Family members in a gang or in serious legal trouble
6. Lower family supervision or monitoring
7. Delinquently oriented friends
8. Friends who accept or endorse violent forms of conflict-resolution
9. Enjoyment from "hanging around" the neighborhood with friends
10. Lower commitment to school, lower expectations for higher education
11. Higher levels of exposure to violence in the neighborhood
12. Higher levels of disrespect for officials, especially police

Kids with a number of such strikes against them are not going to find a happy place at home, in school, in the formal activities provided in the community. But they can find a place in a street gang. I don't believe we have to wait for the gang unit to "document" youngsters as gang members and then crack down on them. We can try to identify them beforehand and try our luck at early intervention. I think Paco was moving in this direction with his early juvenile officer career. It was only later in his gang unit days that he became committed to cracking down on the failed kids.

But this is now, and that was then, so Paco went to work as a gang cop, using the accumulating experience of his new cohorts and his own exposures to street gangs. One of his first assignments was to start lecturing at the police academy on juvenile matters generally, and gangs specifically. Early in the process he asked me to give a talk on street gangs. Naturally, I jumped at the opportunity to "educate" a class of fifty police recruits.

I jumped at it also for a very personal reason. My wife had died some years before from cancer, and I was left to raise two young daughters on my own. I learned, slowly but surely, to be a listener—a good listener. I learned how to take on new attitudes—more nurture, more patience—but I also found a new need, to be listened to myself. My wife, fully engaged as mother and professional teacher, had nonetheless also found time to listen to my ranting about gangs and gang workers and cops and justice systems. I lost that audience with her death. Now I needed my own children to take an interest in my work.

It was a need destined to be unfulfilled, but I was slow to appreciate that. Their world was full of other needs; satisfying mine was a low priority. But for a while I tried. The lecture for Paco was an example. My elder daughter, by then around fifteen, had never heard me lecture (or, more properly, watched me perform professionally). So I invited her to join me that evening; watch Dad do his thing, and be proud! It was a beautiful evening to go out, a subtle sunset and a clear pewter sky as we headed downtown to meet Paco. We transferred to his car—a big old relic that said of its owner, "I'm big, I'm substantial, and I've been around." It was a macho machine.

We drove out to the academy in some silence—I was reviewing my notes and overhead projections—parked in the "Instructors Only" section of the lot and walked, passing jogging and exercising officers in sweats, to the bungalow classroom. In the background were the muffled sounds from the indoor pistol range. Next to the bungalow was an old car with bullet holes ranging from .22 caliber dents to gaping "entrance wounds" inches wide from .45s and God knows what else. It was a display for the visitor, and my Laurie's eyes were wide, indeed; *Dragnet, Adam–12*, all the police TV shows came alive.

The lecture went well, I thought. My performance was before fifty arbitrarily stiff bodies with disinterested faces and bored eyes. They were required to listen to the outsider with his foreign words—cohesiveness, sociopath, functional leadership, group norms, social disorganization. But I spiced it up for them with case examples and a little cop talk—knuckleheads, punks, assholes for gang members; code three for lights and sirens authorized; crackheads and controlled buys in the drug world; hang and bang, throwing signs for gang behaviors. I even threw in St. Michael, patron saint of the police.

I received the required polite applause. On the drive back, I waited for Laurie's comments—I'd have settled for "wow," or "cool, Dad," or "awesome." But nothing came out of the backseat. So finally I turned around and said, "So, what did you think?" The answer, "It was OK, Dad," deflated me fully, and properly so, I suppose. But I was still intent on engaging her in my world, so I turned to Paco as we approached the station and my car: "So, Paco, now you've been through patrol, and lots of years in juvenile. Where do you want to end up?"

"Homicide!" burst forth from his mouth without a moment's delay. I heard Laurie behind me push forward quickly to the edge of the backseat. Her hand reached up to the back of his seat and I saw her with eyes and mouth wide open—Go, *Adam–12*, go!

"Why homicide?" I asked. As best I can retrieve it (no notes taken), his response, tight-lipped but emotional, was: "I wanna take those assholes off the street. I want 'em burned. I want the action. That's what all cops want."

Finally for Laurie, I was in an exciting world after all, if only by association with Paco, a real cop. My lecture was forgotten, but she'll never forget that big guy in the big car with the straight talk. Paco's charisma as crime fighter has to be kept in mind in assessing his impact in our world of criminals and victims. He was tailor-made for community audiences, for news reporters, for police rookies, and even for my students (and, obviously for young, impressionable fifteen-year-olds).

One other episode, this one with my students, demonstrates this dramatic character. Paco came to my class in delinquency on one occasion to talk about the street confrontation between officer and suspect. He emphasized the need for the officer to establish control of the situation— swiftly and certainly—"hands on the car," or "on your knees," or "prone out" (lie flat on the ground), whatever is required. But, my students asked, what about their rights, what about the Miranda rule, they're only suspects after all. Paco's answer was swift. "I'll take control first, anyway I can; then I'll read them their damn rights."

Joining the gang squad and becoming immersed and expert in street gang affairs soon became very serious business and the core of Paco's existence. There are peculiarities about elite units like a gang squad that can create caricatures of its members. This happened slowly to Paco, and I'll describe more of this in later chapters of this book. I could observe this transformation because Paco stayed on the force well past minimum retirement age. After twenty years, he could have pulled out with a pension at half-pay, still young enough to take on another job. But Paco knew he could never be happy as a security guard or an investigator for some attorney who might, of all things, work for the defense. No, Paco stayed in place, rose again to sergeant, and became an expert not just locally but nationally. We both ended up with the same reputation: have lecture, will travel.

9

STREET GANG NEIGHBORHOODS

I don't blame the citizens. I've seen what the gangs can do, and they have every right to be frightened.

—Paco

A recent news item reported a series of gang incidents in which three members of warring gangs were shot and killed. The setting was a metropolitan suburb of mixed ethnicity—Blacks, Hispanics, and middle-class Whites known for their high proportions of artists and older residents who refused to abandon their homes. This had been a gang-involved community for over two decades, with several rival Traditional gangs yielding cycles of increased and decreased violence since at least 1980. Such cycles are the norm; gang activity and gang violence wax and wane, with the quiet periods longer lasting than the explosive ones.

This particular community has been the site of numerous attempts at gang control. One of these, followed by a quiet period, resulted in the first President Bush's declaring it one of his thousand points of light. But the light soon went out as a new cycle of violence emerged. Most recently, a new attempt at control came in the form of a civil injunction imposed by a local judge. The heightened police surveillance claimed success until, that is, three dead gang members betrayed the claim.

There was a poignant epilogue to the story. A female resident, hearing the shots and the sirens, stepped outside her home with her flute, sending soft tones into the air. "I believe music can change things, so I was out there just trying to put some positive mood on the situation," she told a news reporter.

Well, bless her for the thought. Paco's comment about similar situations where residents must respond to a gang attack was characteristically different. "When he's back on the street, shooting up the witness's home and threatening to 'get him' if he shows up in court, a person has a tendency to believe the threat because the kid is loose three hours after he shot somebody." Two choices allegorically present themselves: hide, or play the flute on your front step.

Paco asked me what I thought was the single most important factor in explaining gangs. I gave the question a good deal of thought, but decided I couldn't provide a single answer. On the other hand, if the question had been about the single important factor that has been most ignored, I think I do have an answer, a one-word answer: neighborhood, or community.

These young people aren't born as gang members. The doctor doesn't slap their behinds at birth and announce to the mother, "Congratulations; you've just given birth to a fine, healthy homeboy." Street gangs *emerge*—out of families, out of circumstances, out of communities.

What does a gang neighborhood look like? It's hard to answer that without engaging in some unfortunate stereotyping. There are, after all, some middle-class neighborhoods with considerable gang activity. Skinhead groups can be found in middle-class, upper-class, and rural communities. But if we talk about simply the majority of gang areas, then some patterns begin to emerge. One of them is the abundance of "busy places" where people congregate and seem to draw in youngsters who like to hang around the neighborhood. Look for fast turnover motels, liquor stores, fast-food spots, check-cashing outlets, bars, and local parks, and so on. Busy places are good spots for impressionable youth to come across people at the edges: petty crooks, O.G.s.

That's the gang neighborhood through the eyes of Paco and other officers newly assigned to an inner-city station house. Paco has worked at several of them over the years, including the one where we first started our ride-alongs, and then the Columbia Road juvenile headquarters. He also worked out of the worst of the worst, and had little respect for many of the residents. "When we were contracted to serve that community, five families moved out the next day." In that station house, the whole second floor had to be closed as too dangerous. It took ten years to replace it because bond campaigns for police stations and schools are so seldom successful. A member of the local city council had an answer to that, noting that the public is always willing to pass bond issues for more prisons: "Let's declare all public schools to be prisons," he said. "Then the schools will get their money."

There is a natural ecology that develops around police stations in a good-sized city, and this ecology describes the look of many gang neighborhoods. First of all, Paco doesn't need an exact address to find the station. If he knew the approximate area, he could just look for the building with a roof dedicated to antennas. They stick out above the surrounding structures, coming in various forms: tall, derrick-like structures more typical of radio stations; tall, single spikes; small and large TV dishes; and solid frames with several base-drum forms mounted one above the other. It looks as if some modern artist working in mixed-metal sculpture had been commissioned to decorate the roofs, and his fancy ran wild. The flags are another clue; federal, state, and municipal. And, of course, the parking lots are peppered with patrol cars, vans, and other equipment. But it's the antennas that first signal the station's location. Another constant is the bail bondsman signs and stores, one or many depending on the size of the precinct and the poverty level of the neighborhood.

Then, in various numbers scattered among the apartment houses, duplexes, and small single-family homes are churches—standard, Pentecostal, and storefront; fast-food outlets and delis mirroring the racial, ethnic, and national origins of the community; minimarts and donut shops; garages, auto supply stores, video and alarm outlets; cafes and liquor stores; small law offices, an occasional social service center, and local parochial and public elementary schools. In many of these locations there are small knots of older men outside the store, young kids walking to and fro, and groups of older youth gathered about, some gang and some not.

Some stations seem almost sterile in their appearance, typically two-story buildings fronting on a main street, with little street action to suggest any vibrancy to the community. Others, especially the older ones like Paco's first location, may be several stories higher, dark brick, unimaginative square hulks looking out on streets busy with local color. Pedestrian and auto traffic pass by as if there were no station there at all. Usually, Paco found himself assigned to those older structures with their cramped interiors, sometimes with trailers or makeshift huts in the back parking lot to handle the overflow of special units.

The first constant among the stations in Paco's life is the concern for security. Until the last few years, my visits to the gang unit were informal, often with little planning needed. One merely parked in the visitors' lot or on the street, and walked in. "Hi, guys; Paco around?" But now I must empty my pockets, set the briefcase on the rolling belt, and step through the metal detector. Then they ask my name, call through to the squad room for Paco to come out to meet his visitor, provide an ID badge to pin on my shirt or jacket, and maybe look through my briefcase again. My visit is entered in an official logbook. I walk directly to the gang office; no loitering allowed.

I preferred meeting Paco elsewhere—his car, my office (no security problems there), a fast-food joint—at the loss of the atmosphere that only a squad room can supply. I mentioned this exchange in an earlier chapter: When I started my second gang project, this time on the streets of a Traditional Hispanic gang area, Paco had been assigned to a nearby gang unit, housed in a trailer behind the station house. I told him I was coming into his "hood" to find out more about why kids join gangs and he responded with a sneer: "Why do you want to go there; every kid in there is a gang member." He was already failing to see the community in any more than gang terms. Yet, as my research team soon learned, there were several thousand gang-age youth in Ladino Hills, and only slightly over a hundred were actively engaged in the local gang, the Latins.

For a year and a half, our team—three research staff, two workers, and combined assistant worker/research observer—worked the Ladino Hills area. Our purpose was to reduce gang delinquency through a series of strategies designed to reduce gang cohesiveness. We were convinced, after four years in the first project, that counseling and direct anti-delinquency talk and creation of "club" activities would not reduce delinquency. Rather, we saw that it increased both cohesiveness and delinquency. This was the same result in gang projects in Boston and Chicago as well. So, in Ladino Hills, we set out to reverse things: reduce cohesiveness, and watch to see if gang activity and crime went down.

We were remarkably successful in reaching our early goals. Most of the change took place within the first six months and then continued through the final twelve months of the project. Clique membership dissolved, cohesiveness was reduced by 40 percent, recruitment into the Latins first dropped to zero at six months, and then again at the eleventh and thirteenth months, not to start up again. The number of arrests of Latins was reduced by 35 percent.

But that's not the point of the story; this is about community, in this case a community in which the Latins had thrived for thirty years. Knowing that our project would end after eighteen months, we strove to develop increased community involvement, especially as we were able to demonstrate early on that we had some clear keys for unlocking the door to successful intervention. We wanted to help the community to gear up and continue our progress. We worked with local churches, the local boys' club, the high school in the area, the local newspaper, and volunteer mentors from the fire department and a nearby college. We worked hard on local employers too, finding over a hundred jobs for Latins boys during the project. Finally, we engaged the local Chamber of Commerce, whose members could only benefit from the continued quiescence of the Latins.

We failed—completely. After a year and a half, the boys' club closed to the Latins again; the churches couldn't engage them; the mentors soon disappeared; local employers tolerated our Latins only while we were there to monitor and cajole. The Chamber of Commerce lost all interest. For another year, we monitored the area and the arrest statistics, pleased to see the Latins remain quiet. But three years later, it had all started up again; fresh Latins graffiti splashed the walls and overpasses, intergang rivalries were renewed, and the gang deaths mounted. For a while, we had substantially changed the Latins gang, but we had not changed the community that spawned the gang.

Gangs are spawned by communities. This is especially true, of course, of Traditional gangs. They couldn't continue, couldn't regenerate, if the community or the local neighborhoods were able to control the situation. Compressed gangs come and go; Specialty gangs seem sensitive to changes in community and police pressure. But the Traditional gang hangs in for decades, becoming in some ways a true component of community structure. If the other gang types don't meet resistance in one form or another, they may move toward Traditional gang status in communities unwilling and unable to prevent their growth. And, I should add, there's damn little that all the Pacos can do about it. Paco's stereotype, patently false, is that most gangs are of this Traditional type.

In many, perhaps most gang neighborhoods, there can be quite a separation between gang and community. Compressed gangs are too recent to have established intimate community ties. Specialty gangs sap communities by ripping off material goods or spreading dope into the neighborhood. Such groups get little local support. But in Traditional gang neighborhoods, more complex, even intimate relations may develop. The dividing lines between fringe members and nonmembers blur—after all, these young people grew up together often on the same block, attended the same primary and secondary schools, hung around in the same playgrounds and parks. Further, the long duration of many Traditional gangs that regenerate over several decades means that parents, even grandparents of gang members, may share some of the same gang history and culture. My favorite, most admired gang worker told me of the time he saw a youngster beginning to hang around the gang he was servicing. Tony, the worker, got to know this kid and decided he didn't need gang association; he had other (better) things going for him. Tony went to the boy's home to speak with his parents about keeping him otherwise engaged, but the parents weren't home. Instead, the grandfather answered the door. After he had made his pitch, Tony told me, the grandfather rolled up his sleeve to display his gang tattoo, the same gang the boy was flirting with. It's hard to work against a three-generation pattern when a grandfather tells the worker that what was good enough for him is good enough for his grandson.

We can look at a community, and even more to the point a neighborhood, as constituting a bundle of risk factors. For Tony's gang recruit, his own family constituted a risk factor, upping the chances that the boy would become a gang member. Paco's claim that all the kids in Ladino Hills were gang members was, in essence, his conclusion that that neighborhood was a high-risk area.

Let's put Tony's kid in Paco's Ladino Hills. The family provides firsthand exposure to gang matters. Seeing Latins graffiti displayed all around him reminds the boy that gangbanging is a viable alternative for him. In elementary school, other kids more and less exposed add conversations, fears, exciting reports, knowledge of gang culture, and examples of gang members they have known or heard about in the neighborhood. In middle school, there are younger gang cliques in evidence—the L'il Latins, the Latinettes, and perhaps a baby clique of a rival gang. On the playgrounds and parks and at several busy places, the Latins are seen, are pointed to, sometimes with trepidation and sometimes with admiration but in most cases with some form of respect. The field is ripe for gang recruitment and for voluntary joining.

In my field experiences, I saw many younger kids, and sometimes kids new to the neighborhood, start to hang around in gang areas, connect with individual members, and essentially "try out" the gang life. I watched this closely in Ladino Hills, where half of these wannabes (as the police and press would come to call them) would eventually commit themselves to the Latins, while half simply dropped out of sight. Most kids, of course, never become wannabes because family, friends, school, and their own character protected them.

Given his own upbringing, including the nurturing mother and stern father, Paco has often expressed a common bond with inner-city kids who "came out straight." While he sees these kids as exceptional, they are not. They are the norm. But he uses these resilient kids to demean the gang kids. He has contempt for the gang member for failing to rise up against that bundle of risk factors that Paco can see. He places the fault and blame on the kid, not on the setting.

Oddly, however, he *is* willing to grant more factors in the setting that allow the successful kids to resist the lure of the gang. First and foremost, always, is the family; good kids (like Paco) come from good families (like Paco's). The church gets some praise from him, as do authority figures that provide role models—the priest, the coach, the teacher, the cop, or fireman who gives time to youth groups. He also liked my anecdote from Philadelphia.

In one gang area of that city, a group of grandmothers got sick and tired of the gang members hanging on the street below their apartments. They formed a telephone network, and when one of them spotted a gathering of bangers, she would notify the others. Down the stairs and out into the street would come a group of grandmothers, swinging their brooms and advancing on the boys on the corner, reportedly always running the boys off. I can't imagine a much more frightening sight for a group of youngsters than a group of screaming grandmothers mounting a charge at them.

Paco enjoyed the image, but also worried about payback against the ladies. And, of course, that's the essence of attempts at local community intervention; it can and sometimes does backfire. Peace is not won easily, nor easily maintained. Research has shown that attempts at directly attacking gangs can at best have only short-term effects. Whether the attempt comes from the police, the schools, or from social workers, the positive effect is likely to last only while they are on the spot. The negative effect, by providing attention and notoriety and status to the gang, may last longer, as research suggests. And the community itself may well resent these intrusions. As one older gang member was quoted as saying, "Don't let no white man come up in here waving his finger in the black man's face telling him what he should be doing. Slavery days are over."[1]

What else can be done? The ultra long-term solutions lie in defeating racism, poverty, inadequate resources in schools and agencies, segregation, and the misuse of authority. Obviously, though, this is a tall order and we can't wait around for it. There is an ill-defined middle ground between direct attacks on gangs and complete reform of communities. It goes by many names: community empowerment, local social control, collective efficacy. It all comes back to this: if the community spawns gangs, then it will continue to do so despite our direct attacks. The Latins regenerated themselves. Traditional gangs regenerate themselves over twenty, thirty, forty years, and more.

Local social control, including the use of *but not reliance on the police*, requires some neighborhood stability, interorganizational collaboration, a conviction that neighborhood residents can and wish to work together, the belief that public space belongs to the public. Essentially, it's neighborhood cohesion against gang cohesion. Sounds right, sounds easy. But there are two problems. First, the gang-spawning community has become such in part because these factors are already low or missing. Second, we have only scratched the surface in learning how to bring such factors back through local development rather than imposition from outside. How do we help to initiate social organization in a disorganized community, collective efficacy where the collective has fallen apart, local social control where defeatism and fear have taken hold?

Professor Irving Spergel of the University of Chicago has been trying to do this by developing a comprehensive model and applying it to gang neighborhoods in Chicago, Tucson, Mesa, Albuquerque, Bloomington, and Riverside, California. It's not going well. The necessary model is complex; the problems it must address are far more complex. But in the long run, gang generation will be reduced *in* and *by* the local community. Paco doesn't have a clue. Others of us have a great deal of hard work ahead of us to advance beyond his simplistic solutions, but our directions have far more promise than do his. Meanwhile, it's his efforts that get the press and the political support.

NOTE

1. The quote is taken from page 74 of the *Correction Management Quarterly* (Winter 2001). The reader interested in prison gangs would find that whole journal issue informative.

⑩

GANG MEMBER CHARACTERISTICS

> Bring in one of these kids and ask him: "How do you feel about this guy
> you killed, his family, the fact that he just got married and wasn't even a
> gang member?" Maybe he'll say, "So what's to feel; it ain't no big thing."
>
> —Paco

If the community is often the most ignored aspect of street gangs, the character of the gang member is certainly not. To the contrary, one hears and reads a great deal about the nature of gang members. Unfortunately, this nature is often seriously misunderstood and limited to caricature. Paco's comment above is a good example of such a caricature.

Another is the journalist's common suggestion that gangs and cops are flip sides of the same coin. Yes, there are some interesting parallels, but that's about all. Camaraderie is common to the gang and the force; both develop and practice a mythic rhetoric about the other; both can be heard using the language of the embattled minority. There have even been examples, exaggerated in the Rampart gang unit described later, of gang units deliberately mocking gang styles by adopting special logos and language for their unit. But it doesn't go much farther than that. Rather than trying to find caricatures or "typical" gang members, it is far more realistic to note their variety.

In Chapter 6, I introduced you to the other Paco, the gang member whose girlfriend died in childbirth, the gang member who went to court

and obtained custody of his newborn baby daughter. That Paco was eighteen years old, an intelligent youngster, just finishing high school when I
knew him, quiet and reserved but frequently seen with his compadres. He
was, unknown to the police, a very delinquent young man. This Paco was a
member of the Latins and a very popular leader; he had the largest number
of ties to the members of the central clique of the Latins. In figure 10.1, I've
illustrated the clique to show you how central this quiet youngster was in
this twelve-person clique. Another thirty or so members, mostly fringe,
were clustered around this clique.

Each circle is a core Latin. The lines connecting them indicate close associations between each. My quiet Paco is obviously at the center of things,
yet he was virtually unknown to the local police or gang unit.

Now let's contrast this to sixteen-year-old Nando, also a clique leader
connected to young Paco but with his own network of core members. He
was the opposite of Paco. Probably equally bright, he was also hyperactive,
a high school dropout, a troublemaker with an extensive juvenile police
record. He was also charming, responsive, and had a quick mouth and fast
hands. Note that there are four other core members connected to him.
They followed; he led.

When we came to recognize Nando's character, we decided to use his
central position to get to the other four. We found Nando a job; he was one
of forty-nine for whom we did this. Within three weeks he started missing
work, was allowed to return, and then quit a month later. We found him a
second job at which he lasted a month. There followed four months with no
"bread" in his pocket, a girlfriend who urged him to get serious, and some
persistent counseling by our staff. And then the magic happened!

We found Nando an apprentice job in a one-man printing shop. The
printer became a mentor, and Nando starting coming home with printer's

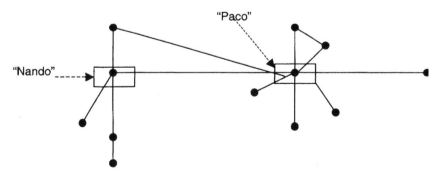

Figure 10.1.

ink on his hands and arms to display his new status. He started learning the trade and became interested in night classes at the trade school. Even more importantly, his four core homies now begged us to get jobs for them. Georgie said, "I gotta get a job. Nando's been working so long now." He was second; the other three soon followed. Understanding the clique structure is what made this possible.

Paco Domingo would not have been aware of young Paco. He would have busted Nando and never have thought about what else might be accomplished for Nando or his core homies. Knowing who is core and fringe can be vital to any control attempts. Recognizing the different personality types that can compose a street gang is equally vital to constructing alternative approaches to them. Paco's approach is only one and correctly so.

Variety among street gang members, just as among other large groups of young people, is truly notable when you get up close to them. They are bright and dull, tall and short, strong and weak, confident and shy, very criminal and mere dabblers in illegality, courageous and chicken, active and inactive. This is not to say that a few broad generalizations cannot surface through the variety. I can hazard a few of these.

- Despite some increase in the tendency for members of Traditional gangs to remain affiliated for longer periods of time, street gang members are drawn primarily from our youth populations. On average they are youngest in Compressed gangs—adolescents and very young adults with a range of perhaps twelve to twenty. The range is wider in Neo-traditional gangs and wider still in Traditional gangs. Here the ages are more likely to range from the same twelve to the thirties in some instances, with an average in the early twenties. Thus, Paco was quoted in the news as saying that the average age of a gang member was twenty-three years, an overestimate based on his usual stereotypical stance that most gangs are Traditional gangs. The oldest average, more likely, is among the Specialty gangs (other than Skinheads), where some maturity is required to maintain a criminal enterprise such as drug distribution or auto-stripping in chop shops.
- Gang members, at time of entry into the group, are on average more delinquently oriented than their non-gang peers. However, the bulk and the peak of their illegal behavior occur *after* entry, and before leaving the group. It is gang participation on top of their predisposition that makes them, on average, far more criminal than others in their schools and neighborhoods.

- They are, as noted before, far more likely to come from marginalized populations—racial, ethnic, and national minorities. Even Skinheads tend to come from marginalized segments of the white communities. This marginalization brings with it ancillary characteristics; a sense of fate and hopelessness, lack of self-confidence, and an "oppositional culture" that suggests to them that they live in a hostile world. As one of them put it succinctly to me, "bein' poor's a motherfucker!"
- Keep in mind the age factor of such street gang members; one of my first and most lasting impressions of them when I was doing street observations was of their "ultra-adolescence." They were caricatures of adolescents—shy, self-conscious, with exaggerated humor used mostly to call attention to themselves, and consumed with concerns (and braggadocio) about sex far more than about crime or violence. Issues of self-image and self-esteem constantly seep through the wisecracking, confrontational veneer. As gang scholar Diego Vigil has observed, they made up for weak self-esteem with stronger group esteem. In Paco's defense, I grant that it's sometimes hard to keep the adolescent caricature in mind when you face a gang member charged with serious violent acts. Too often, the character and the behavior coexist.
- In much the same vein, street gang members typically feel very uncomfortable when out of their own territory. I've heard them express genuine fear at unaccustomed animal noises when they are taken on field trips to the mountains. I've seen them group together with wide eyes when brought onto a university campus for interviews and visits. I've watched them hang back from other human contact on a suburban beach or a museum visit. In such exposures, their first instinct, like small kids, is to group tightly together. But listen to them when they get home, and they tell the bravest stories imaginable.

A gang worker, after laboring mightily to set up a journey for his boys, reported to me, "The day of the trip they all found excuses not to go. Later they admitted they were scared to go out of their environment. They might have confidence in me, but not in themselves." Yet these are the same boys of whom Paco said, "They just rape, rob, and pillage." This phrase—rape, rob, and pillage—became a favorite of Paco's. I heard it on several occasions, usually when he was with other gang cops. Mutual support, group support, comes from group rhetoric: rape, rob, and pillage.

Leaving aside Paco's perspective for the moment, researchers have found two useful ways to draw a further picture of gang members. One is to contrast the characteristics of core and fringe members of the gang. The other is to compare gang members with non-gang members from the same neighborhood. After I've done that, I then want to return to the issue of gang leaders, because it's the gang leader—the O.G., the shot caller, the Veterano—that Paco uses to create his stereotype of gang members and thus his justification for cracking down on the lot of them.

CORE VERSUS FRINGE

Since commitment to gang is a question of degree, the dividing line between a committed core member and fringe or peripheral member (similar to Paco's "associate" or "affiliate" member) is necessarily a bit arbitrary. And, of course, many fringe members become core, and then later revert to fringe. It is best, then, to think in terms of a major time slice, perhaps a year or more, and ask which members maintain a central, core status over much of that time, or fail to do so (fringe).

We've done some analyses in our own projects of the characteristics that seem to differentiate core from fringe members. When we compare these data with impressions from researchers in other locations, we find general agreement. Keep two constraints in mind: boys are more likely than girls to be core in a mixed-gender gang, and older youth (prior to desisting from gang activity) are more likely to be core than younger youth. However, since young people tend to congregate with *same-age* peers, there will be core members seen at the lower end of the age range—core to their age clique, if not to the entire gang.

There's one other constant. Since core and fringe members of a gang will usually come from the same neighborhoods, perhaps the same blocks, one should not expect much difference in their social circumstances. And this is indeed what our analyses showed. While gang members differ markedly from the general youth population in poverty, unemployment, housing quality, broken families, and educational levels, core and fringe members do not differ from each other on these factors. Level of gang membership is not understood by reference to the sociologists' or the economists' variables. We have to turn, instead, to clinical psychologists and social psychologists for our clues.

Psychological research suggests two characterological routes to core gang membership. First are youths with a combined deficient and aggressive set of traits. The deficiencies most likely include lower intelligence and therefore troubles in school and more truancy; lower impulse control, fewer outside interests or skills, more emotional disturbance, and more dependence on peers. Behaviorally, they engage in more delinquency, are more likely to get others in trouble, and are more willing to fight. This "deficient-aggressive" kid is the psychologist's delight but, in our experience, more of a handful than the psychologist can manage.

The second route to core membership fits better in the social psychologist's arena. The kid on that route is a very social kid—think of Nando—more often participating in spontaneous activities, more accepted by core members. He has greater clique involvement, like young Paco, contributes more to group goals, and has a greater desire to lead. This "group involvement" route may or may not involve a major commitment to illegal behaviors; it's socializing and group identity that are important.

What of fringe members? It's just the opposite. These were lower on the deficient-aggressive factor and lower on the group involvement factor. However, our analysis revealed that the two factors are somewhat independent. This means that a member could be core by virtue of being high on one factor, or the other, or both. Fringe members were lower on one or the other, but more likely lower on both.

Some illustrations may help. Captain Blood was a short, skinny kid with excellent school skills to compensate for his small stature. He was also an epileptic (he went into a grand mal seizure during an interview I had with him). He made up for his deficiencies through extreme aggressiveness and his intellect, which, among other things, led him to be an extensive diarist of his very famous gang's exploits. Oh, how the police wanted his writings! Captain Blood took the deficient-aggressive route to core status.

Richard was another deficient-aggressive core type. The gang worker who had known him for four years labeled him a "gang psychopath." During the twelve-month period that I came to know Richard, while he was seventeen and eighteen years of age, he exhibited just about every conceivable facet of the deficient-aggressive pattern. He went through ten job placements, most arranged by our staff. He lost those jobs through a combination of absenteeism, fighting on the job, and failure to perform. As a marijuana user and heroin experimenter, he was given two appointments at a rehabilitation center and one at a psychiatric unit; he refused to participate in all three. He quit school after a drunken episode. He supplanted one girl, from the Latinettes, with another from a rival gang, and then turned to a third from the same rival gang and ran away with the third to live in a garage. He then assaulted her, causing her to have a miscarriage. He joined the Job Corps, but soon quit, following fights and a stint in jail. He flunked a Marine's entry test and failed to appear for a retest. During this same period, his own family was evicted from their home, and then had to move again from new quarters.

This same year, we learned of Richard's six arrests prior to the final one. One led to jail time, during which he spent two periods in solitary confinement for fighting fellow prisoners. The arrests were for petty theft, drug possession, riot and disturbing the peace, interfering with the police, failure to appear, and joyriding. Other events, which we knew about but the police did not, included escape from a drug bust, firearm possession, purse snatch, robbery, housebreak, and five assaults or gang fights (both within the Latins and outside). He was also a victim in an additional six assaults, mostly by rival gang members. In one he was stabbed and in another he was clubbed over the head with a tire iron, which resulted in chronic dizziness and headaches.

On the anniversary, to the day, of the killing of Manny, the Latin I described in an earlier chapter who had been gunned down at the head of the stairs, Richard got loaded on wine and pills. With a companion as driver, he cruised the rival gang area for a payback. He stabbed a fourteen-year-old found alone on the street, and then shot two older (non-gang) adults, killing one of them. After several years in state prison, I heard of Richard once again, accused of involvement in the murder of a fellow inmate. It occurs to me every now and then that Richard was one of the two brawlers I described in Chapter 5 who had me encased between them in my vain effort to stop their fight just a year earlier.

Manny, the boy whose death was avenged by Richard, was a core member of the Latins by reason of his group involvement pattern. He leaned heavily on his gang relationships. Within two weeks of his return from a probation facility, he joined with others in a raid on a rival gang. He was constantly seen on the street with his homeboys for over a month—never alone—right up to the day of his death. He and Richard, victim and killer, present dramatic contrasts of routes to core gang status.

Most examples, of course, are far less dramatic. Paco would dwell on these two, and overlook all the others who did not kill or get killed. And they are the norm, not Richard and Manny. The other Latin who was fighting with Richard when I tried to intervene was a younger deficient-aggressive named Eddie who desperately wished to be accepted by the Latins. He was accepted by some and was given teacher's pet status by the gang worker who felt sorry for him. Eddie came from a terrible family situation and had little going for him other than his peer friendships. The fight with Richard, I later learned, was caused by too intense an attempt by Eddie to be accepted and a disdainful response from Richard. With Richard's departure for court and prison, Eddie became a familiar figure at the core of the Latins. He was far more the norm than was Richard.

For contrast, let me cite just one further example of core membership via the group involvement route. Fourteen-year-old Bonnie, a short, five-by-five bundle of female energy, had become the most prominent member of the Generalettes, an auxiliary group to the large Traditional Generals gang. I always saw her on Wednesday evenings on the playground outside the Generals' weekly "club" meeting, marching her group of a dozen or so girls in formation, doing drills and cadence counts: A regular little drill instructor who might have warmed Paco's heart. But Bonnie's need for the group became too strong, too demanding, and she was ousted by the girls.

In response, she went to a public park a dozen blocks away, recruited a number of girls who were "hanging but not banging," and formed a new independent girls' group named—naturally—the Bonnettes. Her own needs seemingly required fulfillment by a strong group affiliation. The other side of the coin, of course, is that there were recruits available and amenable to gang development. Although it had been Paco who ran the video of the female fight and stabbing described in an earlier chapter, he had done so to display the violence, not because he took groups like the Generalettes or the Bonnettes seriously.

GANG VERSUS NON-GANG

Earlier, when I described Paco's assignment to find early identifiers of kids most likely to join gangs, I ended with a listing of a few variables that have by now been shown to do that to some extent. These variables are *predictors* of gang joining; the more of these variables that describe a youngster, the more likely it is that he will join the neighborhood gang and thus separate himself from the others in the neighborhood who are not so high on these predictor variables.

I want to be clear, however, that there are other variables that describe differences between gang and non-gang youth. Many of them develop *along with* gang membership and are thus correlated with it but not causes of it—leaving school, promiscuity, poor work performance, and increased crime levels are examples of gang-relevant factors that may *result* from membership but are not gang-joining predictors. There has been quite a bit of research about these factors—let's call them gang *descriptors* as opposed to gang predictors. They allow Paco and us to draw some generalizations about the nature of gang membership, but not to explain it. Paco has trouble with this distinction. For him, they all run together.

As with the twelve predictors noted in Chapter 8, these gang descriptors include individual, family, school, peer, and neighborhood variables.

Individual gang variables include positive attitude toward delinquency and alcohol and drug use, weak behavior norms and standards toward family and peers and school; also, being labeled as bad or disturbed by teachers, a negative self-concept, perceived barriers to success, the importance of having money, and "street smarts" such as knowing where to dispose of stolen goods.

In the family area, we can add frequent changes of residence, lower family cohesiveness, deviance among family members, family arguments and fights, and inconsistency in parental punishment of the children. School variables include lack of full-time school attendance, higher numbers of school days missed, lower school achievement, and non-participation in school sports. To these, we can add larger numbers of peer friends and various attitudes toward one's friends, the accessibility to guns in the neighborhood, and lower perceptions of police fairness in the neighborhoods.

Taken together, these individual plus family plus school plus peer plus neighborhood descriptors, along with the twelve predictors noted earlier, constitute a heavy load. And keep in mind that they describe gang as opposed to non-gang members in the same neighborhoods. If we were to compare gang members with other youths in clearly non-gang areas, then we could add racism, poverty, employment opportunities, school resources, and a host of other obvious social factors.

Given all this, it is no wonder that tough and frustrated gang cops like Paco throw up their hands and respond that they are not, and cannot be, social workers. Whatever brought the gang member to drug use, car theft, assault or homicide, in the final analysis the cop has to respond to *the behavior* and get that guy off the street for as long as possible. Decrying the ineffective family control of his gang members, Paco said, "Y' know, they have to be afraid of us; if we don't make them scared of us, they'll go out and do whatever they want. We've got to keep them scared—that's our job." So Paco goes willingly to court to testify as effectively as he can, even at the borders of truth.

And just as obviously, it is no wonder that the defense attorney draws on these background predictors and descriptors to lessen the degree of guilt assigned to his or her client, and to lessen the severity of punishment to be meted out by the judge. Thus, Paco and I have been brought into court increasingly to face off against each other, he for the prosecution and I for the defense. We don't differ about the defendant's guilt so much as about how he got to that point and what to do about it, as I'll show in a later chapter.

GANG LEADERSHIP

Let's look at one additional aspect of gang membership that separates Paco's view and what research has taught us, the nature of gang leadership. As noted earlier, Paco's notion of the gang leader is the shot caller, the O.G. or Veterano with a long record, probably including incidents of violence. Richard would be a gang leader for Paco, but, in fact, Richard had little influence among the Latins: core, yes; leader, no.

Nando was a clique leader; Paco might select him. But he'd miss the Latins' Paco, the most popular member of all, and probably select Manny, the violence victim. If he cared about the girls, he'd correctly pick Bonnie. She fairly announced herself (but remember that at one point she was ousted from her leadership).

Paco's stereotype favors older leaders over the younger, the violent over the nonviolent, the male over the female, the loud-talker over the spokesman, the incarcerated over the nonincarcerated, and the one prominent in crime over the one prominent in sports activities, party-giving, sex, or drug supplying. He would call Gregory a gang leader, but Gregory was a sociopath with a boxer's build and a mind to match, who argued in a gang meeting that the group must seek retaliation before a truce. "Ya win the last fight; then ya conversate," he said, and headed out the door to be followed by his homies. But no one followed him out.

Sometimes gang leaders understand more about these affairs than Paco. I interviewed one young man specifically because he had shown leadership and had been nominated by others as having a "high rep." I pushed him for half an hour to admit his status, with little luck. "We all equal," he repeated. And then, finally, he explained that in his world, if you're known as a leader, it's like sticking your head up. The higher head becomes the target.

Mad Man and Narco—both monikers being excellent symbols of their dominant characteristics—could ordinarily lead nothing. They were known for their weaknesses. Yet one evening they rushed into a gathered group of a dozen Latins playing the piano and sitting around talking war stories, and shouted excitedly to the group that the Gaylords and High Riders were going at it down the street—everyone up and out. For that brief, exciting moment, Mad Man and Narco exercised leadership, as a dozen Latins and two gang workers and a gang researcher rushed out to the fray.

Captain Blood, the diarist, was an intellectual leader, admired by gang members and police alike for his leadership in documenting gang exploits. Bonnie led through dictatorial exuberance, but only with respect to her group's social activities. Red was, for a year, "club" president because he had gone back to school at night and was holding down a steady job. He was clever with words, urging his group in a contentious meeting not to emulate Gregory—"hanging on the corner, all loaded up with the booze"—but to go back like him "and get your smarts." However, when challenged by a violence leader in the group who asked about the rivalry that had triggered this meeting, he responded: "If they come over here, we gonna go through them like a hot knife through butter!" Leadership in one area, followed by leadership in another, seemingly opposed area. Red was perhaps the most effective street gang leader I ever knew. He was arrest free, as well—no Pacos in his world of adults.

Social scientists distinguish between different concepts of leadership. For instance, many people believe leaders are born more than made; they have inherent characteristics that allow them to rise to the top. Social scientists are more likely to stress that "leaders are made, not born." People rise above others in response to situations. Harry Truman was not an admired person until forced to replace one of history's great men. He became a significant leader out of necessity.

But Truman had an organizational position to fill. What about groups without an organization? Informal groups, such as street gangs, require a different conception of leadership. Two terms are used in informal groups: "functional" leadership and "distributed" leadership. Functional leadership suggests that different gang members will serve leadership *functions* at different times and places, with respect to different activities, in order in some way to serve the group's goals, to keep it viable. Mad Man and Narco did that one evening; Captain Blood did it over some years; Red did it for a year, and demonstrated it in two different functions at one meeting.

It follows that if different functions must be filled, and not all by the same individual, then leadership will be *distributed* over a number of members—not all members, but some. And that is why Paco doesn't recognize so many leaders and misunderstands the broad nature of gang leadership. He concentrates only on one or two functions—leadership in gang rivalries, leadership in criminal activities. If he can help bust these leaders, he believes, he can seriously weaken the whole gang structure. He overlooks that the functions still need to be served, that there are other "leaders" and potential leaders. Only in the most simple gang structure such as the Specialty gangs are you likely seriously to disrupt them by busting the few—the main drug suppliers, the connections to the fences or the chop shops, the individuals whose *function* is *critical* to the gang *goal*. Those italicized words are peripheral to the nature of Traditional, Neo-traditional, Compressed, and Collective gangs. Street gang leadership is distributed rather than concentrated.

You break up a gang not by busting its leaders, but by working on its group processes and its neighborhood context. These skills are not in Paco's hands, nor should we expect them to be. But it would be nice if he could understand this. That's why I wrote earlier about the neighborhoods and will write in a later chapter about group processes. Neighborhoods spawn the gangs. Group processes continue them. The gang's advantages for the *individual* member, if highly varied, may have been captured best by one seventeen-year-old member during an interview on the TV program *Frontline*:

> If you're in a gang, you're hated by many, loved by a few, but respected by all.
>
> *January 30, 2001*

⓫

STREET GANG CRIME PATTERNS

If it's a drive-by, it's automatically a gang shooting.

—Paco

Paco's statement above epitomizes how far he has come over the years in stereotyping gang crime. He offered it one evening when we were poring over monthly arrest logs in the station during research on gang crime versus non-gang crime. On those logs, every incident that involved a gang member, either as a perpetrator or as a victim, was designated by the investigating officers as gang related. By comparing those incidents with those not so designated, we could go to the incident files and compare the nature of gang and non-gang crimes.

That evening we noted about twenty drive-by shootings that had no gang designations, as compared to many others that did. When these twenty were pointed out to Paco as part of our collaborative process, he looked at the log entries and changed each one, without further study, to a gang-related incident. For him, every drive-by was gang related, by definition. He liked to quote the police saying: "Gangs are self-cleaning ovens; the members wipe each other out."

Several months ago, while reading on the couch in my decidedly middle-class home in my far-from-gang neighborhood, I heard a loud car zoom down the hill outside, followed by half a dozen gunshots as it passed my plate glass window. I ducked automatically, heard nothing further, and then went outside and retrieved several shell casings. It was a drive-by shooting (probably into the air; I found no damage) and I called 911 to report it. "Anyone hit?" I was asked. I responded no, and the lady said, "Well that's nice." I offered the address, time, etc., but heard nothing further from the police.

A gang drive-by? Not at all, and many shots are fired from cars in my large city that have nothing to do with gangs. But Paco had lost sight of this. Drive-bys, for him, typify what he has come to think of as gang crime: "One kid we had in here," he said at the station, "he'd just look at you with a smirk and describe how he and his gang go around shooting cars and people, with no feeling, no emotion at all."

Driving home one afternoon through a part of our old first gang project area, I witnessed a very angry young man in the second car at a stoplight rush out of his car with a lead pipe. He screamed at the front car, and then proceeded to smash in the side and rear windows to the echo of wild female screaming from inside the vehicle. He then reentered his own car, looked over briefly at me, smiled, and drove away.

The assailant was young and black; the screaming girls were young and black. A gang incident? Road rage? Family feud? There's no way to know. Paco would have said gang related: gang area, black assailant and victims, street setting; gotta be gang.

How does this happen? How does a shrewd, experienced gang cop come to develop a narrow, stereotyped image of gang behavior? There are several answers, I think. First, the stereotyped offense pattern provides Paco with a meaningful antagonist, a challenge to his image as street cop and "tough cop." The list of offenses includes murder, aggravated assault, drive-bys, rape, robbery, arson, witness intimidation, shooting into an inhabited dwelling, and—of course—battery on a police officer. These are all felonies, and the most serious felonies. They fit the public image of street gang crime. They fit nicely with Paco's character needs.

Second, arrest and conviction for these "gang-type" crimes bring rewards to Paco. He gets support from the troops, "well dones" from the "suits," and attention from the media. Interest in thefts, graffiti, burglary, disorderly conduct, and the like simply doesn't compare.

Third, serious gang-type crimes provide Paco with the opportunity to prepare technically sophisticated affidavits for search warrants in which he must attest to his expertise as the "affiant" (legalese for the writer of an affidavit) as well as appear in court as the prosecution's gang expert. Search warrants and expert testimony attach to the stereotypic crimes and are far less frequently called on for the lesser crimes.

Finally, special anti-gang legislation rapidly appearing across the country usually lists most of the same gang-type crimes as the ones justifying special enforcement and sentencing practices. Paco gets more bang for the buck in concentrating on these crimes.

All these factors serve to demonize the gangs, with cops like Paco holding the line between the "gangsters," as he now often calls them, and the rest of us. It allows him to say to the media, as he did on one occasion, "We're caught up in an experience of violence—murder has no meaning; killing has become a game, a way of life."

Paco, in this sense, is *not* typical of the many gang unit officers with whom I've talked over the years, and this is worth remembering. Paco started off with less prejudice, with less stereotyping, more attuned to the variability one finds among gangs and gang youth. Talking with other gang cops always reminds me that the hard chargers like Paco are more the exceptions than the rule. Examples of more qualified perspectives are illuminating:

- "Originally we nipped it in its bud in one or two years."
- "They think of themselves as a gang, but the cops don't. They're not serious enough."
- "We all got excited about it, but it was superficial; small fight, graffiti; poorly organized, and so on."
- "We got wannabes and copycats in the projects. They just can't pull it off."
- "They're pretty wimpy."
- "No drive-bys, no organization, no leadership, no colors, no migration."
- "I say we don't have a gang problem, but I'll deny I ever said it."

These comments come from gang unit officers in seven different communities, including several with chronic gang problems and Traditional gangs. In my 250 interviews with gang cops across the country, I came to respect the more reasoned approach taken by many of them and realized how guarded I must be in assessing Paco's increasingly narrow perspective. Many of these others, in commenting about their gangs, noted how few homicides they had logged, how drug use was far more common than drug sales, especially organized drug sales, how their gangs were commonly composed mostly of adolescents rather than adults, and how disorganized many of the groups seemed to be.

But, unfortunately, Paco's views on the principal kinds of crime gang members commit are quite similar to common notions among the general public. I suppose that's not too surprising; the public view derives mostly from the media, including dramatic movies like *Colors*, and the media portrayals come primarily from dramatic pictures provided by cops like Paco. The officer describing "wimpy" gangs gets no press coverage, but when Paco reports that "killing has become a game, a way of life," he gets on TV.

In fact, it would be an interesting exercise to work backward, from media portrayals to Paco's views, to see how well they correspond. The media tell us that all gangs are violent, that they often dominate a neighborhood—even "own" it, that they are heavily involved in organized drug markets and drug "franchising" across the country, and that they prey on the weak and the innocent. Paco has told them all of this, although as to "the weak and the innocent" he also knows that the most common target of a gang's violence is the membership of other gangs. A common sardonic suggestion heard from many officers says, in effect, "Let's put them all in the Rose Bowl to shoot it out; that'll solve the gang problem."

I want to illustrate the stereotyping of street gang crime, and contrast it with the realities of each crime, by reference to two common misperceptions about gang crime patterns: those having to do with drug sales and those having to do with violence. First, let's consider street gangs and drug sales. Until the early 1980s, there was no special attention paid to this connection because the gang world and the world of organized drug sales were thought to be relatively separate. Gang officers and narcotics officers existed side by side but interacted only occasionally. There was no particular need to collaborate or, more notably, to cross over into each other's carefully guarded turf within the department.

Then, in 1982, Los Angeles area police officers began to come across small, crystalline forms of cocaine that looked like little rocks of salt. Indeed, they called it "rock cocaine." Further investigation revealed a rapidly developing, new drug market. "Rocks"—later to be more generally referred to as "crack cocaine"—consisted of relatively pure cocaine, easily and quickly ingested by smoking and easily prepared with the use of powder cocaine, baking soda, and some boiling water. Any house with a supply of the powder could produce a quantity of these rocks, sell them at $10 to $25 for a quarter of a gram, and produce a customer whose quick "rush" or euphoria was rapidly followed by a depressive state that demanded another hit. Fast turnover was the key, and rocks could be sold in small quantities, easily hidden and easily destroyed at the approach of the police by swallowing or crushing underfoot.

Special "crack houses" were developed. Small homes or apartments dispensed the goods, often from behind reinforced doors and windows hard to penetrate by police before the dope was flushed down the toilet or dumped directly into the main line sewer pipe.

A new industry was born, and because the product was easily created and rapidly consumed, it moved from the West Coast to the East Coast in about two years. Crack dealers appeared everywhere, and Paco was on it. He later told an educational television audience, "Bloods and Crips are going national, franchising, distributing crack cocaine across the country. There are Crips and Bloods in every major city."

Paco's world suddenly doubled: gangs plus drugs. He and his department and departments across the country made the connection between gang members and drug sales, because a number of low-level street dealers were recruited from street gangs. He told me, "These gangs could exist without crack, but crack sure is a helluva chunk of it, a helluva lot of it." Now Paco was a gang cop in a new and challenging world of narcotics, of crack houses and undercover "buy and bust" operations, of sting operations where cops became suppliers to catch the higher level distributors, where task forces with other departments and federal agencies opened up a new world of evil for the gang cop to handle. He told me that raids on crack houses could be very dangerous affairs for the police, since "every crack house has armed dealers" ready to resist either the police or rip-offs by other dealers. In court one day, Paco described a new gang in his area:

> It started off with just the drug dealing, and that's the crack cocaine. It got more organized. And when I say "more organized" it got reckless. The kids quit going to school. They started selling drugs during the wee hours of the night and the early morning. Alcohol was involved. And the gang situation . . . started to flourish and the gang situation in the [rival] area began to flourish. And so, to protect their turf, they began to flex their muscle; I mean they began to repel anybody that wanted to come into their area. If they seen a blue car coming down the street, they would shoot at it.

This is dramatic stuff, and it fueled Paco. He added in this particular case that one of the gangs had "a huge cake at a party with all their names on it. It was purchased by the gang at a pastry shop. We researched the cake," he told me with a wink: Paco the gang researcher!

Then came the invitation: would my colleague and I be interested in going on a crack house raid? My colleague was Dr. Cheryl Maxson, and naturally we both accepted the invitation to what would turn out to be a very major operation. Cheryl is an attractive as well as very competent gang researcher, and her take on Paco soon assumed a different flavor than mine. While collecting data from police files, she found Paco at first to be surprisingly cooperative. But she soon realized that his cooperation involved peering over her shoulder to look down, supposedly, at the files in front of her. The view from above, plus other suggestive looks during their encounters, led her to refer to Paco thereafter as Sergeant Sleaze.

Following some days of undercover operations and interdepartmental planning, a major task force was to sweep out to raid ten crack houses in one night. I would accompany one group to five targets while Cheryl was to join the second group to the other five. The year was 1985, at the peak of the early excitement about the gang/crack connection.

On a chilly March evening, we gathered—rather ironically, I thought—in the huge empty parking lot of a giant rubber tire plant that had been abandoned years before. The thousands of jobs lost when this and other plants were emptied out in the inner city had gone to distant suburbs and foreign countries. Local workers were left behind to swell the ranks of the unemployed and raise children whose lack of job prospects would help fuel street gang development. Now we gathered in this site of gang spawning to mount ten coordinated raids on crack houses reputedly providing street dealing jobs for otherwise unemployed gang members. I didn't share the irony with Paco, my host for the evening's festivities.

The command post consisted of numerous trailers and communication vehicles with antennas reaching high above us. This was a gang operation; no narcotics officers in attendance. Our fellow observers were an ABC-TV news pool group, representatives from the D.A.'s office, the city attorney's office, the parole department, and liaison officers from the largest neighboring police department. Most of the targets, in fact, were in the neighboring city, but not divulged ahead of time for fear of interference from the department's black and whites (patrol cars). "If it goes badly," Sergeant Sleaze said, "we'll drop their calling card and run!"

After dark, we had accumulated over fifty vehicles, some "motors" (motorcycle officers) cavorting around the lot, and two SWAT team vans and trucks. We totaled 120 or more people, and, although we were two miles from the nearest target, it was hard to understand how we could remain unannounced in the community. All the coordination, it seemed, had been oriented to getting everyone together, but not sufficiently organized for the raids themselves—how many cars, with what personnel, using what radio codes, and so on. I did learn, however, that gang squads would hit most houses, with SWAT teams remaining available because of anticipated armament.

The scene around the command post was movie material—of the Keystone Kops variety. The motors were charging around, SWAT teams were displaying their special equipment, officers were offering quickie lessons on the use of "picks" for forced entry of steel-enforced doors, weaponry was being exhibited, everyone was donning green flight suits and caps. We were shown the Winnebago they were customizing with reinforced siding. There was a lot of griping about lack of the "best" equipment, borrowing cars, "suits" failing to support joint gang unit/narcotics unit collaboration, and most of all, the inadequate supply of coffee.

Yet with all this, there was a general air of camaraderie and anticipation—"who brought the beer?" was heard on more than one occasion. There was also the pleasure felt when it was learned that the local city council members and staff had not been notified of the operation because of the rumored corruption there. On the other hand, as one wandered through the maze of parking attendants, tables marked here for report writing and there for evidence to be logged, trailers and generators, there were happy comments about overtime pay for the night's activities, one of the benefits of special operations.

Finally, Paco announced it was time to mount up and head out. I was his passenger—by now I no longer signed waivers to indemnify the department in case of my harm or demise—but we got only a half-mile out when the radio went silent. It went dead in our car and in all the others in the group. It turned out the communications center at the command post had been set up without regard to dead spots in the community; we and our target were in a dead spot. One officer, after everyone fiddled with his mikes and receivers, got out at a public phone and reached the command post to report the problem. Forget coordination, was the decision, just hit your target!

Our first house was small, nondescript, and unfortified. It was also abandoned before we got there. First entry took at most thirty seconds, thanks to the use of a "key to the city," a heavy cylinder with a handle used to bash in locked doors. A search revealed no dope and no weapons, but garbage and mold all over. The toilet was piled high with feces, because water and light bills had gone unpaid. The place was a cesspool, more appropriate to the sanitation department then the police. In the backyard, a gang cop stepped into a hole and injured his leg, the night's principal casualty.

The second house was similar; small, very messy, and already abandoned. We found no dope, no weapons, but $1,500 in cash and traces of cocaine powder. The third house was much the same, but yielded two suspects and one gun. Forget the fourth house; the communication screwup left several teams simply trying to locate it.

Number five was more in line with expectations. We laid back a block away as the SWAT team threw flash-bang grenades through the windows. If you're exposed to these—flash bangs—you are stunned, your hearing is temporarily gone, and you're at the mercy of your assailant. The team flushed seventeen suspects out of the house and lined them up, all dazed, sitting on the curb with their hands behind their heads. But when we entered, again there was no dope, but more of a crash pad for users. Sixteen of the seventeen suspects were released on the spot, while the owner was detained. The house inside was another pigsty: filth, garbage, windows and doors barricaded only by furniture. Another commode was filled to the brim with feces. There was no plumbing, no lighting inside, an abandoned car and a gallon jug of hydrochloric acid outside.

If this is how gang unit intelligence mounted its attacks on the scourge of crack sales, it seemed that, indeed, drug busts should be left in the hands of the narcotics units. But Paco says a 50 percent night is a good one, as these things go. And we finally got a report from the fourth house that provided a better yield; explosive chemicals, a half-pound of cocaine, three gallons of PCP, an increasingly popular hallucinogenic. Paco suggests the abandoned houses resulted from a leak in the neighboring police department, then amplified; by a "leak" he meant a crooked cop "on the take."

Dr. Maxson, it turned out, got to only two targets, one of them a two-house location. Her notes include the following:

We caravaned to a Sears parking lot, waiting for the SWAT team to make entry. Some confusion about location and directions. No one had a map; someone outside our search team provided directions. Forty-five to sixty minutes waiting to hear that SWAT team had secured entry. Many comments about political nature of this operation. "The other department does it, so we do it, then they do it," "there's no reason to be doing this at night."

Second location at the end of dead-end street; most houses on block had bars, this one included, but it was not "fortified." SWAT team departed shortly after our arrival. Small, two-bedroom stucco, unkempt yard, door and screen banged up. SWAT had used flash-bang; it broke out windows and totaled the TV in the bedroom, but not much other damage on entry. Search was incredibly thorough. House was somewhat messy and definitely dirty (a mouse ran over my foot?), but after search it was totally trashed. Large scales (for dope) in living room; shotgun propped against wall, $130 in cash found under bottom drawer of cabinet, small amount of cocaine powder (less than 1/4 gram) and marijuana stems in a few places. Officers retained bankbooks, gang artifacts (picture of homeboy in casket, others with red bandana, gang hand signals, and two letters with lots of gang terminology). About ten or fifteen minutes after our arrival, the resident's brother came in and was handcuffed, rambling on in a PCP haze about his brother and his violent tendencies and about bombs.

About an hour after arrival, they found a large glass jug, more than a gallon, of PCP buried outside by the fence on the side of the house. Everyone went out to look; there was an air of excitement at the find. Ten minutes later the searchers in the garage yelled out that they'd found C4 plastic explosives and to cut all police radio traffic (apparently these explosives can be wired into a police radio band). They called the bomb squad and talked about evacuating the area. I left the area.

Because this was a gang unit operation, it was not the few confiscations of narcotics that interested the officers but the explosives and the gang pictures. They had some new gang intelligence and some new reasons to suspect corruption in their neighboring department. For these reasons, Dr. Maxson's host was pleased with the evening. For us, it was something of an eye-opener about police inefficiency. It also helped to confirm, even in the crack house setting, findings from other research as well as ours that Paco's joy in the gang/drug sales connection emanated more from his needs than from the facts of the connection.

Research on street gangs and drug trafficking, done in many different locations around the country, yields the following results:

1. There have indeed been a number of locations in which drug traffickers have employed street gang members as street dealers, and some others in which gang members themselves have graduated to become major midlevel dealers. These instances are occasionally dramatic, and often used to overgeneralize about the connection between street gangs and drug sales. They are more the exceptions than the rule.
2. The majority of gang unit officers reporting on the gang/drug trafficking connection in national surveys report either no connection or, most prominently, a weak connection. A smaller minority reports a stronger connection, and the smallest number of all report street gangs fully devoted to drug sales and distribution. These latter are the "drug gangs" that fall under the specialty gang category described earlier.
3. There have been some interesting ethnic patterns. In the 1980s and into most of the 1990s, Blacks—and black gangs—were far more involved in crack sales than in sales of other types of drugs. Hispanic gangs, when involved, showed higher involvement in marijuana, heroin, and PCP. And since there are more Hispanic than black gang members in the United States, the above fact argues against the proposition that the gangs have come to control the crack market.
4. Contrary to public views, and contrary to media portrayals and Paco's personal conviction, street gang involvement in drug sales, where it has occurred, has generally *not* led to increased levels of gang violence. In our own research in Paco's department, for instance, we found a *decrease* in gun seizures among gang street dealers as crack

sales increased. The oft-noted violence increase is there all right, but it tends to be among the non-gang dealers, the more normal run-of-the-mill drug traffickers. Thus, we have another gang stereotype that fails to hold up to careful scrutiny.

5. The reason that there is such a strong presumption of gang control of drug sales has to do with another stereotype about their nature: that street gangs are well organized. But as noted before, and as we shall see in the next chapter, the group processes that can amplify gang crime and violence tend to be short-term, immediate, impulsive processes that defeat the kind of organization needed for sustained drug marketing. Street gang processes generally defeat good business practices. The drug gangs, whether spin-offs of other forms or independently developed, are the proof of the pudding. We can distinguish them from Traditional and Compressed gangs by the very nature of their organization; for stable marketing—small, tight, hierarchically led, secretive, with well-understood rules and sanctions for breaking the rules. Drug gangs exist, and are good targets for intervention, but they are quite clearly distinguished from the majority of loosely organized street gangs.

Most street gang members don't have the heart, the ambition, and the steadfastness to become successful drug dealers. I cannot imagine the typical street gang member putting himself (or herself) through the crack routine described in court by Paco:

What they would do is, they started holding these drugs, because they were so small, in their mouths. And they could hold about maybe ten at a time, and they would hold either a bottle of water or a soda. And if the police came they'd just take a drink and swallow everything. And either they would let it come through their system and get it out that way, or they would use epicac and throw it up and gather it and sell it again.

And they also stick it in . . . well, up their butt cheeks would be another place they stick the crack cocaine . . . and the kids were afraid to keep it in their mouths in the beginning; but as things evolved certainly it was the place of choice to hide or conceal drugs was in somebody's mouth or up their butt.

The other major stereotype about street gang crime, of course, is about violence. If I wanted to make the case that gangs are violent, I could do so easily, just as the media do. Simply cite a few instances, that's all it takes. I would, for instance, offer the examples of police officers killed by gang members—in Los Angeles, in Lynwood, California, in Oakland, in Omaha.

Or I could cite the politicians' children assaulted in Columbus and Denver. There are the famous cases of Karen Toshima in Westwood and three-year-old Stephanie Kuhen in Los Angeles, both shot and killed accidentally and both publicized because they were so obviously innocents. I could cite the well-meaning gang worker in Los Angeles whose attempt to mediate a feud went too far; when I saw him the next day, his face looked like a plate of scalloped potatoes from the beating he took. There's drama in the gang world, but not often because, in truth, most street gang activity is dull, languorous, boring. Most of what gang members do is sleep, eat, drink, hang around, and talk big. It's boring. I've said before, the only thing more boring than gang life is being a research observer watching gang life.

But don't gangs kill? Don't gangbangers carry guns? Yes, to both, but on occasion, not daily. Most gang homicides, when they occur, result from firearms, usually handguns. But, as even Paco notes, the importance of the gun is not in its use, but in its possession:

> In the gang world it's kind of like a subculture. Guns are like a status symbol. The gang with the most guns has the most power on the street. They are the most feared gang.
>
> So when a gang member has a gun, he's usually very proud of it and he shows everybody: "Look at the gun I have," and "I have all these guns." And it's really a status thing like the way when someone—a regular person, non-gang member—has a nice car in the garage here for the weekend. It's a status thing, maybe a nice Porsche or something that they're not going to drive to work every day. When they do take it out, they're showing off their new car. It's a status thing, much like a gang member showing off his gun.

Even Paco acknowledges that gang members don't go around "packing" or "strapping" (carrying a gun) most of the time. Rather, he notes: "It's important for everybody to know where they can access the gun; the gun's a great equalizer. One person with a gun can kill fifteen people with fists." And, as noted, most gang homicides result from guns, but it's equally important to remember that most gunfire does *not* result in death. For that matter, most gunfire hits no target at all. Just try driving forty miles an hour down a street, spotting a human target, pointing your weapon out the window, and hitting that target. You'll miss. Most people will miss. But the mere act of doing it is worth excited telling and bragging afterward.

There's an appellate court ruling that claims a reasonable person should know that the probable, likely outcome of an aggravated assault will be the death of the victim. That's just judicial ignorance and arrogance. In the very worst gang cities, there may be fifteen recorded gang assaults for every homicide. When you recall that most gang assaults are *not* recorded (gang members don't turn to the police for retaliation), the ratio is probably closer to 50 to 1 or 100 to 1. The likely outcome of assault with a gun is injury, but not death.

The gang-related homicide, like any homicide, is a terrible and tragic thing. But to understand it, it helps to put it in context, not treat it as the common event. Gang violence is not homicide; it's assaults for the most part. There are some interesting aspects to gang violence. One of these is the weapon, and another is how it differs from non-gang violence.

When guns aren't used, what is? The answer comes in a series of categories. Most common are tools, body parts and clothing, alcohol-related objects, and auto-related objects. Think of hammers, pipes, screwdrivers; fists and feet, shoes and belts; beer bottles, mugs and glasses, bar stools; tire irons, bumper jacks, and cars themselves. Next come things readily found around the home such as vases, forks, brooms, and flowerpots, and items around the neighborhood: bricks, boards, tree branches, and chunks of asphalt. Sports items are next in order: bats, pool cues, barbell weights, and golf clubs. All of these plus the more traditional knives, blackjacks, fire bombs, and canes. Some of my personal favorites in the police investigation files are milk crates, handcuffs, a cash register, and a parfait glass.

Assaultive action tends to be more impulsive than planned. Thus, weapons other than firearms are naturally going to be what is readily at hand. Since gang fights are even more likely to be impulsive, the readily available item becomes a weapon. Of all of the items noted above, none approaches the gun in lethality. So, if we look only at homicides, we become impressed by the gang's firearms. When we expand our search to the other, far more common forms of violence, then the gun recedes in its predominance. Every gang member (and many others of us as well) has felt the fist, but relatively few have felt the bullet. Among those shot, the vast majority have lived to show the wound to his homies with some pride.

And make no mistake about it: gang-shooting targets are first and foremost other gang members and their friends, and predominately within their own race or ethnicity. In Los Angeles County, home to the largest number of street gangs in the world, Hispanic gangs prevail, followed by black gangs. Of all the gang-involved homicides recorded during the ten years between 1980 and 1990, 71 percent were Black-on-Black and Hispanic-on-Hispanic. Only 3 percent of the victims were White, and fewer than 2 percent were Asian and other victims. Thus, 24 percent were Black-on-Hispanic or Hispanic-on-Black incidents. These ethnicity data may be of some comfort to Whites and Asians, but they most certainly are not to the African American and Hispanic communities. Gangs are, by and large, killing their own community residents, mostly the young and mostly fellow gang members.

This is a singular feature of the gang world, this turning on one another. Analyses of gang homicides and assaults compared with non-gang homicides and assaults reveal even more of the character of gang violence. This "gang profile" of violence allows street cops like Paco and other investigators to guess quickly whether or not a new incident is likely to be gang related. Compared to non-gang incidents, as in many robberies, domestic assaults, street and barroom fights, and so on, the gang event is more likely to:

• occur in the open—on the street, in a park, etc.;
• involve an auto, as in drive-bys;
• involve a firearm;
• involve additional offenses such as an assault (but not robbery);
• involve injuries to multiple victims;
• involve unidentified assailants;
• involve fear of retaliation;
• involve more people on both the victim and suspect sides;
• involve victims and suspects unknown to each other;
• involve gang members as victims;
• involve males only;
• involve Hispanics and Blacks.

Thus, there is a profile, a signature to the gang event. It is more likely a chaotic event with multiple participants and effects, visible to witnesses, and stereotypically convenient for labeling as "gang related." Paco's stereotypes do, after all, have some factual basis, which he then expands and generalizes to form a caricature rather than a factual profile.

Having said all this, let's put this violence back into its broader context, the one that Paco and his prosecutor friends tend to ignore. Violence is the rare crime. The term "violent gang" is a misnomer if by calling it violent we mean that violence is what the gang is all about. Most street gangs, if we were to label them by their more common questionable behaviors, would be called loitering gangs, or drinking gangs, or graffiti gangs, or petty theft gangs. If boasting about real and exaggerated events were against the law, we could add "boasting gangs."

What *is* clearly true is that gang members contribute disproportionately to many kinds of crime. This is shown most clearly in recent studies that follow gang members over several years. Depending on the crime, gang members have been shown to commit three times, five times, seven times as many acts as non-gang kids from the same areas. They often account for half or more of all serious juvenile offenses in these areas. So gang members are indeed very active.

However, gang members, like most chronic offenders, are not specialists (except in the specialty gangs described earlier) in any one kind of offense. They are generalists; their crime and delinquency is versatile. Paco knows this, but ignores it in public discourse in favor of stressing the stereotyped and violent gang crimes. More and more, police departments as a whole reflect the newer anti-gang legislation by recording as gang crimes only those offenses that fit the stereotype, thereby reifying it very effectively.

Let me share with you the offenses specifically recorded against gang members in two police departments. The first is Paco's. The second is a large southwestern department with a serious gang problem. Both departments provide data on "gang-related crimes."

Paco's department records only eleven offenses for gang members; murder, attempted murder, felony assault, robbery, arson, kidnap, rape, extortion, shooting into an inhabited dwelling, witness intimidation, and battery on a police officer. Paco's department, using statistics gathered from him and the other officers in the gang units, paints a very ugly picture of what gang members do. It appears as though they specialize in violence of all kinds. Oddly, they don't seem to commit other kinds of crime, at least according to official police department statistics. The second department shows a similar pattern. In a special analysis of recorded crimes in an area with five gangs, its listing does not include forcible rape, auto theft, arson, vandalism, curfew violation, loitering, graffiti, or stolen property. Only violent offenses, drug crimes, and serious larcenies are recorded.

A third department has not yet bought into this stereotype. Its gang-related crimes in one year include twenty-seven categories of offenses; murder and attempted murder, assault, robbery, kidnap, sexual assault, and shootings are included from the list above. But in addition we find auto theft, burglary, carrying a concealed weapon, possession of drugs, criminal mischief, disobeying a lawful order, discharging a weapon, disorderly conduct, providing false information, felony menacing, graffiti, harassment, possession of an illegal weapon, interference with police, menacing, reckless endangerment, shoplifting, theft, receiving stolen property, trespass of property, and trespass of an auto.

The contrast is striking; stereotyping versus versatile offending. The second department records nonreality; Paco's records its own bias. The third department has a much better fix on what gang members do. It is more likely to arrest and detain gang members because its concern is broader. Its

rap sheets on gang members will be longer, leading to more certain and severe sanctions for gang members. I find this ironic; the nonstereotyping department, all other things being equal, will do a better job of repression
than will Paco's.

It will also do a better job of informing the public of the dangers of street
gangs. Just compare a few statistics: in Paco's department, the figures show
assault to comprise 54 percent of all gang crime, and murder and attempted
murder another 13 percent. In the other department, figures reveal assaults
at 10 percent, and murder or attempted murder at less than one offense in
1,000. The pictures of gang crime couldn't be more different. Paco's department portrays gangs as violent and vengeful, and scares its citizenry half
to death. But some of the *least* common gang crimes are murder, rape, kidnap, arson, and felony assault, as shown by the broader statistical collection
of many departments. If you really want to be concerned about gang crime,
think about loitering, drinking, graffiti, and petty theft.

One other point about gang crime will lead us into the next chapter,
where we consider the group dynamics, the social processes that are so important to gang behavior. Gang ethnographers and observers have known
for decades about two important factors of gang member crime: that kids
already inclined toward delinquent behavior are the more likely recruits to
gangs and that once a kid joins a gang he becomes considerably more involved in delinquent and criminal behavior. Now survey research done in
the 1990s has shown this even more clearly. In projects in Rochester, Denver, Seattle, and Montreal, researchers have followed hundreds of youth in
each city over many years, with repeated measurement of crime over those
years.

These studies follow the offense patterns of kids in the same schools
and neighborhoods who either do or do not join gangs. For those who do
join, there are measures of offending before joining, during membership,
and after leaving the gang. Comparisons to the offending of non-gang kids
provide solid evidence about gang-related crime and confirm our earlier
beliefs. Gangs tend to recruit more delinquently oriented kids and then
amplify their crime involvement heavily. The attraction of the gang is
more effective with delinquents; the group processes then augment criminal involvement and leaving the gang allows a return closer to pre-gang
levels.

Certainly this finding is a powerful argument for working on barriers to
gang involvement. Prevention is likely to be far more effective than trying
to reduce crime when kids are active in the gang. Further, inducement to
leaving the gang for other alternatives seems worthy of attention as well.

But beyond this, it is clear that we must consider and understand those processes during gang membership that amplify criminal activity. This should help us to intervene more effectively and also help us to avoid doing those things that group processes will twist to the gang's purposes, rather than to ours. This latter point is critical, because the usual gang interventions, from detached workers to gang cop crackdowns and anti-gang legislation, are likely to exacerbate the very group processes that, in turn, amplify gang crime.

⑫

STREET GANGS ARE GROUPS

I can't even tell you if there was a first assault—might not even be the truth. If they feel their gang members were actually jumped, that's as good as gold for them; they're going to go out and retaliate.

—Paco

For most of us, it is the crimes they commit that make street gangs a major concern. As Paco's comment above illustrates, there is something special about gangs that amplifies their crime involvement. It is that special something that we must address in dealing with gangs, and that special something is *group* process or *group* dynamics. Group processes affect more than just crime, but let's start with that issue.

Since the last chapter demonstrated some differences between gang and non-gang crime, let's look at some crime levels that gang and non-gang kids admitted to in hundreds of interviews with us. These admissions, called "self-report delinquency," came from a large city with a history of street gang problems over the past several decades. These differences are pretty typical of what results from the selection into gangs of delinquently prone youth and then the crime amplification that group processes in the gang produce.

These data come from a study of admitted violence from gang and non-gang kids, ages thirteen to fifteen, from the very same, high-crime neighborhoods. The kids, both gang and non-gang, come from exactly

Table 12.1.   Percent Reporting Involvement in Violence in the Last Six Months

	Gang	Non-gang
Set fire to building or car	5	1
Attack with weapon	29	3
Throw objects or rocks at people	42	25
Gang fights	56	9
Hit someone	45	28
Use weapon or force	15	5
Hurt or threaten someone to have sex	0	0
Had sex with someone against his/her will	2	3

the same blocks and neighborhoods as each other. They went to the same schools. Our interviewers had maps of small areas into which each respondent's residence had to fall. Thus, the differences in violence levels reported by the gang members and the non-gang respondents cannot be attributed to their living in different areas; they are functions of gang membership, yea or nay. Look first at the percentage of each group admitting involvement in eight forms of violence in just the six months prior to the interviews.

With the exceptions of sexual violence, young gang members clearly outdo their non-gang counterparts. To these very large differences we can add some information about weapons. Over a third of all the respondents, gang and non-gang, had carried a weapon in the last six months—39 percent of the boys, and 30 percent of the girls.

However, the figure is 59 percent among gang members, and only 17 percent among the others. Gang members also carried their weapons twice as often, almost once a week but not every day as press reports might lead us to believe. In these gang-involved neighborhoods, almost three-quarters of gang members say it is easy to get a gun, compared to 44 percent of the non-gang respondents. Even among the girls, fully a half report that it is easy to get a gun. Finally, these kids report first carrying a hidden weapon on average at the age of twelve. Data such as these remind us both that gang membership is violence related and that it develops in neighborhoods that already contain plenty of violence potential. It is this potential that allows group processes to amplify the violence through the social norms of the gang. Here is Paco's prepared comment on a court case, carefully exaggerated for effect but illustrative of his perspective:

> As with all gangs, retaliation is the key to dominance or status in the gang world. If one gang does something to a member of your gang, it's your responsibility to retaliate against that gang. And usually it's two-fold. If someone

beats up one of your guys, you go stab one of their guys. If someone stabs one of your guys, you go shoot two of their guys. It's always one-upsmanship. It could start from name calling and escalate all the way up to multiple murders.

This kind of escalation may well be more common in gang situations, but criminologists have often commented on its rather common character in non-gang situations as well. While minor confrontations don't usually escalate to serious damage, when serious damage does occur, it can often be traced back to something far less severe. While I was cruising with Paco one evening, we received a radio call of trouble in a bar nearby. Paco volunteered to respond. In a few minutes we pulled up across the street from the bar. Instructing me to stay in the car, Paco entered the place and soon reappeared with a fairly drunken Hispanic male in tow. When they reached the car, Paco motioned me to stay in the front and began to place the drunk in the rear seat.

But down the block, several other men were watching, and when he saw them the drunk started to scream at Paco and at them. Everything was in Spanish, leaving me out of the loop, but the response was clear. Not only those men, but within a minute at least twenty people, male and female, were approaching us in a clearly threatening manner, demanding that Paco release or not manhandle their *carnale*, their brother, their *compadre*. I saw a riot about to occur, but Paco quickly and effectively got his man in the car, turned to the approaching group with one hand on his gun and the other in a stop motion. Keep in mind, Paco is an imposing figure of a man. He then entered the driver's seat, started us up, and took off before anything more organized could take place. He handled the whole affair very effectively, by himself. But he was sweating, and I was a bit shaken; escalation from minor to major events can happen quickly. It was just such an escalation, starting with a traffic stop, that led to the famous Watts riots in Los Angeles in 1965.

Group processes affect us all—in clubs, in teams, in work groups, in families. If we understand the dynamics in groups like these, we can easily translate that experience to the situation in street gangs, remembering that the members of that particular group usually have less going for them outside the group. Thus, the group processes within the gang can take on even greater importance for the members.

Consider the matter of group norms, the standards that groups accept for guiding members' behaviors. Gang graffiti often symbolize some of these norms. Graffiti are used to mark gang territory *and* to warn off rival gangs. Scratch out *our* graffiti, says the gang norm, and we will come after *you*. Graffiti are variously used to express status, mourning of a dead homeboy, turf locations, and challenges. The number 187 next to a name suggests that the named individual had better watch his back; 187 is the California penal code number for murder, and it is found on gang walls across the country and even in Europe, on a park bench at Heidelberg Castle.

Paco came across a wall that, in the large block letters of local Hispanic gang graffiti, spelled out "187 Domingo." This was the ultimate threat for Paco Domingo, whether real or not. For two months, Paco took no action, nor did his fellow officers, who were well aware of this *placa* (graffiti). But then Paco spotted the graffiti writer, who had stupidly put his own *placa* with his moniker elsewhere on the same wall in the very same style. Paco chased him down, arrested him, took him to the station, and had him charged with conspiracy to commit or to solicit murder. Don't mess with Paco Domingo.

I got the impression over the years that gang norms, of all the group processes, were the most notable to Paco. He came back to them time and again, particularly when testifying in court where his exaggerations might have the greatest impact. For instance, the famous "code of silence" so prominent among police officers who will not rat on each other captured his imagination as descriptive of gang members as well: "It's my opinion that someone who would break that code in a gang would be forever looking over his shoulder for retaliation. He would probably be killed or attempted to be killed soon."

Mind you, he testified to this while knowing full well that he and his fellow gang officers often enticed arrested gang members to become informants on their gang in return for release or reduced charges. Are they setting up gang members to be murder victims? Of course not; they know that most informants are not found out by their homies; officers sometimes go to considerable lengths to protect them. But also they often don't respect gang informants enough to be bothered by the consequences. Let 'em shoot it out among themselves! Here's Paco testifying about this again, and once more overstating the case:

> Members of a gang—any gang—are very strictly bound by their code, by their gang code, not to talk and not to cooperate with the police and other authorities regarding criminal behavior. That's part of the gang culture; you just don't cooperate regarding your own gang members. But any gang member, it's the same thing; you don't want to be testifying against another gang member, not even a rival gang.

What Paco refers to as a code, a rigid standard for gang behavior, is more correctly seen as a group *norm*, and group norms are stretchable.

They define a band of behavior that is altered by circumstances. We all ascribe to a norm of not lying, yet we do stretch the truth quite often to fit the circumstances: "I did not eat it all, "I didn't say that," "He wasn't speeding, officer," "It's in the mail," and so on. Norms have boundaries. Gang norms have boundaries, and they're not well fixed. Many gang members, in certain circumstances, tell on others; many fail to participate in a fight or a payback; many keep a portion of their drugs or stolen goods; many try for sex with other members' girlfriends. Gang norms are rhetorical, not hard-and-fast rules. Paco loses sight of this.

A related group process in gangs has been called status enhancement in the criminological literature. "It's a status thing," Paco recognized. The status of the group reflects on the individual who often has few other sources of status. Putting your *placa* on the wall gives status; wearing your gang's colors or tattoos gives status. Retelling gang "war stories" offers status. Talking to reporters and speaking on TV about your gang provides status, especially if you exaggerate the group's solidarity and importance. "The gang is our family, man," "We the baddest gang they is," "Cops can't touch us, man." Gang members often carry in their pockets news clippings about their gang's exploits. Even having a street worker assigned to them becomes a source of status: "We're so bad they gotta give us a sponsor."

So I often tell Paco, and any officer who will listen, not to feed the need for status. Don't call them by their street names; don't harass them for hanging on the corner. Don't try to impress them with how much you know about them. Don't legitimate the gang member, but individuate him or her. Any status enhancement received from gang membership solidifies that membership.

This is particularly the case with gang leadership. Terms like O.G., shot caller, and Veterano attached to a gang member only reinforce his status. Some gangs try to achieve status by posing as "community leaders," calling themselves "community service groups" and the like.

Normally, street gangs are not so organizational, so formal in nature that they require designated leaders. Gang leadership is more often a matter of influence, reputation, and respect. This is earned, not assigned or elected. The member who checked out my credentials, making sure I wasn't hanging around because I was a narc or a pedophile, was exercising a form of leadership for his homies, but he wasn't a chairman or a president or designated enforcer for the gang. It is in the sense of fulfilling functions that gang leadership is usually expressed. It's a group process, not a quality of a few strong characters as Paco sees it. He wastes a lot of time trying to bust up the gang by arresting so-called leaders, failing to see that leadership *functions* are processes that are shared by different individuals in different circumstances.

Similarly, those well-meaning practitioners in the community who try to resolve gang rivalries by arranging truce meetings are probably doing more harm than good in the long run. First, they enhance the status of the warring gangs, and even the war itself, by working for the truce. They officially legitimate the conflict. Second, they attempt to empower the gang "leaders" they designate as such to go back to that group and tell them to "cool it." The leadership mantle is thereby bestowed.

On this matter, Paco and I are in complete agreement. "Truce meetings are high risk prevention," he said. He hates gang truces because they legitimate the gangs and give them the respect and publicity he never wants them to have. I, too, worry about the legitimization, the confirmation of leadership status, and the likelihood of increased cohesiveness that may result.

In Omaha, the ultimate status enhancement for a gang leader was conferred when he shot and killed a patrol officer who had pulled over his van on a summer evening. Six youths were in the van when it was stopped, and two teenage girls were nearby, along with others in an adjacent yard. The twenty-year-old shooter leapt from the van, looked directly at the two girls, then fired three times at the officer still seated in his car. The gang members had been cruising the area, looking for robbery victims and rival Crips. When the shooter reentered the van, his feat of "bravado," as he undoubtedly saw it, was greeted by his homies with laughter as they drove off.

Further investigation revealed the shooter to be a core member of a local Bloods gang. He was said to be both respected and feared by youngsters in the neighborhood, buying them candy and soda pop. He had a long rap sheet: burglary, shoplifting, disorderly conduct, obstructing justice, distributing crack cocaine—the typical cafeteria of offenses. Time in both a juvenile reformatory and in prison did no good. A month before killing the officer, he was himself the victim of a drive-by shooting.

This young man, as it turned out, had developed what the Omaha *World-Herald* investigation described as "a great deal of animosity toward authority. Police are the enemy." And here he was, in a police traffic stop, already hopped up by his homies in the van who were out looking for trouble in any case, with a firearm in hand, and reputation to be confirmed. Group processes combined to make him a shooter; the officer's vulnerability made the shooting a murder, and they drove off laughing, group cohesiveness raised to the extreme.

This business of group cohesiveness is pivotal to understanding street gangs. It is the ultimate group process in that it results from gang norms, status needs, leadership patterns, rejection by society, the scorn of officials, and the deficits in character of the deficient-aggressive and group-dependent kids who join in the hanging and banging of gang life.

Group cohesiveness in the gang is almost as hard to define as the gang itself; tightness, mutual commitment—"we're a family," "we watch each other's backs"—the priority of member relationships over all others, pride in group, "all for one and one for all." I've seen it in action in a wide variety of settings:

- The quiet gathering of the Latins that was so quickly stirred into action by two hopheads reporting the presence of rival gang members;
- The response to the leadership challenge when the speaker said, "We're gonna go through them like a hot knife through butter";
- The tight grouping around me at a taco stand in the anticipation of a rival drive-by;
- The excited gathering in the park of a large gang segment expecting an attack from their rivals;
- The massive gathering of 100 members (and my research assistant) at the site of a rumored drive-by about to take place, a rumor that most certainly would have scared off most of us.

These are the dramatic instances that immediately impress the observer, but equally important is realizing the extent to which these young people come to depend on one another, in so many settings, for emotional support and a common identity. It is seen in group meetings, in informal sports events, in school, on the street, and at parties. It's not stable. Cohesiveness rises and falls. It's greater in some gangs than in others, higher among some cliques than others, and always responsive to outside pressures as much as internal needs.

Among the five types of street gangs outlined earlier, cohesiveness is probably highest among the Specialty gangs where mutual dependence and loyalty spells the difference between successful business and court conviction. It is probably lowest in the Collective gang, that rather amorphous collection of neighborhood youths so well described by Mark Fleisher's account of the Fremont Hustlers in Kansas City. One of Paco's errors is in attributing high cohesiveness to the Neo-traditional and Traditional gangs, but imagine the difficulty in maintaining high levels of bonding among hundreds of young people broken into subgroups by virtue of their own size.

This attribution of high cohesiveness to the best-known gangs is common to a number of gang officers, and certainly to the media and to filmmakers. It stems, at least in part, from our general notion that cohesive groups are productive groups and therefore that high cohesiveness is to be expected, even fostered, to obtain the groups' products. We work hard to develop group cohesiveness—we commonly call it group spirit—in sports teams, in work groups, in hobby groups. We like the product of these groups, so the greater the cohesion, the better.

But the "product" of the street gang—the graffiti, thefts, threats of violence that are amplified by group processes—is not like the positive products of these other groups. So gang cohesiveness should be discouraged by police, by gang workers, by teachers, by parents. We *can* foolishly increase it by intervening in knee-jerk fashion, as shown by Paco and by gang worker programs. Research data reveal that cohesiveness, and thus the criminal product, increases as we intervene in gang processes more directly.

Reducing gang cohesiveness is not easily accomplished because the inadvertent effect of almost any intervention is to *increase* it by providing attention, notoriety, and legitimization to the gang's structure, its leadership, and the members' attachment to it. The best advice is to *avoid* doing things to *or* for the gang that has such effects. Don't hold gang meetings or truce meetings. Don't single out gang members for special attention among all youth in the community *because* they are gang members. Provide resources—jobs, tutoring, counseling, parental help, and so on—because they can benefit from these as *individuals*. Mount neighborhood youth programs, not gang member programs.

For the police, productive acts would be to arrest gang members just as they do the rest of us, for the offenses committed. Don't single them out for special treatment, don't harass them as gang members. Don't show off by using their street names and disrespecting their groups to them. Avoid the simplistic we-versus-them war games mentality. Cohesiveness breeds enhanced gang crime; the data clearly state: don't grease the skids. Paco's strategies too often provide the grease.

Yet other data suggest that the gang itself can increase its own cohesiveness when things are too quiet. Decreasing levels of cohesiveness can threaten the gang's life and the importance of core members who become dependent on the gang's strength and reputation. Deliberate action, criminal or social, can be undertaken to stir things up again. Thus, interventions that successfully reduce the group spirit of the gang may inadvertently trigger off new actions—attacks on rivals for instance—that serve to reassert gang status. What a paradox! And what a warning that we must understand and respect group processes in gangs before we meddle with them.

Paco understands cohesiveness at a basic level. He takes pride in his own life in the Marines—"the few, the proud." Police departments generally count on group cohesiveness: the brotherhood of the Corps and the brotherhood of the department are not far removed. On occasion, it gets even closer to our concerns when elite police units such as gang units develop their own special cohesive bonds, as in the gang unit that called itself the Vikings and as in the LAPD's Rampart division anti-gang unit whose corruption blew holes in that department's armor.

But just as a gang unit can go bad, Paco reinterprets gang cohesiveness to twist it into an evil. Now it becomes a conspiracy, not group spirit. It becomes planned antisocial behavior, justifying pulling out all the stops to combat it. Mind you, to *explain* the nature of gang cohesiveness is not to excuse it or to justify it. It helps to understand, but Paco has grown increasingly impatient with understanding. He distorts a process into an inherent evil. I've always found irony in the parallels between police cohesiveness and street gang cohesiveness, between the twist that Paco gives to the gang process and the twist that the gang process gives to anti-gang messages. He epitomized this distortion of the message charmingly for me in discussing the anti-gang movie, *Boyz N the Hood*. He described the general anti-gang message, and then the single scene in which the retaliatory drive-by ends in the downing of several rival gang members. At the end of that scene, the cool "hero" of the action approaches each injured rival and calmly administers a single "head shot" to each victim, execution style.

"That's what the guys get off on," said Paco. "That was a righteous gang execution; and they really grab their jocks on that one; forget the rest of the movie." Group process led this gang to see glory in the head shots, rather than the dire consequences of gang activity.

Group process is what you make of it. For Paco, gang cohesiveness becomes an evil, a conspiracy. For the gang, it is the means by which anti-gang forces, including the messages of the police, the media, and the social reformers, are turned into gang supports. For the criminologist, it is neither conspiratorial nor self-justifying, but rather a complex key to understanding the gang and beginning to frame intervention ideas that will not be inherently counterproductive.

⓲

STREET GANG VICTIMS

The man was terrified. We had six policemen there, but it
took us two hours to convince him to sign a complaint.

—an anonymous chief of police, 1976

The victims of crime, especially violent crime, hold a special place in our
society. Almost without exception, we feel for them, we pray for their re-
covery, we know that we may be next. Yet 60 percent of the victims of gang
violence may not earn our sympathy. Why? Because they themselves are
gang members, predators turned victims by unpredicted turns of events.

Paco, we have learned, has little sympathy for gang members. If a gang
member becomes a gang crime victim, well, he asked for it. Let 'em all kill
each other off. Yet one of my most memorable exposures to Paco involved
his ironic display of concern for the parents of a gang crime victim. I was
sitting in the back of a courtroom waiting to testify in the case of a gang-
related homicide. Paco was there as well, waiting his turn. In his opening
statement, the defense attorney was doing a rather effective job of explaining away the gang shooter's alleged behavior, saying there would be testimony that seemingly might either free him or at least produce a lesser
charge against him. The prosecutor had not as yet been active.

As the defense argument steadily advanced, a small group to my left became increasingly disturbed, with tears and head shaking clearly indicating
their unhappiness. This was quite obviously the victim's family. The case

against the killer of their son was not going well. When the noon recess was announced, Paco and another officer, who turned out to be the principal investigating homicide detective on the case, rose and went directly to the family, mother, father, and several siblings or cousins to judge by their ages. Both officers, with Paco being the more solicitous and forceful, sought to assure the victim's family that this was only a temporary setback. They knew the case, they noted, and it was "a done deal." The D.A. would put this guy away for good. "Don't worry, please. I promise you, this guy has no chance. Your son's murderer will pay, big time."

They spent fifteen to twenty minutes reassuring the family, telling them the D.A. had a very strong case and the defense couldn't get the killer off. There was much hands-on comforting and words of assurance from both officers. I had never seen Paco like this; he was warm, supportive, actually hugging the mother. I was quite taken by the solicitous attitudes of both officers for the bereaved family.

And then I remembered who the victim was, a hard-core gangbanger from a rival group. The case materials I had read in preparation for my testimony revealed shooter and victim alike to be highly committed gang members with long rap sheets and few mitigating factors. Paco was going to help burn the shooter, while the equally despicable guy—in his mind—had suddenly aroused his deepest sympathies. Was he being honest? Hell, no. It didn't matter which "gangster" had been the shooter. Paco would line up with the victim's family against the defendant. The irony of his embracing the case of the dead gangbanger, and literally embracing the member's mother, struck me as almost ludicrous, given what I knew of Paco's view of hard-core bangers. But he had a role to play here, and he played it well.

Late in his career, as this case was, the arena of victim's rights had come to interest Paco more. It was a legitimized, backdoor way of expressing his denigration of the victimizers, especially in cases of what he termed "random" or "senseless" gang predation.[1] (He has also become fond of words like predation and predator, to go along with "gangster" and "hoodlum.") State and federal laws protecting and promoting victims' rights, encouraging victim testimony at time of sentencing, and compensating victims for their losses all made the point for him. The Bill of Rights now applied to victims, not just to the rights of the predators.

Understandably, his viewpoint expanded to include crime witnesses, whether or not they were victimized. "Witness intimidation is stated or implied in each case we handle," he overstated. And indeed, which of us hasn't wondered on occasion whether we might be subject to retaliation if we made a crime report identifying the perpetrator. This can take on added significance in gang cases, since we may assume that the gang perpetrator has plenty of homies to come to his aid in order to discourage our testimony. Paco told a news reporter, in his usual exaggerating fashion: "They have an inexhaustible supply of guns and a penchant to use them. These kids are willing to take revenge. That's a thing you used to see just on television. They will retaliate against the report of a crime, so people don't want to talk to us when we go to a scene, not even the victims."

He said this some years ago, before firearms had become one of the gang stereotypic offenses of principal concern to the police and encapsulated in anti-gang legislation like the STEP Act. But by the 1990s, witness intimidation had become a major issue. A study in one Midwestern city, for example, reported intimidation of victims and witnesses reaching 34 percent in gang cases but nonexistent in non-gang cases. Recall from Chapter 11 that most gang violence among gangs involved victims of the same race or ethnicity as the perpetrator and mostly from the same communities. Victims and witnesses have to assume a greater vulnerability when they are close by. With 60 percent or more of assault victims being gang members themselves, intimidation is an expectable corollary to crime. Certainly the perception of its likelihood is ever present, whether it takes place or not.

Victims of gang homicides differ from other victims in several significant ways. Even in areas where gangs are a part of the neighborhood, clear differences emerge. Victims of gang homicides, in a large study reported by Cheryl Maxson, are on average twenty-four years old, while victims of other homicides are a full ten years older. Ninety percent of the gang victims are male, while 77 percent of other victims are male. Gang victims are far more likely to be killed out in the open—on the street, in a public park or a shopping area—while other victims are most often found in a residence. And, while in the long run it makes little difference to the deceased, gang victims succumb to firearms in 95 percent of cases, compared to 75 percent in non-gang cases.

In the study reported in Chapter 12 of gang and non-gang youths from the very same neighborhoods, even there the victim patterns among thirteen to fifteen-year-olds was different. Non-gang girls reported being beaten up more often, and beaten or abused within their own families more, but it was the gang girls who were more often robbed, stabbed, shot at, and sexually assaulted. Paco once testified about the response of a gang suspect being charged with assault on a girl. Told that the girl's mother reported suspect and victim had been living together for a while, the boy told Paco. "Fucking her doesn't mean I was dating her." The exploitative attitude is similar to the occasional use of "strawberries," girls who offer all forms of sex in return for a hit of crack or heroin.

Among the boys, the gang members uniformly reported higher rates of victimization for all offenses than did the non-gang boys. Being a gang member can be hazardous to your health.

The often-cited reports of innocent victims, random or senseless violence, or even assaults on drug sellers are gross exaggerations of gang victim realities. The bulk of gang violence victims are the result of intergang rivalries, intragang disputes, turf battles and threats, and similar internecine affairs. This does not deny the existence of other victims; they are many. And a few have captured our imagination, like Karen Toshima in Westwood or three-year-old Stephanie Kuhen in Los Angeles. These are the cases that galvanize public outrage and political reactions. The rest, the "run-of-the-mill" gang killings and other events, are the ignored background.

Most of us have been crime victims—a house burglarized, an auto stolen, a pocket picked, something taken from the office. Victimization is common. It affects our lives. When we hear about gangs and their victims, we are likely to applaud the efforts of the gang cops. My beef is not with them, only with those, like Paco, who lose their objectivity and deliberately demonize the street gang. I am no friend of any criminal, gang or otherwise. I am, in fact, more a victim than most of my readers.

I've never been accepted as a jury member for two reasons. First, I usually get kicked off because I know and have worked with too many cops, too many judges, too many attorneys. But second, even if I get beyond these items in the voir dire stage of jury impaneling, my victim status finishes me off. In one instance, there was the following dialogue:

Prosecutor: Juror number 4, have you yourself ever been the victim of a crime?

Juror: Yes, I have.

Prosecutor: Could you tell us what the crime was?

Juror: Sure. Which one?

Prosecutor: Oh. Well, just tell us what the crimes were.

Juror: Ummh, let's see. My car was stolen once, and vandalized on two other occasions. On two occasions I've had personal items stolen from me. Over the years I've had, I believe the number is now up to ten home burglaries. And I was the victim of an attempted armed robbery.

When he stopped laughing, the judge assured me I would not be an appropriate juror and dismissed me. I was also let go by the defense attorney once when he asked if I had any friends who were attorneys and I responded: "Good lord, no!" Would I be biased as a juror because of my various victimizations? I really don't know. I have found the home burglaries particularly aggravating. In one instance, the burglar broke in through a bathroom window and accidentally cut himself quite deeply, using one of my towels to staunch the flow of blood. I freely admit I felt considerable pleasure in his injury (and I had more than one towel, in any case). So, as I said, I'm no friend of the criminal.

Paco, of course, is aware of my many exposures as a victim. They put me on his side. He assumes that I, too, must want to see all predators put away. What I have never brought myself to share with him is that I am a "card-carrying" member of the American Civil Liberties Union (ACLU). The ACLU is anathema to most police, because ACLU attorneys uphold the rights of criminals in court proceedings. The ACLU has argued strongly against anti-gang injunctions and has persistently raised questions about police handling of gang matters as in the infamous Rampart gang unit affair. If I had told Paco of my ACLU connection, that alone might have severed our relationship.

NOTE

1. Of course, gang attacks are neither random nor senseless. They are not random events because they follow a pattern, even if the wrong target is hit. Nor are they senseless. They make sense from the attacker's view, even if not from ours.

14

GANG CONTROL: PACO'S WAY
AND OTHER WAYS

Let me tell you what the justice system is. It's me and my partner. We
have a car, a radio, a backup unit, two .38s, one shotgun in the rack. That
is the justice system on the street. To make it complete, you add one
criminal. There isn't any D.A. or public defender in that system, no probation officers, no judges. Just me and my partner . . . and some assholes.
. . . A lot of people aren't carrying their weight.

—Paco[1]

As one part of interviews carried out with officers across the country, I
asked, "What do you do to handle the gang problem?" Paco's answer was
short and sweet: "We do harassment." In a more public setting, he would
have called this "selective enforcement" or "directed patrol." Other responses indicate just how widespread are Paco's views.

Arizona: We let patrol hammer at 'em.

Connecticut: At one point, some major gangs were dissipated—the leaders
were killed.

Alaska: Gang migrants started showing up at the airport. We jumped on 'em,
violated the hell outta their rights—and they left.

Illinois: Our shakedown is one step below harassment. It probably violates
their rights quite a bit.

Florida: At one point we mounted a county-wide task force and knocked the shit out of them.

Texas: Sometimes we do "air strikes" (street sweeps, directed patrol, and the like).

As I've indicated, Paco is basically a loner. He knows his gangs and feels more than competent to deal with them. But when they expand, proliferate, spread their wings to other locations, he knows there are these other cops out there, other Pacos, to whom he can reach out. There is a network of Pacos, sharing gang intelligence and glorying in similar war stories. Yet, with few exceptions like cross-department task forces, as a loner he cannot connect and share with others who also have an interest in gang control and prevention.

Paco and his counterparts don't give much thought to alternative approaches to these gang situations. Gang suppression is the key to their thinking, and often the limit to their thinking. But there's a panoply of other approaches out there. We need to consider these first, and then look as well at various forms of suppression.

I mentioned in an earlier chapter that gang prevention captured Paco's attention briefly. Like many police officers, he sees the clue to most crime prevention in the family. "Before you have a delinquent kid," he told me, "you usually have a delinquent parent."

Prevention has become a central value to the police, but only in restricted senses of the word; think about Police Athletic Leagues for instance. *Early* prevention is OK; get to the kids before they head for trouble; clean up the physical neighborhood before its own deterioration encourages crime. Juvenile officers and community relations officers can engage in these activities, but not Paco's gang cops. They clean up afterward.

"Top management," Paco told me, "can try to talk themselves out of having a gang problem here, but meanwhile *we're* out in a community under siege. They can say what they want, but we got the job of getting Sneezy and Dopey and Doc and the other gang dwarfs off the street and put away." And when I responded in terms of community residents wanting more attention to early prevention and neighborhood improvement, his response was, "They can't say it to me direct, you know. But I look in their eyes and I know how grateful they are for me getting these scumbags off the street."

So Paco doesn't work with gang prevention programs. His greatest distaste is for those who espouse prevention through denial of the problem. Their notion may be that by calling the problem a *gang* problem, they may make it worse. "Major league denial," Paco calls it. They may feel that admitting to a gang problem is bad publicity for the community or its elected officials. In my national interviews, I found that the first response, even by police, was official denial of gang problems in over 40 percent of the cases.

"As long as criminal conduct goes unnoticed and unpunished, or we rationalize the fact that kids are shooting each other because of some television program . . . violence is going to grow," noted Paco. He could have pointed out that in some cities denial of gangs lasted only until a public official's family member was assaulted, as in Denver and Columbus. His personal example was of a similar sort: "A couple of weeks ago, a football quarterback was killed by a gang member and all hell broke out; lots of media attention, a task force against youth violence, and so on."

He might have acknowledged another problem of denial, but I doubt it would have occurred to him. When a community denies its own street gang problems, it prohibits itself from undertaking prevention activities. Paco doesn't care about most of these, but they are widespread in communities that have tried to come to grips with their street gangs. The most comprehensive of these are attempts at community and resident mobilization or community organization that might decrease the need for local youths to turn to gangs for their own fulfillment. Famous examples include the earlier Chicago Area Projects and New York's Mobilization for Youth. Neither undertook research evaluations that might have demonstrated their success.

A more recent example was launched in the late 1990s in Los Angeles. Called L.A. Bridges, this citywide prevention program was budgeted at over forty million dollars over four years. Unfortunately, it failed to concentrate on gang-prone youth for its many prevention programs, and then it allowed its independent research evaluation first to miss the mark and then to fade away after only a year. Thus, as in Chicago and New York, a major opportunity to learn "what works" in community organization was lost.

Cops like Paco have minimal interest in community organization programs. They are, however, more willing to support, if not become directly involved in youth recreation and service programs like Big Brothers and Sisters, Boys' and Girls' Clubs, and other programs more designed for conforming youngsters and of little appeal to gang-prone youth. Even more congenial to Paco are programs like DARE (Drug Awareness and Resistance Education) and GREAT (Gang Resistance, Education, and Training). Both of these are programs run in the schools—usually upper-elementary or early-middle-school grades—using uniformed police officers to deliver a multiweek program of life skills and social values to "ward off" involvement in drugs and gangs. But Paco gets angry, once striking out at me vocally in a public hearing, when I reported the results of independent research evaluations of both DARE and GREAT. Both, although widely accepted by the public and enforcement agencies, have proven to be almost totally ineffective in preventing drug use and gang joining.

In an earlier chapter, I mentioned Paco's disdain for gang truces. He distrusts any program that gives any credit or recognition to a gang member whom someone suggests is a gang leader. A number of programs, beyond truces, do just that, enrolling members respected by gangs as youth counselors and gang workers. These enrollees are often the Veteranos or O.G.s whom Paco cannot accept as "reformed" in any real sense. Anecdotal evidence is often offered to "prove" either the success or the failure of such programs. Research evaluations have been mixed; one in Philadelphia suggested total failure of the effort, and one in East Los Angeles reported some limited reduction in intergang violence.

Another, almost romantic, vision of gang prevention, and the one most distasteful to Paco, is the so-called "Hoodlum Priest" approach. Here, one charismatic individual, often church related, takes on the world on behalf of gang prevention and reform. He embraces the gang members as part of his flock, to be nudged, taught, encouraged, preached at, and eventually turned from gang activity to more positive pursuits: family, education, work, service back to the neighborhood. Probably the most famous of these individuals is Father Gregory Boyle of East Los Angeles, subject of a very sympathetic book by journalist Celeste Fremon, *Father Greg and the Homeboys*. Over many years, Father Boyle has organized job programs, a special school, and parent groups for the gangs in his parish. But at last count, he had administered last rites to over a hundred of his gang members, a horrific number and one that does not make one sanguine about his approach. Many cities have counterparts to Father Boyle (famous as "G-Dog" to the homies), and in each there are cops like Paco to whom they are anathema, bleeding hearts who tell gangsters that God loves them despite their crimes. Paco is not in the resurrection business.

Beyond gang prevention there lies an additional set of approaches that could be called "gang intervention." These approaches are designed for situations in which gangs and gang activity are already established, too late for prevention (or at least for "primary prevention" as the public health field terms efforts to avoid the emergence of a problem).

Professor Irving Spergel, at the University of Chicago, has provided a useful summary of the many approaches, from prevention through intervention to suppression. He has a comprehensive approach to gang work that has been implemented in locations across the country. Funded by the U.S. Department of Justice, the "Spergel Model," as it has come to be known, stresses the simultaneous, though not equal application of five major strategies to reduce the street gang problem.

Two of the strategies fall under the general rubric of prevention. The first is community mobilization, which involves integrating the efforts of grassroots organizations, social agencies, community service groups, and individual neighborhood residents and businessmen. Since leaving the Juvenile Division, Paco has separated himself from all such efforts, wary of "community activists" and people with agendas different from his. He aligns himself with the police chief in one city who noted increased activity of the Baker Street Gang. The chief reportedly decided to have the street name changed to Pansy Lane; no self-respecting street gang member, he suggested, would want to associate with the "Pansy Lane Gang." Whether this change was actually made, we don't know; it's the spirit of the thing that counts.

As a juvenile officer, Paco had seen the likely benefit for delinquency prevention of groups like Big Brothers and the Boys' Clubs. Police officers and police departments across the country have to greater and lesser degrees endorsed such early prevention efforts. As I noted earlier, Paco still approves of such groups, but not for gang problems. These are too serious to be placed in the hands of volunteers, social workers, or well-meaning agencies. "Law enforcement officers," he told a newspaper reporter, "just don't have the time or ability to get into psychology and cultural-type issues" with street gangs.

A second strategy in the Spergel Model is organization change. This includes better integration between such groups as police, schools, probation, and human services, something Paco resists, but also changing these organizations to be more responsive to (or even tolerant of) gang members. You can imagine how this would strike cops like Paco.

Over the years, Paco has not altered his views about the value of the schools. He sees school completion as important to the making of solid citizens and as a potential control mechanism by keeping kids busy and notifying police about troublemakers. Other public agencies, however, get little respect from him:

- The courts: "Some kids with fifty arrests and maybe twenty or more convictions are being handled like Sunday school children."
- Corrections: "There was a time when kids were afraid of the courts, afraid of going to the juvenile camps, afraid of being labeled a hoodlum and sent away to someplace where they'd be miserable and lonely."
- Street work programs: When I discussed findings that some street workers' evaluations had shown an *increase* in gang cohesiveness and crime

and should probably not be continued, he praised my "objectivity" and said: "If it had come out the other way, we wouldn't be talking together."

He was appalled by my report of a street-working probation officer who on one occasion saw a gang member killed right in front of him. The officer failed to take any action. On another occasion, this probation officer looked out his driver's window at a parallel car to see a pistol pointed at his head. Again, other than freezing, this probation officer took no action. Paco's derisive comment was, "Well, what the hell; all probation officers are incompetent."

Yet, in recent years, Paco has come to appreciate the work of some probation and parole officers because these correctional agencies nationwide have been increasingly taking on the role of "peace officers." They are becoming "thumpers rather than helpers," as Paco put it, revoking probation and parole for violations and returning clients to correctional facilities. In my state, probation and parole officers have a special prerogative not available to police, the power to conduct searches of their clients' residences and workplaces without warrants from the court. This is a very formidable hammer, and Paco has teamed up with these officers to conduct such searches of gang members on probation or parole.

The Pacos of the world are not only found in gang units or police departments. They can be probation officers, they can be parole officers, and they can be guards in correctional institutions. And, of course, they can work as agents of the FBI, DEA (Drug Enforcement Administration), or ATF (Bureau of Alcohol, Tobacco, and Firearms). Yet there is balance here. Many probation, parole, prison, and federal officers express disdain for cops like Paco. They see these police "cowboys" as limited in their skills and their ability to control the bad guys by anything other than force. Such cops, they know, don't work well with people in the community, even though community members can be intelligence sources about gang members who could be returned to incarceration.

None of this bodes well for Paco's involvement in helping to bring about organizational change on behalf of gang prevention. This is a long-term strategy in the Spergel Model, and Professor Spergel himself has noted communities applying the model in which the police have to be brought kicking and screaming to the table. It only takes one cowboy to stampede the herd.

The third strategy in the Spergel Model is called "opportunities provision." It is more of an intervention than a preventive strategy in that it is aimed at active gang members. It comes in many guises: providing tutoring and other help with school work and counseling to remain in school; developing job training and job placement for gang members; helping them to enter the armed services; opening up recreational centers that normally shun gang members; and enhancing access to health services, especially for female gang members. Paco has no special problem with opportunities provision, and many of his fellow officers occasionally refer gang members to agencies providing these services. But it's not Paco's bag.

The fourth strategy is called "social intervention," but in essence it refers to the use of outreach workers, and especially street gang workers. They are assigned to gangs, develop rapport with individual members, counsel them, work when possible with the parents, intervene in pending intergang hostilities, try to connect members to job and other opportunities, and often develop group activities such as gang meetings, ball games, outings, car washes, dances, and so on. Street gang workers usually become advocates for gang members, sometimes even in court hearings, and because they seem to "sponsor" the gang or its members, they generally draw the ire of law enforcement. Some gang workers are former gang members themselves; nothing pleases Paco more than hearing of a gang worker busted for illegal activities and, since it happens more than occasionally, he is often pleased.

The fifth Spergel Model strategy is suppression. While many agencies can and do attempt to control gang behavior, it is left to the police to initiate or play a major role in suppression activities. Suppression here means more than the normal range of enforcement procedures. This is enforcement above and beyond the usual call of duty. It is based on the idea of deterrence, or the use of punishment to reduce or eliminate future crime. The more certain, the more swift, and the more severe the suppression, the more effective it is supposed to be. Paco and most police believe strongly in the certainty, swiftness, and severity of arrest, conviction, and sentencing. They are less concerned with two corollary aspects of deterrence: that it be seen as legitimate by those who are suppressed and that it offer positive alternatives to criminal behavior. Paco automatically assumes the legitimacy of his procedures, of most anti-gang procedures, and couldn't care less about providing positive alternatives to crime.

But here's an irony. Professor Spergel undertook a survey of law enforcement and other officials in some forty-five gang cities. He asked which of the five strategies was most and least common, as well as which was believed to be most and least effective. The most common strategy was suppression. Believed to be least effective? Also suppression! We should keep this in mind as we review various gang suppression approaches. While there are virtually no competent evaluations of the various suppression approaches, a program in central California may be instructive. As reported to one of my graduate students by a deputy chief probation officer, he developed a gang suppression program to "tail 'em, jail 'em, and nail 'em." They targeted 200 gang members, concentrating on the "shot callers" with the idea that tailing, jailing, and nailing the leadership would disintegrate the gangs. Thirty-two were put away, and the gang numbers increased thereafter from 200 to 400.

The effectiveness of gang suppression programs is virtually always determined by selected anecdotal reports and by the certainty among the suppressors—including cops like Paco—that what they do works. If they didn't think so, goes the rationale, they wouldn't be doing it. This is not a position peculiar to the police, of course. Recall the counselor who declared, "I can't believe that fifteen minutes with me won't help a kid." We all become convinced of the efficacy of our efforts. The major difference with law enforcement, unfortunately, is that it is so resistant to independent evaluations of its efforts. Effectiveness is assumed rather than objectively demonstrated, and that's a pity. Here then, within Professor Spergel's fifth strategy, is a list of basically untested suppression procedures.

- *Neighborhood Sweeps:* At their extremes, sweeps are exemplified by Operation Hammer, in which 1,000 police officers on successive nights swarmed through gang areas of the city to "send the message" that the police, not the gangs, were in control. Typically, neighborhood sweeps result in few useful arrests or convictions but are assumed to have a deterrent effect on visible gang activity. They are not designed to foster positive community relations.
- *Saturation Patrols:* Like small sweeps, these are temporary task force efforts, a show of force over a few days or more, designed less to sweep up gang members than to prevent open gang activity through sheer patrol visibility. Both sweeps and saturation patrols are highly labor-intensive and cannot be maintained for long without serious depletion of normal enforcement activity. A study in Dallas indicated no effect of a saturation patrol program there.
- *Selective Enforcement:* This is the targeting of "hot spots" of criminal or gang activity, often seen from the recipient's point of view as police harassment. "Motorola cops"—patrol officers responding to coordinated radio calls—make repeated visits to street corners, pool halls, taco stands, and other habitual gathering spots for gang members. On one occasion, when asked by a group of gang members why they were being hounded at an amusement center, Paco responded, "You're too ugly to be seen in public."
- *Cul-de-Sacs:* These are small areas, usually short streets or alleys heavily used for drive-up drug sales, which are closed off at one end so as to trap dealers or buyers. The number of drug-related arrests peaks

quickly, but then subsides as dealers and buyers alike develop alternative sites for transacting their business.

- *Illegal Stops and Searches:* On a visit to Philadelphia to determine whether a widely touted gang prevention program was responsible for a dramatic drop in gang violence, we spent some time with the local police. Highly critical of the prevention program, the head of the police gang unit took credit for much of the improvement. Saying he would deny it if we quoted him, he admitted that the principal strategy was a series of illegal stops and harassment of gang members. In another city, a police spokesman said, "So I say it's time for a real crackdown. I say we throw every acknowledged gang member out of the county parks on sight until they can learn to behave like decent gentlemen." And in Los Angeles, it was revealed that the police in the Rampart Division and elsewhere were illegally detaining undocumented immigrants and, in direct violation of department policy, turning them over to immigration officials for deportation. The immigrants targeted for these activities were often gang members and, in one highly publicized incident, a former gang member active in a group called Homies Unidos involved in arranging intergang truces.

- *Hard-Core Targeting:* On the theory that incarceration of so-called gang leaders is not only a worthy pursuit in its own right but also an effective deterrent for other gang members, special programs are developed for those leaders. One example is "Hard Core" prosecution programs—a favorite of Paco's—that use special search warrant procedures, continuity in prosecutor personnel ("vertical prosecution"), witness protection programs, and refusal of plea bargaining to achieve high rates of convictions and long sentences for gang leaders and serious felonious gang criminals.

  A second example at the police level is gang enforcement teams (often involving more than one city and coordination with prosecutors' offices) that use departmental data to predict which gang members are most likely to re-offend. These members are then put under heightened police surveillance and arrested for even the most minor offenses. They may then, in addition, be subjected to hard-core prosecution.

- *Fear Spreading:* Here, communities facing possible gang activity for the first time turn to the police in traditional gang cities for help. Gang cops like Paco are then sent from Chicago or Philadelphia or Los Angeles to "inform" the new location of what they might expect. In numerous incidents, the message from these Paco prototypes is strictly of the suppressive sort, sharing police crackdown strategies and sharing war stories about "killers in the classrooms and predators on the playground." If the new community doesn't arm itself, it, too, can come to look like Chicago, is the message.

• *Correctional Gang Units:* Occasionally in prisons and jails, but more importantly in probation and parole departments, special gang officer units are established. In the latter, the officers have low caseloads of released gang members only. This permits unusually heavy surveillance, including the use of warrantless searches of homes and property. The avowed purpose has little to do with postincarceration adjustment, but rather with discovering violations of the provisions of probation or parole. Such violations permit a return to court, or immediately to lockup. Here, corrections for gang members is defined as keeping them off the streets and in lockups.

Paco's favorite probation officer was a member of an anti-gang probation unit. The two of them often went out on "warrantless search" patrols with the intention of catching gang members in violation of their probation conditions so they could be returned to incarceration. This officer's office, where he interviewed and "counseled" gang members, had its walls festooned with gang logos, pictures, jackets, and other gang emblems that signaled his total disaffection for gangs and their members. This message of hate and disdain could not have been lost on his "clients"; it was also a message of brotherhood for gang cops like Paco.

• *Anti-Gang Legislation:* Various state legislatures, responsive to police and prosecution lobbying, have passed laws specific to street gangs. Generally, they provide for more serious sentencing for convicted gang members, specify particular (often gang-stereotypic) offenses for these sentence "enhancements," and spell out the criteria defining "criminal street gangs" and gang members. The STEP Act is a prominent example. Many of the court cases in which I have served as expert witness involve whether the defendant and/or his group falls under the STEP definition and therefore produces additional years of incarceration.

Another example is Proposition 21 passed by the California electorate and immediately subjected to appellate and Supreme Court review. Proposition 21 allows for up to ten years of additional prison time for violent gang-related offenses, adds gang-related homicide as eligible for a death sentence, makes it a crime to recruit youth into gang membership, and provides indeterminate sentences (no fixed periods) for selected gang-stereotypical crimes. It also authorizes wiretaps for gang activities, and requires anyone convicted of a gang-related offense to register with local police, much as sex offenders are so required. Clearly, gang membership and offending are given special treatment and the increased armament of judicial suppression. Paco and other gang officers are called on more and more to testify on these matters in court, as shown in the next chapter of this book.

• *Civil Injunctions:* While these prior statutes deal with criminal offenses, a corollary legal approach has been taken at the civil level. Pioneered by the city attorney's office in Los Angeles and then expanded elsewhere, civil injunctions are court orders, sought by prosecutors, that prohibit specified behaviors by "documented" members of specific, named gangs. Such behavior, in various injunctions, has included early evening curfew violations, carrying beepers, appearing on rooftops, appearing in specified public parks, approaching or signaling or talking to people in vehicles except buses and police cars, and being seen in public with other members of their gangs. On occasion, there are also civil abatement clauses having to do with residential zoning ordinances, cars parked on lawns, and other factors that might suggest drug sales in the vicinity. As one overly optimistic city prosecutor put it, such restrictions "will force these gang members to make a permanent change in their lives and give up their gangster behavior." Now *there* is a prosecutor totally out of touch with the realities of street gang life. Two research evaluations undertaken to assess the effects of these gang injunctions, one by the ACLU and one by the University of Southern California, indicate the failure of these programs. A third study reported a 5 to 10 percent reduction in assaults, but no effect on other crimes.

A similar process, in the form of a civil abatement, did not require a criminological assessment. It was ruled unconstitutional by a 6 to 3 majority of the U.S. Supreme Court. Enacted in Chicago in 1992, the ordinance gave police officers the power to disperse any group of two or more people in a public location if any one of them *might* be a gang member. This was "gang" sweeping in its rawest form, and for over three years it led to more than 40,000 arrests, mostly of black and Latino residents—40,000 unconstitutional arrests, as it turned out. The police, of course, were strong advocates of the law because it gave them so much discretion in harassing presumed gang members. I call it "Paco's law."

• *Federal Intervention:* Street gangs, by their very nature, are usually local groups acting locally, although gang member migration has become an increasing problem. When the Berlin Wall fell and the end of the Cold

War was signaled, the FBI ("Fairly Busy Incompetents" as one wag spelled it out) decided it could turn hundreds of agents into street gang fighters. Along with agents of the DEA and of the ATF, these federal police brought to the local gang scene a set of beliefs and legal tools heretofore reserved principally for organized crime and drug cartels. With expanded investigative tools, stiffer sentences, RICO, property seizures, and a tendency to seek and see criminal conspiracy underlying gang activities, the feds offered to collaborate with local police to suppress street gangs further. Many departments accepted the offer. Many did not see the need or did not value the federal intrusion into their turf.

An unusual window on all this was opened when an experienced (very un-Paco-like) gang unit supervisor was provided with an internal street gang assessment of his area, written by the United States attorney on the basis of quick reports from FBI offices in the area. The assessment was designed to justify direct federal involvement in local street gang control. It included such clear overstatements of fact as:

- "The criminal activity . . . has concentrated itself primarily in narcotics trafficking, especially of crack cocaine, and weapons-related crime" (compare this with what was described in Chapter 11 of this book).
- In black gang neighborhoods, "the gang activity makes them unendurably bleak" (compare this to sections of Chapter 9),
- "The Crips and Bloods sets . . . , represent a genuine 'organized crime problem'" (compare this to Chapter 6),
- "California penal statutes are extremely weak," but federal laws "can easily result in sentences of 20, 25, and 30 years for relatively minor (2 ounces of 'rock') drug convictions" (compare this to sections of this chapter and Chapter 15).

The gang unit supervisor responded with an internal memo to his department bosses detailing the way that federal procedures designed for organized, structured, conspiratorial criminal gangs were ill designed for the typically disorganized, poorly structured, often impulsive nature of street gangs. Further, he spelled out ways in which the federal approach might in fact give "undeserved status to the gang." He noted that "it would seem that federal law enforcement agencies are fixated on the belief that local gangs are organized and, additionally, that most of the gang violence that occurs is over gang/drug disputes . . . it simply is not the case here."

After offering more specifics about street gangs to illustrate the inappropriateness of the federal approach, the supervisor concluded,

"This report (the federal memo) does not break new ground in gang investigations. . . . The report is obviously influenced by the federal perspective that gangs require structure for successful prosecutions. It relies heavily on narcotic trafficking to give the federal government the necessary 'hooks' to pursue" local street gangs. Paco, it seems clear, would not share this supervisor's summary of federal suppression as based on the conspiracy "fixation"; rather, he tends to share the fixation.

- *Gang Migration Suppression:* Because of the assumed "conspiracies" underlying street gang control of the increased narcotics, especially crack distribution in the 1980s and 1990s, gang units across the country paid increasing attention to gang member migration. Our own and other research found drug sales not to be the dominant force in such migration. While the majority of gang officers we interviewed across the country reflected the same conclusion, others like Paco became very sensitive to the issues and found gang member migration to be a fitting target for suppression.[2] Here are some of the strategies suggested by Paco and his counterparts.

1. Assign teams to highways coming from major cities to watch for "gang-suspicious vehicles."
2. Roadblocks: Stop "any vehicle with four to five Black males inside."
3. Saturation patrols combined with aggressive enforcement: "get out of town or go to jail." Meet with new arrivals "and tell them they won't be tolerated. Be very strict against outward displays like clothing, hand signs, beepers, etc."
4. An interdiction team identifies outsiders and points of origin at entry points such as bus and train stations and airports.
5. "Gang enhancement laws and aggressive enforcement of jaywalking, loitering and other such city ordinances deter migrant interest in the city."
6. "Kill them dead and let God sort them out."

It seems clear from all the foregoing that Paco has available to him a wide assortment of very specific suppression alternatives, far more direct than the more diffuse, complex, and ambiguous programs available to prevention and intervention advocates. Most of these suppression procedures are perfectly legal. Some are taken to excess. A few are obviously illegal. But our criminal justice system has built-in checks and balances. One of these, perhaps the most critical one, is the criminal court. This is where we try to guarantee that overzealous suppression will be highlighted and its effects mitigated. Since Paco has become an experienced expert witness on behalf of gang suppression, we will look at this in the next chapter.

NOTES

1. From an interview cited by Robert Carter in 1976.
2. Note that gang *members* migrate; gangs do not.

(15)

PACO GOES TO COURT

I do admit that a few of my good friends are involved with gangs. But does that automatically make me a part of the gang life?

—Michael Duc Ta, convicted and sentenced to
thirty-five years to life under new anti-gang legislation,
rather than the eight years allowed previously.
Los Angeles Times, April 9, 2001

I've noted in prior chapters that Paco exaggerates gang issues, misstates the nature of gangs, or twists his evidence and experience to get convictions of gang members. What I want to illustrate in this chapter is that this approach of Paco's is not a function of his zeal alone. When he enters the courtroom, he lands on the turf of zealous prosecutors and sometimes biased judges. In addition, the case against the gang member defendants is considerably advanced by specific anti-gang legislation that all but invites the exaggerations and misstatements that Paco provides. When Paco goes to court, he becomes part of an ongoing balance in justice that favors the prosecution.

This book started with a court case in which Paco's testimony, late in his career, went way beyond reality in order to improve a gang member's chances of a long prison sentence. It wasn't only a matter of Paco's loss of perspective. He was also responding to the invitation of special anti-gang legislation.

Anti-gang legislation has gotten even more suppressive since that court case. The young man, Michael Duc Ta quoted above, is one of the many subjected to this increased suppression. His case and others illustrate just how far unfettered suppression can go, especially with gang cops like Paco Domingo to grease the skids.

A second example is provided by a group of five youths who attacked a seventeen-year-old boy with a beer bottle as well as their fists and feet. Prosecutors said it was "gang" behavior because the assailants shared an interest in 1950s dress and music, labeling them the "Slick 50s" gang. A judge in a similar case where gang elements were seriously exaggerated by the prosecutor finally vented his exasperation. He complained:

> I just don't understand why there isn't some documented evidence of this gang, why there isn't some testimony about perhaps graffiti of this gang or the common sign or symbol that supposedly this group uses, which I haven't heard anything about.
>
> And there are so many layers of hearsay involved here, that it is mind boggling. I mean, it just seems like this is this big morass. It is a nebulous mess.

Let's look at a third example. A young man in his midtwenties drove away from a bar in the early morning hours, together with his girlfriend in her car. They stopped at a railroad crossing while a slow moving train passed by, and engaged in some rather passionate kissing to pass the time. A second car pulled up next to them, also waiting for the train to pass. The couple in the second car glanced over, noted the actions next door, and smiled knowingly. On seeing this, the first driver—soon to be the defendant—pulled out a handgun, leaned out his window, and fired five shots at the tires of the second car. Two shots missed, one hit a tire rim, and two punctured a tire. The train passed, and the two cars separated.

The facts of the case were in little dispute. The prosecution charged the defendant with five counts of "discharging a firearm at an occupied motor vehicle," and one count of "possession of a firearm by a felon." The shooter had two prior felony convictions as a juvenile and three as an adult. He was on parole at the time of this event. Clearly, his life on the street was about to end; three strikes and you're out. No further charges could add to his anticipated sentence of life without parole.

But the prosecution added two more charges because the shooter was a documented gang member, being an "active gang participant having a concealed firearm" and violation of penal code section 186.22, the STEP Act, undertaking the shooting to "willfully promote, further, and assist" the goals of his gang. That is, the act had the intent of furthering gang pursuits.

Paco was brought into the preliminary hearing specifically to support the P.C. 186.22 gang enhancement charge as directed by the prosecution. Cross-examination by the defense attorney tore the allegation apart: the victims were strangers, and not gang affiliated; there was no exchange of gang challenges ("where are you from," calling out of gang names); the incident took place outside of the shooter's gang territory and outside the territory of any rival gang; Paco could offer no evidence that the shooter was still an active gang member, and no evidence that the incident was communicated to other gang members, by anyone, to enhance the reputation of the gang. In short, the attorney showed that there was no evidence to support the STEP Act allegation of intent to further gang goals. Indeed, he almost tripped Paco into saying that *any* crime committed by a gang member adds to the gang's reputation and therefore was committed for that purpose. No reading of P.C. 186.22, no matter how broad, would allow this.

The attorney asked that the 186.22 charge be dismissed. But the prosecution nonetheless elicited from Paco his (obviously unfounded) opinion that "the shooting that was committed was done with the specific intent to further, assist, or benefit" the gang.

Asked on what his opinion was based, Paco responded "I base it on the fact of what would come out of it," and then cited an incident several months after this shooting in which an intergang confrontation, not involving this defendant in any way, involved the firing of a gun. It was the best Paco could do, and this time his best simply couldn't hold water. The prosecutor was overcharging and trying to use Paco to justify it.

This chapter is based on my involvement in almost a hundred court cases as a consultant for the defense. The prosecution has never—not once—consulted me. I presume this is principally because they have their own gang experts, police officers like Paco, who are fully attuned to the values of the prosecution. I suspect as well that I have not been called because prosecutors so often have misgivings about the values and attitudes of college professors and criminologists. We tend not to bill ourselves as advocates of suppression.

In these cases, I have been given materials such as police investigation reports, background data on the defendants, probation reports, witness and informant interviews, copies of physical evidence, and rap sheets on the participants' criminal histories. Most pertinent to this chapter, I have received transcripts of grand jury, arraignment, and trial testimony of police witnesses. A number of these transcripts include Paco's testimony. In other cases, I have actually sat in court as Paco testified, as preparation for my own testimony.

This has constituted a marvelous learning experience for me, opening yet another research window on gang affairs to go along with my street time, interviews, and forays into police and court records. It has also yielded some prime anecdotes, courtesy of Paco:

Question: "Do you drink when you're on duty?"
Answer: "I don't drink when I'm on duty, unless I come on duty drunk."

I should add that most of the cases in which Paco or officers like him have provided grist for my mill have been quite serious in nature: convictions for assaults, robberies, and homicides. The lesser cases generally don't require the use of gang cops as expert witnesses. A number of my involvements have been in capital cases in which the defense is legally obliged to argue against a sentence of death. These can be tough cases to handle because of the seriousness of the act for the victims and the seriousness of the out-comes for the defendants. A lot of emotion is involved, and one's personal values become quite salient. This includes Paco's and mine. It also draws forth, in the nature of gallows humor, some of Paco's lawyer stories. In the only reference to classical literature I ever heard from him, he quoted the poet John Keats: "I think we may classify the lawyer in the natural history of monsters." Of course, for Paco, "the lawyer" refers to defense attorneys. Somehow he forgets that prosecutors are also lawyers; defense attorneys are lawyers, while prosecutors are prosecutors.

It has been my distinct impression that gang cases in court are out of bal-ance. The bulk of the armament, both evidence and jury assumptions, favor the prosecution. Further, on average, the prosecution has greater resources to call on, including gang experts, officer credibility, case investigators, and special technologies. And beyond this is the indisputable fact that in most instances the defendant is, in fact, guilty of one or more of the charges lodged against him. These defendants have not been innocent victims of a cruel society, but, at the same time, some of them have been subjected to an overabundance of prosecutorial power.

My contributions to the defense have little to do with guilt or innocence. I am certified by the court as an expert on *gangs*, not on the crimes charged. I prefer it that way. I'm on safest grounds as a gang expert. When I testify in opposition to Paco or other officers, I know I can do so with confidence; they're on my turf now.

What the defense wants of me, and therefore how I come into conflict with Paco as the prosecution's expert witness, differs from case to case but some patterns have emerged.

- The defense wants to establish that the defendant had little choice but to join his local street gang; growing up in his neighborhood all but required this. My testimony would harm, not help the defense since in most gang neighborhoods the majority of youth do not become committed to the gang. I could help the prosecution here, but, as I noted, I've never been asked. As Paco told me in the corridor outside a courtroom on one occasion, "The prosecution never calls on someone like you because the police officers know what's needed to be known; you'd be wasted time." He added, on another occasion when I asked if he had ever testified for the defense, that he would never do that: "I just couldn't do that to my buddies."
- Similarly, the defense wants to establish that the defendant's gang status required him to participate in the crime. He could have been shamed or beaten if he did not. Again, this is usually a great overstatement. Many gang members choose to avoid involvement in planned events, or hang on the edges if things develop suddenly. Of one hundred or more members of a gang, how many are present at or involved in the crime? Gang membership is a crime opportunity, not a crime compulsion.
- Occasionally, the defense wants to suggest that the defendant's status or role in the gang makes it unlikely that he was the guilty party, unlikely to have been the shooter or the shot caller, as charged by the prosecution. Usually this is hard to establish, but in some instances due to age (too young, too old), lack of recent participation, involvement in job, family, or other pursuits, or diminished capacity, I can suggest that the defendant is unlikely to have been the correct suspect.
- Similarly, in the sentencing phase of a trial, especially a death penalty case, the defense hopes to exhibit "mitigation" (i.e., that the defendant's situation or background helps to explain his participation and this should reduce the severity of the sentence [or put him in juvenile court rather than adult]). In most cases, I am unable to be very helpful; gang members as individuals are not so different from other perpetrators of criminal acts. In a very few cases, however, I can argue that the defendant was unusually susceptible to gang suggestion and pressure due to the absence of any positive values in his life. His father, a former member of the same gang, has spent more time in prison than out. His mother is a drug addict and occasional prostitute in their own home. He has been shunted through a series of ineffective relative and foster homes and he has serious intellectual deficits reflected in persistent school failure and transfers. He has been

physically abused in the family and assaulted by rival gang members. In other words, this kid has little going for him but his local street gang, and therefore he has diminished responsibility for responding to the pressures applied by manipulative fellow gang members. These next four patterns are where Paco and I are most likely to cross swords.

- First, as in the case cited in the Introduction, there are instances in which the defense wishes to challenge the prosecution's definition of the defendant's group as a criminal street gang, thus permitting sentence enhancement.
- In like fashion, the defense may wish to challenge the prosecution's contention that the defendant is a bona fide gang member, or "gang associate," or is still a gang member after some years of inactivity. Remember, for Paco a gang member and a gang associate or affiliate (whatever those terms may mean) are one and the same. And "once a gang member, always a gang member."
- The defense may believe that the police officers' descriptions of gang structure, gang purposes, and gang norms have been exaggerated in order to imply greater guilt or responsibility of the defendant. I am brought on to impugn this exaggerated testimony. In most cases, gang officers stay pretty close to reasonable descriptions and I am of no value to the defense. But Paco and some others provide overstated descriptions that require rebuttal.
- Finally, in some instances the defense may want a brief discourse on the nature of street gangs to dispel the normal stereotypes likely to be held by jurors (and occasionally by the judge). Identifying a defendant as a gang member, in and of itself, can be prejudicial to his case and some judges recognize this. They can either allow a gang discourse, or prohibit the prosecution from allowing gang elements into testimony, or do neither.

Paco, of course, has never been pleased to learn of my scheduled appearance in court. These conflicts, more than anything else, spelled the end of our long-term if tenuous relationship. My defense lawyers and I are an interference to justice, as he defines it. "More researchers," he told me as another of his jokes, "are de-emphasizing white rats in favor of lawyers as laboratory subjects. There are three principal reasons: (1) there are so many of them; (2) you're less likely to become attached to them; and (3) there are some things that rats will just refuse to do." For Paco, I've left the classroom and joined the defense bar.

The case I least looked forward to was one in which a gang member was accused of shooting and killing a gang cop. I had images of sitting on the witness stand and looking out over a courtroom jammed with police officers. While I waited in the hallway to be called, I was treated to similar displays of family stress. On one side of the corridor was grouped the defendant's family—mother, brother, young niece, several other family members, their priest, and a defense attorney. On the opposite side was the victim's group—wife, mother, aunt, brother, several uniformed officers, and an assistant prosecutor. Down the hall, fourteen jurors stood chatting, watching both groups bonding separately. Quite a scene.

There was some question about whether the shooting was deliberate or accidental, but I was there on a different mission: to rebut Paco's testimony, as offered in the preliminary hearing, on the nature of Traditional gangs such as the one involved in this case. My name was on the witness list given by the defense to the prosecution, and the prosecution decided not to put Paco on the stand, much to my relief. Asked Paco, "What's black and white and looks good on a lawyer? Answer: "A pit bull."

And indeed, sometimes attorneys can look pretty silly in court, giving Paco a slam dunk response as in this case where gang involvement is obvious:

> *Question:* "Do you have an opinion as to whether or not that shooting was done in association with a street gang?"
> *Paco:* "The fact that the shooter was a gang member, the fact that he attended a gang party armed with a handgun, the fact that he had backup there other than members of his same gang, and he shot a gang member!"

As demonstrated earlier, the definitional issue posed to gang cops in court is usually answered with some variation of the terms found in the STEP Act. Typical of the responses is this one from Paco: "A gang is three or more individuals who share a common name or symbol, who meet on a regular basis, and commit criminal activity in furtherance of the gang." This is a boilerplate response, available in slight variations to gang officers across the country. It is the prosecutors' requirement rather than a realistic description of most street gangs.

Perhaps the most serious, if flawed, recent attempt to determine who is a gang *member* is provided by a California police agency, incorporating criteria for entering a gang member into CalGang, a statewide roster of several hundred thousand gang members. Judges and prosecutors generally accept a person's listing in CalGang as "proof" of membership, yet often reject a defense attorney's stipulation of nonmembership if a defendant's name cannot be found in the roster.

GANG DEFINITION

A gang is a group of three or more persons who have a common identifying sign or symbol, or name, and whose members individually or collectively engage in or have engaged in a pattern of criminal activity, creating an atmosphere of fear and intimidation within the community.

Acceptable additional criteria for the identification of a gang member for the CalGang file:

1. Subject admits to being a gang member during the incarceration classification procedure. *(This is the only criterion that will stand alone for entry into CalGang; all others must meet at least two of the following.)*
2. Subject admits gang membership in a noncustodial situation.
3. Subject has been identified as a gang member by a reliable informant or source. This criteria encompasses when a subject is required to register with law enforcement as a gang member by court order per Section 186.30 PC. The court shall be considered a reliable source.
4. Subject has been identified as a gang member by an untested informant or a source with corroborative evidence.
5. Subject has been seen wearing gang-type clothing.
6. Subject has been seen displaying gang symbols and/or hand signs.
7. Subject has identifiable gang tattoos.
8. Subject has been seen frequenting gang areas.
9. Subject has been seen affiliating with documented gang members.
10. Subject has been arrested with known gang members for offenses consistent with usual gang activity.

Note: One must keep in mind that federal law requires that there is an established criminal predicate for the individual before that individual may be placed into an intelligence file. Criminal predicate is established when a law enforcement officer can demonstrate a reasonable suspicion that the concerned subject is involved in criminal behavior or criminal enterprise. Street gangs, by definition, are criminal organizations due to the propensity of its members to commit criminal acts and therefore criminal enterprises. In California, law enforcement officers are held to the same reasonable suspicion standard; however, in addition to that standard, if the concerned subject is to be placed in the CalGang file the officer must also meet the established CalGang criteria.

Acceptable evidence in court differs markedly from acceptable evidence in social science (including criminology). The latter requires information on both sides of an issue, preferably established according to scientific criteria. The idea is to give a theory or a hypothesis an equal chance of being supported or discarded. But legal evidence is far more one-sided; evidence is used to support one's positions, be it prosecution or defense. It's up to the opposition to offer contrary evidence (with the exception that deliberately withholding exculpatory evidence is not allowed). The acceptability of a gang officer's testimony is therefore important, but normally easy to come by. "Based on your training and experience, Officer Domingo," is standard language in court to admit the officer's opinion as credible evidence. And to establish the case, the prosecution takes the officer through a brief review of his training and street experience. It's usually easily established, sometimes assumed, occasionally mutually stipulated, and rarely—truly rarely—successfully challenged by the defense. Field experience is usually enough for the judge, with or without proof of special professional or academic training in gang matters. Here's an example from one officer in court, asked to explain the source of his expertise:

A lot of my training is just stopping, talking to gang members I have interviewed over the years.

I have been in the gang unit since the start of it. And I have interviewed over—in excess of a thousand gang members, informally, stopping them on the street, asking them questions about, you know, who they are, what gang they're in and, you know, just different little interviews with them.

And, then, probably around 100, or so, I have sat down and conducted formal interviews with them, where we will go into the structure of the gang, names, different gang members, how they plan a drive-by shooting, how they plan the sale of narcotics, or other things they do.

The judge in another case accepted an even more succinct response: "A lot of these guys I know and I've known for several years. I know where they're at, who they're with, and I basically know that they're with this gang and I don't question them all the time about stuff we already know."

Criminal court judges are not necessarily impartial arbiters in gang justice. Sometimes the very nature of the criminal court fosters Paco's prosecutor-oriented testimony. From the early 1980s on, judges have more and more come to represent the conservative, law-and-order mood of the country; increasingly they have been drawn from the ranks of the prosecutors' offices. Charles Linder, past president of the Los Angeles Criminal Bar Association, has commented: "One result is that it has been ten years since I heard a judge say, 'I do not find the officer's testimony credible.'" Applying his thoughts to LAPD's Rampart gang unit scandal, Linder notes:

the virtual merge of judge and prosecutor [has] contributed to an environment in which cops assigned to the anti-gang CRASH (Community Resources Against Street Hoodlums) unit at Rampart believed they could break the law with impunity. Cops can lie on the stand because they fear no judicial sanction . . . no police officer in modern times has been prosecuted for lying under oath, as long as he lied for the prosecution.[1]

This may be hyperbole, but I've seen it in action. Many gang cops do not take advantage of the situation. Increasingly, Paco found that he could, so he did. He was not alone.

It is also the case that on occasion I have been limited in my testimony by judges who did not want to hear generic information on gangs, only information on the gangs involved in their particular court case. In those instances, the gang cops' testimony about the nature of gangs went unchallenged. The advantage is to the prosecutor.

On two, and only two, occasions, I found that a judicial ruling was simply incorrect and inappropriate. In the first, a gang-savvy prosecutor convinced the judge that my testimony would be inappropriate because the shooter and the victim were members of the same gang and "only intergang homicides are gang related." This judge was either naive or prosecution oriented.

The second case revealed the judge's bias even more clearly. The issue was whether the defendant, the driver of the car but not a participant in or observer of the murder committed by his passengers, should have known that the "likely and probable outcome" of a gang assault is the death of the victim. I was prepared to offer strong empirical data to the contrary, data the prosecutor clearly didn't want offered.

Out of hearing of the jury, the defense established my generic expertise and the judge accepted it, even commenting on my accomplishments. But the prosecutor established that I had not done research on the gang in question and had not interviewed members of that particular gang. This, it was claimed, meant that I could not be an expert witness in the case. The judge, a former deputy prosecutor, amazingly accepted the prosecutor's argument. This ruling was in direct opposition to well-established case law and has been derided by other judges I have queried, even at the state appellate level.

Further, this ruling, if generalized, would mean that the prosecution would always have a gang expert witness—there's always a cop who knows something about the gang—but the defense almost never would. There are over 30,000 gangs in this country, and only a score of researchers with direct knowledge of individual gangs. This would really stack the deck in favor of the prosecution. In what some have called "the politics of prosecution," the legislation has opened the door, the judges have propped it open, and the prosecutors have walked through using the gang cop as their support. The case cited in the Introduction to this book is a prime example where a legislative gang definition was used by the prosecutor, with Paco's strange testimony, to try to turn a party crew into a criminal street gang.

In a later case, before a different judge, quite the opposite and correct ruling was offered. I made the following notes immediately on reaching the corridor outside the courtroom:

> Judge W. today informed both attorneys that he would accept only *generic* expertise. Knowing the gang in question is not relevant. The police must reveal generic gang knowledge. Then, if the prosecutor wishes, he can elicit testimony that this gang is *typical* of other gangs in the area. But that's all that expertise can attest to about them. This fits with comments from other judges that have certified gang cop experts on specific gangs *as well as* generic expertise. Legitimately, gang patterns as I know them can be applied to the gangs in specific cases; that's what Judge W. means by generic expertise.

Let me be clear that Paco, being his own boss in his professional role, did not always give the prosecution what it wanted. In a case already cited in Chapter 5 that backfired on the prosecution, a fringe gang member killed an informant for the local police and the DEA. The prosecutor wanted to package this as a Mexican Mafia hit. He counted on Paco to make his case and thus get the death penalty for the shooter (first-degree murder, conspiracy, and so on). However, Paco showed some good knowledge of the Mexican Mafia workings, having been involved in a major conspiracy case, and did not fall into the trap. He tried to support the prosecutor's position, but he was not convinced that the fringe member defendant was a likely recruit for a mob hit. As a result, the prosecution settled for a plea to a five-year sentence, hardly the stuff of mob retaliation. In this case, my testimony was unnecessary. It would merely have corroborated what Paco said and he was the prosecution's own witness.

Another instance of such attempts by prosecutors is much more typical. The case involved a drive-by shooting between rival gangs. Asked the prosecutor, "Now, is assassination of rival gang members by firearms a principal activity of this gang?" Paco: "Yes." "Was that a principal activity back there in those [four days, two and a half years ago]?" Paco: "Yes." By now, the reader knows that a drive-by "assassination" is the rare event, not a "principal" activity. The prosecutor invited, and received, a lie. Further, such words as "assassination" are clearly inflammatory. The defense objected to it; the judge overruled.

PACO GOES TO COURT

Let me offer just one other illustration of prosecutorial zeal. Again, it was a case in which the prosecutor tried to go beyond her own expert witness's testimony. The situation was complex as I testified in the fourth trial in a series of five. I had prepared by reading the prosecution gang expert's testimony in the first three. It was almost identical in each trial. This time the gang expert was not Paco.

Once again, the defendant was in a car when one of his fellow passengers got out and killed a young man in a retaliation or "payback" affair. The defendant's presence was enough to elicit a charge of murder by "aiding and abetting" the shooter and because he should have known that the "likely and probable outcome" of an assault was the death of the victim. Again, I was armed with data to the contrary, but my argument got lost in the ensuing wrangle.

The prosecutor confronted me, and I mean this literally, as she was visibly angry and antagonistic toward me, to the point that defense objected to her "badgering the witness." The judge sustained the objection. The prosecutor proceeded to misstate the testimony of the gang cop as asserting that the outcome of a gang fight was that someone would be killed.

"Did you read his testimony or not, Doctor Klein?"

"Yes, I did."

"And he testified to that outcome, didn't he."

"No, I don't believe he did."

"Are you saying he didn't testify to that?"

"Yes, my reading is that he did not. I refer you to pages 552 and following in volume 5 of the testimony."

This is where she lost her cool. I was disputing her statements of fact. She fairly cried out, "If I call that officer up here today, Dr. Klein, if I get him to testify in front of you," and this is where the badgering objection was made and sustained.

What had happened was that in her zeal to use expert testimony about "likely and probable outcome," she had misread or didn't remember or misstated the officer's comments. I don't know which. Here's what the transcript shows (I will emphasize the relevant phrases that she lost):

- Gang members, and I know this from having spoken to them, the probable consequence of getting involved in a gang fight is somebody *might* get hurt or killed.[2]

- They know that *sometimes* what may start out to be a fistfight ends
  . . . where a fistfight leads to something more serious.
- Although their intentions go to retaliation and get into a physical confrontation that somebody *could* get killed.
- They know there is that *possibility* when they go out that things are going to escalate *or could*. There are times when they say I will beat up
  "Killer" from the other gang and *they beat him up and walk away*.

Finally the officer is asked, as shown in the transcript, if the likely outcome isn't greater "if you are confronting a rival gang, wouldn't you say that
would be true?"

Answer: "It all depends on the circumstances."

Question: "If your answer is no, you can say no."

Answer: "Yes, I would say no."

So here we have a gang cop being very careful in his prior trial testimony,
not falling for the "likely and probable" trap, and a prosecutor so intent on
mounting the maximum charge that she seriously misstates his testimony.
She then so poorly confronts the defense witness on this same testimony
that she both loses her point and embarrasses herself in front of the court
and jury. Maybe this is where Paco would have offered another of his lawyer
jokes: "What do you have when three lawyers are buried in the beach up to
their necks?" Answer: "Not enough sand!" She didn't have the advantage of
Paco as her witness. To judge from other cases, he would have given her the
testimony she wanted. And my clear impression is that juries *want* to believe their police witnesses.

And so Paco doesn't merely appear in court, provide simple testimony,
and then leave. Rather he steps into a complex context that draws from him
a posture, an attitude, a set of values honed both by his experience and by
the puppet masters at the prosecutor's table and behind the raised bench.
He has a clear role to fill: to testify with a view toward conviction and maximum sentence. This is serious business to him, and you sense it as you observe him when his name is called.

Paco comes to court in "protective coloring," like a predator quietly approaching his unsuspecting prey. He is dressed in casual formality: slacks, a
dark sport jacket or blazer over a dark dress shirt. He never wears a suit;
captains and lieutenants wear suits. But his tie exposes him as a bit out of
place—wide, broadly patterned in too-bright contrasting colors. I got the

impression of a man saying "I'm not at home here; I'm from the street but I've accommodated to you as a courtesy, so hear my words."

In addition, what sets him apart is his posture and demeanor. The shirt and jacket seem ill fitting over that upper body pushed out of proportion by his constant bodybuilding exercises. He is "buffed up" in the weight lifters' terminology, and the shirt and jacket seem ready to bust their seams, the tie ready to pop out as in a cartoon sequence. Paco answers the call to the stand by rising slowly from his seat, walking in measured step through the swinging wooden gate and directly to the side of the witness stand. He raises his hand to be sworn in as if telling us, "I've been through all this many times, no big deal." He swears to tell the truth, the whole truth, and nothing but the truth so help you God and settles firmly into his seat, looks over confidently at the jury box, then at the approaching attorney ready to do the latter's bidding to get that conviction. The oath is history.

My procedure is always to look directly at the attorney as I respond, unless specifically asked to address the jury's interest on the nature of street gangs. Paco, by contrast, often aims his responses at the jury, turning directly to them as a sincere teacher might. This is very deliberate; he is their mentor; he has the message. He speaks with the authority of one who's been on the front lines; his knowledge is "real" knowledge and he dispenses it with the certainty of an experienced professional. "I once had three murder trials going on at the same time," he told me, "bouncing from court to court for days and days. I hate the time, but it's OK, as long as we get the convictions."

Paco works that jury to get the convictions. Does he perjure himself? The answer to that involves interpretation: is it perjury to exaggerate, to overstate, to use incidents to frame generalizations, to omit qualifications to general assertions? Maybe this is a legal question, but I certainly view it as an ethical one. Rafael Perez, the corrupt LAPD gang cop who blew the lid on his unit's zealous pursuit of convictions, admitted that he perjured himself several hundred times. Many of his arrest reports, he said, were fabricated and more contained "smaller lies." Paco is not Perez, but we are talking about matters of degree here. Paco has his own truth, and he has to get beyond those interfering defense attorneys. "What do you have with 500 lawyers on the bottom of the ocean?" Answer: "A good start."

How does all this play out in court? When faced with the knowledge that the defense will also present an expert witness on gangs—me, or someone like me—Paco is a bit cautious. It's when he does not expect this that he feels free to exaggerate. Most of the examples I cite throughout this book, then, come from transcripts of preliminary hearings and trials that I am given later in order to prepare my testimony. In most instances, Paco expects to testify unchallenged.

In one such instance, an attorney provided me with testimony from several cases. In one of these, Paco testified that during a gang war members will deliberately misidentify rival gang members in order to hang crimes on them. Yet in several other cases, the transcripts showed that Paco used members' identifications of others as proof of guilt. Sometimes you can have it both ways. The issue, it seems to me, is whether the *presence* of gang indicators, as proof of gang membership, is matched by the *absence* of such indicators as proof of nonmembership. Paco emphasizes positive gang indicators and shies away from negative ones. But critically testing a witness like Paco is not easy. He is the certified expert; he has a kind of street smarts unknown to jurors, and he comports himself with full confidence in his expertise. And the prosecutor simply has to set him up:

> *Question:* "And are you of the mind, based on your training and experience, whether or not one of the primary activities of that gang is to commit drive-by shootings and intimidation?"
>
> *Answer:* "Yes, it is."

This goes unchallenged, even though it's nonsense. No gang has drive-bys and intimidation as a primary activity. These are way down the list. Many, perhaps most, street gangs engage in them rarely or even not at all. A response like Paco's should be listed with one of his jokes:

> *Question:* "Any suggestions as to what prevented this from being a murder trial instead of an attempted murder trial?"
>
> *Answer:* "The victim died."

The next case offers a variation on the theme of unchallenged assertions of gang membership. Here is the summary of evidence about gang relevance as I offered it to the defense:

> The only things I find of direct relevance to the STEP Act are the opinion of Officer Domingo on page three of the search warrant report and pages 124 to 126 of the transcripts. These are redundantly stated opinions and are not corroborated by any other evidence in these materials. The gang unit sergeant's testimony clearly fails to suggest your client is a member (to say nothing of active member) of the local gang. There are no FI (field interrogation) cards

showing stops with gang associates. There is no entry from the gang roster system. The prior record as reported by probation is devoid of gang-related or gang-like incidents. There is no evidence presented that any past or intended marijuana sales are in furtherance of the gang. Indeed, individual sellers and entrepreneurs carry out most such sales for their own benefit, not that of a street gang. In the absence of such evidence, even weapons possession *may or may not be* gang related.

I have no doubt, from these materials, that your client has been a gang member. I do have doubts that he was one at the time of the incident, or that he was sufficiently ganged up that his actions were for gang purposes. His living arrangements, his job situation, and particularly his educational achievements do *not* fit a picture of an active gang member acting in furtherance of gang goals. I believe Officer Domingo's opinions are in furtherance of prosecutor goals despite the absence of supportive evidence.

Now contrast this with the way Paco uses his generalizations about street gangs to turn this same defendant into an active gang member pursuing the goals of a "criminal street gang" (Penal Code 186.22):

Based on the suspect's statements regarding his gang membership, the victim's statements, and the weapons and marijuana we found in his bedroom, coupled with the fact that the suspect is not employed,[3] it is our opinion that the suspect is selling marijuana for the benefit of his gang. This opinion is based on the fact that it is common for gang members to sell narcotics for the purpose of supporting the gang, and it is also common for gang members to possess weapons to protect themselves from rival gang members while selling narcotics. It's also a known fact that gang members possess weapons such as sawed off shotguns and pistols because they are easy to conceal when committing other crimes such as robberies and assaults. Based on that opinion ,we additionally charged the suspect with 186.22 (a) PC.

Section 186.22 is the STEP Act, defining "criminal street gang" and allowing increased sentences for members whose actions support the gang or are in furtherance of gang goals. "Support" and "furtherance" in my court experience are assertions made by the prosecution *and never proven*. The court accepts these assertions. Defense seldom challenges them. How, after all, can you prove that a gang member's action is purposefully designed to further gang goals? There's no gang treasury to enrich via drug sales, no totem with notches for each successful drive-by, assault, or murder. There's no score sheet on which to record a unit increase in gang status attributable to a payback. Indeed, to assert furtherance of gang goals is a statement of faith and nothing more. Having the phrase entombed in the legislation and the penal code does not make it anything more.

Sometimes logic flies right out the window, as in the following case when Paco got too caught up in the gang *qua* gang terminology.

> *Question:* "In your experience, are gang-related crimes committed by individual gang members?"
>
> *Answer:* "It's happened. Generally it's by the gang itself, not one person."

This response is especially ludicrous because the case involved a notorious gang, or gang conglomeration, with several thousand members. Such a gang does not commit a murder: individual gang members do, or a few members together do.

Sometimes Paco gets caught up in the prosecution's attempt to use this gang-as-unit mentality in prison gang cases:

> *Question:* "Would you include the prison gangs as a criminal street gang" (i.e., falling under PC 186.22 that deals specifically with *street* gangs not prison gangs)?
>
> *Answer:* "Yes."

This response permitted the application of the STEP Act to prison gang members, never the intention of the original legislation. Paco went on in this case to identify six defendants as prison gang members and "therefore" as members of a "criminal street gang" and subject to the enhanced sentencing under P. C. 186.22.

Then the logic goes full circle as prison gangs, generally far more organized and violent, are identified as the puppet masters of street gangs. Paco testified in one such case, "Prison gangs have manipulated the street gang and that's why now they are so rampant." He then offered as an example a large Hispanic street gang whose numbers he claimed quite falsely have risen to 20,000 members. Oh, my!

Once I was involved in a case in which Paco testified to a whole series of overstatements and generalizations in a veritable barrage of untruths. In preparation for my own testimony, I was sitting in the back of the court furiously taking notes. The italic is mine, to draw the reader's attention.

- Shot callers are the leaders; they *dictate* what's going to happen. They give the orders and others follow through. *This applies to all gangs.*

- *All* gangs, or the majority of them, are vicious.
- It's *incumbent* on them to carry a gun for protection.
- [This gang] has *hundreds* of cliques—they're *statewide.*
- There are leaders and there are soldiers.
- That attack *demands* a response from ADW (assault with a deadly weapon) to homicide. This would be a *planned* response.
- The *majority* of gangs are vicious and violent in nature.
- [About another Hispanic gang] Most of them [the members] are vicious, *because they're coming from other countries.* They are immigrants who are being recruited *on a daily basis.*

I'd like the reader to keep in mind that while almost all serious gang cases have police expert witnesses available to the prosecution, it is the unusual case that can call on an equally expert defense witness. There are few constraints against Paco and others testifying at the limits of reality if they so choose, or are led to do so by zealous prosecutors and sympathetic judges. There is little humor to be found in all this, but I can offer this one example cited by a colleague.

Prosecutor: "When he went, had you gone and had she, if she wanted to and were able, for the time being excluding all the restraints on her not to go, gone also, would he have brought you, meaning you and she, with him to the station?"

Defense Attorney: "Objection. That question should be taken out and shot."

NOTES

1. From a column in the *Los Angeles Times*, March 19, 2000.

2. My data, taken from police records, put the odds at somewhere between 15:1 and 50:1 against a lethal outcome. In two recent cases, my providing such data to the defense attorney, and shared with the prosecution, led to the prosecutor's decision not to press the issue of "likely and probable" consequence. In each case, plea bargains were reached for lesser charges. Said one of the attorneys: "They saw you coming."

3. This was an error of fact.

16

ELITE UNITS, GANG UNITS, AND PACO

Locker room mentality pervades what happens on the street, and that is different from a department's core values.

—Los Angeles County Sheriff Lee Baca, March 6, 2001

When Paco joined the force, he was characterologically predetermined to become a "tough cop," a "hard charger" as Steve Herbert describes the type in his book, *Policing Space*. But that predisposition wasn't enough, by itself, to produce the highly focused, single-minded anti-gang officer Paco became over the years. As we have seen, frustrations with his time in the patrol and juvenile divisions set him up for the enticements of the increasing street gang challenges, along with the rewards of feeding the appetites of prosecutors and many judges.

But there was still more. Paco's development found fruition in the fertile ground of the gang unit. In the "troops versus management" spirit described by Herbert, Paco became a trooper, an outsider whose narrow world within the cohesive gang unit provided the final, validating context for his John Wayne attitudes. He wanted autonomy and discretion beyond the ordinary; location in the gang unit fit the bill. He didn't respect management and never took the exams to become a manager, a "suit." He preferred to avoid supervision, and the gang unit was an avenue to avoiding it. As described by Professor Charles Katz of Arizona State University–West, the principal analyst of gang units, these groups tend to be autonomous, gung-ho teams, proactive, unsupervised, and secretive with "confidential information." Unit officers tend to be handpicked for the pleasures of hard charging. Paco found the right niche for himself.

Since most police departments pride themselves, as did Paco's, on a strong, hierarchical, almost militaristic structure, the autonomous gang unit would seem to be an anachronism. Yet gang units exist across the country, allowing the Pacos to emerge and flourish. To fully understand Paco, we need to understand his unit, the validating setting for his place in the crime-fighting arena.[1]

When Paco joined the gang unit, it was one of very few in the nation. Gang matters (where recognized) were generally handled by normal patrol and investigative divisions, and occasionally by juvenile divisions. But the increase in street gang problems through the 1970s and at an accelerating pace in the '80s and '90s signaled the need for concentrated expertise in gang matters. A 1993 survey found that three-fourths of departments with 100 or more officers had gang units, yielding a figure of roughly 370 units in these larger departments across the country. According to Katz, the continuing explosion of street gangs in smaller communities led by 1997 to the existence of almost 1,000 gang units, room enough for lots of Pacos as well as less aggressive officers. The growth has been so great that various regions of the country now have professional gang investigators' associations, holding annual conventions and periodic seminars and workshops. The gang cop is now an institution in our criminal justice system.

The growth in gang units is far from an anomaly in law enforcement. The growing professionalism among the police has led quite naturally to increased specialization of many sorts. One form of such specialization has been the establishment of elite units in response to particular forms of crime. The gang unit is merely one variant of these elite units and tends to share with them certain expectable characteristics. Commenting on the Rampart scandal, the nationally respected expert on terrorism, Brian Jenkins, described a number of these, among which are a special esprit de corps and separation from the normal policing operations.

Jenkins, writing in the *Los Angeles Times* (March 27, 2000), notes that elite units come to experience a sense of mission and danger. They tend to approach their world as combatants—"knights against dragons, good versus evil." Rules are bent and broken for the greater good of achieving unit goals—"we know what we have to do." The "desks" and suits of the police bureaucracy are avoided, and the "wink of approval" from the top brass is assumed. "Cops and soldiers are clannish," notes Jenkins, "elite units doubly so." Finally, Jenkins's analysis predicts a Paco within this elite unit context because such units "lure the mavericks, the misfits, the adventurers, the cowboys." They become, in his words, "the shock troops to reduce crime."

Not that Paco and his gang unit are alone in this. The pattern is well established by other elite units: narcotics, SWAT, antiterrorism, and street crime units typify the general model. Special challenges, special tactics, and special intelligence combine with remote supervision to produce cohesive bands of specialists inclined to write their own rules and bend others in the pursuit of righteous goals.

New York City's Street Crime Unit, the one that fired forty-one bullets at unarmed Amadou Diallo, has as its motto, "We own the night." How reminiscent this is of the gang cop's challenge to the homeboy, "This is our territory, not yours." When the Manhattan North Drug Initiative unit officers went on trial for the infamous Batista beating but were acquitted because fellow officers adopted the code of silence, seventy-five off-duty officers cramming the courtroom embraced each other in victory.

Boston's City Wide Anti-Crime Unit could take pride in being told by its superiors to "go in, kick butts, and crack heads." LAPD's new SWAT team took on heroic proportions when it torched the house hiding members of the revolutionary Symbianese Liberation Army, killing all inside. Another SWAT team, acting more like a college fraternity, recently used a local mud hole for the initiation of its new members. Cohesiveness does not exist among street gangs alone.

In Los Angeles, it was the LAPD's narcotics officers in 1988 who smashed and trashed two apartment buildings in a massive search for drugs on Dalton Avenue, leaving their own graffiti on the walls: "LAPD Rules," "Rollin' 30s Die." Twenty-five officers were fired or suspended, and the city paid out four million dollars to the citizen victims. The Red Cross offered aid to the twenty-two people left homeless; none of the officers was charged with a crime. "We were delivering a message," said one of the raiding officers who used an ax to smash furniture and walls; "I looked at it as something of a Normandy Beach, a D-Day."

Such incidents are, in no stretch of the imagination, typical elite unit operations. Yet they can occur because of the poorly supervised nature of such units and the cowboys they attract. The LAPD had a Public Disorder Intelligence Division (PDID). It became a paranoid operation, spying and storing personal data on political leaders, Quakers, entertainment figures, clergy, judges, and even police commissioners. One member, who kept classified data in his home and lied to the investigators of the unit, later became police chief in a nearby suburban community. The PDID had to be disbanded after front-page coverage, court orders, and lawsuits.

Next door, as it were, elite units in the L.A. Sheriff's Department also went beyond the normal limits. One called itself "The Regulators" and sported a logo of crossed pistols. Another, a gang unit, became "the Vikings," reportedly taking on the special argot and symbols normally attributed to street gangs. One of the unit officers, a "cowboy" according to legal reports, may have contributed by his own excessive behavior to his shooting death at the hands of a threatened gang member. When I thought those days were over with, I visited a sheriff's station and was given a tour of its two gang unit trailers in the parking lot. One featured a logo of a sharp-tooth-bared shark; the other logo was an emblem with long daggers through it. Said my host, a former gang unit officer, "The Sheriff has decided to get rid of these logos, but that would be foolish." Two years later, the logos were still there.

This, then, was the world to which Paco graduated, and the world in which he could flourish. In one such station he inhabited, there was a community holiday raffle to raise money. The prize offered by the department, at one dollar a ticket, was a brand new, shiny, semiautomatic 9 mm Beretta handgun. No one, seemingly, questioned the symbolism of the prize.

One of the interesting sidelights to this elite unit situation illuminates just how secretive, cohesive, and autonomous they can become. This is the pronounced tendency for each to resist collaboration with each other. To paraphrase Paco slightly, "I don't want their shit on my turf." We saw this in action when, in the midst of the crack explosion of the mid-1980s, Paco's unit and other gang units in the city were commanded by the top brass to coordinate their efforts with the narcotics units. The brass didn't say how—I'm sure they had few clues—they just said to get it done.

But it simply didn't happen. Gang units take their time raiding crack houses, for example. They're after the intelligence to be reaped there—graffiti, diaries, photos, weapons. The narcs care little about such intelligence. They want the quickest possible entry, to grab the dope before it's flushed down the toilet or dumped into the opening of the sewer main line.

Gang units have informants, gang members "turned" into snitches to avoid serious charges. Narcotics units also have informants that can trip up dealers in "buy and bust" operations, or lead officers to distributors. But the gang unit is not given access to the narcotics informants, any more than they offer their informants to the narcs. The turfs are separate in operations if not in geography. Said a lead detective in one of the narcotics units, "Who the hell has the time to interact more with the gang unit people?" Paco loved to make his own drug busts, and his unit tried to hit crack houses on their own. The narcotics detective, impatient with the slower pace of Paco's boys, talked about "taking a place down," thoroughly trashing it and violating civil liberties when necessary. His lieutenant, telling me about a failed meeting with Paco's group, talked about interunit coordination in terms of control ("who's in charge?"), turf, credit for arrests, jealousy over the effort expended, and the imputation that one or the other group wasn't doing its job properly.

Gang units tend to come out worse in the attempted coordination between competing elite units. For the most part, the gang unit has less prestige, is in less favor, than the more dramatic units such as SWAT, anti-terrorism, or narcotics. All the more reason for Paco's disdain for the others and his desire for him and his crew to go it alone.

There are, of course, some rogue cops, some corrupt cops, some really mean cops among the hundreds of thousands of well-meaning and properly behaving police officers. There have always been some of these rogue cops, and there always will be. We'll meet some of them in the next chapter. But theirs is not Paco's story. Rather, his is the story of a tough cop led to excess by his context—the departmental culture, the zealousness of anti-gang legislation and prosecution, and the character of elite units into which he fits so fortuitously. Paco's story, then, is one of the *interaction* between character and context.

Yet even this is not the full story. There are gang units and there are gang units. They are not carbon copies, but vary significantly in attitude and operations. Paco, placed in a group with emphasis on intelligence over enforcement, might never have become the narrow, hard charger who rousted the homeboys on the street and demonized them in the courtroom. It was Paco's fate to be in a militaristic department with a pervasive law-and-order culture that encouraged and then ignored somewhat unfettered anti-gang operations.

Not all gang units look like Paco's and not all gang cops look like Paco. In their comparative study of four gang units, Professor Katz and his colleagues found that enforcement time among the four sets of officers ranged from 12 percent to 32 percent; intelligence operations ranged from 3 percent to 43 percent. Most notably, administrative, travel, and non-police-related time reached as high as 65 percent. This is not Paco's image of how gang cops should spend their time. Perhaps more telling yet, the study showed that the typical eight-hour watch yielded an average of only 1.8 field stops per officer. Paco would gag on such figures; no wonder gang units are seen as being less elite than some others are. A book on gangs quotes a veteran officer: "Gang units are like every other special unit in policing—full of bullshit and totally political."[2] Again, it all shows that Paco Domingo, gang cop, is an exception, not an exemplar. He's out there and real enough, but he's not your average gang cop.

How do gang units come to be so varied, and so far from normal administrative expectations? How can Paco's kind of unit flourish amid these more numerous but less extreme groups? The answer lies in part in what Katz and his colleagues report about the "decoupling" of gang units, that is, their separation from the normal operations of their departments. The research suggests three different ways in which gang units become separated and isolated.

1. In some instances, the unit is *operationally* isolated. Although physically located in a central location, they're left alone. This leads to less investigative activity, less collaboration with other units, and more leeway for senior officers like Paco to hold sway and for individual officers—again like Paco—to choose their own priorities.
2. In other instances, the unit is more *socially* isolated. One may even need a special key or code to enter the unit's offices. This social isolation leads to reduced information sharing. Supervision and accountability are lower than normal, often yielding the absence of operational goals and guidelines. A gang unit subculture, as in the Rampart scandal, can easily develop. Remember the "Vikings" and "The Regulators?"
3. Finally, gang units are often *physically* isolated. In some instances this merely means the trailer in the parking lot. In others, as in Rampart, it means location in a separate building distant from the station and normally close to the turf claimed by troublesome street gangs. Here, anything goes, "community policing" turns into "policing the community," and supervision is almost totally internal. This became Paco's heaven. "It's like having the Marine Corps invade an area that is still having little pockets of resistance. . . . We can't have it. . . . We've got to wipe them out," his chief was quoted as saying. And this sort of department attitude, often noted in depictions of the LAPD, is what allowed Officer Rafael Perez to tell the court at his trial, "In the Rampart CRASH unit, things began to change. The lines between right and wrong became fuzzy and indistinct. The us-against-them ethos of the overzealous cop began to consume me."

With all this, it sounds as if gang units are more trouble than they are worth. Yet, that's not been our research experience. Sophisticated gang units yield distinctive advantages to a department. As I noted earlier, criminal investigations of gang-related crimes are more effective with input from the gang unit. The gang unit gives the department brass an extra, close-up look at the street gang situation in the city and can usefully affect deployment of resources.

For the officers in the unit, there are several advantages. In many cases, they get the status of "investigator" or "detective," not just officer. For some there is a pay increment. They get to wear civilian clothes. They are often stationed away from headquarters and (too often) away from supervision by the suits. Thus, Katz notes, they spend as much as 40 percent of their time in nonpolicing activities, "such activities as eating, resting, watching television, reading the newspaper, visiting, and running personal errands."

But such freedoms have costs as well. They can engender disrespect from their fellow officers. They can develop a bad "rep" (reputation) on the street. They can get pretty loose with confidential information and, as the Rampart scandal teaches us, the path to brutality and corruption is eased in the decoupled unit. And, oh yes, there is danger: gang cops have died at the hands of gang members.

But ask Paco how these things balance out and he comes back again and again to the advantages of his position. The gangs must be challenged; the community must be protected from them; the streets must be cleared. And only the gang cop can do the job unchallenged. Indeed, as Paco makes clear in his unchallenged presentations to the court, the media, and the community—"a gang is a bunch of thugs"—his expertise is his coin of the realm. He has stories to tell, and the public eats them up. In his case study, Katz illustrates this with a series of "war stories" related to their audiences by his gang cops. These are stories both truthful and fanciful, bringing drama and glamour to the job, and legitimating it in the public eye. As one of Katz's officers reported to him, "I try to bring the gang subculture to the community. . . . We are the best ones to do it because we are the experts."

Most important, the unit is there to justify the effort, the stress, the special requirements, and to provide the psychological support that gang cops need. If group cohesiveness is important to the street gang, it is also important to the gang unit. Just as in Rampart, it started as shown in Katz's study of gang units with the selection of fellow officers. The unit seeks out its new members based on experience, networking, attitude, and sometimes ethnicity. Most don't need to apply. This kind of self-selection gets cohesion off to a jump start. Notes Katz: "[They] take pride in the fact that they were 'chosen' to be part of the gang unit."

Cohesiveness in groups is generally a good thing. Cohesive teams play better; cohesive work groups produce better products; and cohesive families attend to the needs of each member. But in street gangs and in police gang units, cohesiveness can have clear drawbacks. The more cohesive gangs may indeed produce better member interaction, but they also produce more crime and more violence. Society does not like the group product.

Similarly, the more cohesive gang unit may well produce better results, and members may serve each other's needs better. But they may also go beyond the bounds suggested by police department regulations and societal norms. The gang unit that creates its own special logos, or takes on other counterpart trappings of the street gang is a unit to watch. The Rampart CRASH unit members adopted tattoos and a logo that went beyond those cited earlier: a grinning skull, topped with a cowboy hat with police badge attached, displayed against a hand of playing cards—aces and eights, known as the dead man's hand. CRASH units, Rampart and others, were reported in the press to hold "shooting parties," with plenty of beer, and special plaques awarded to officers who shot gang members.

To the officers involved, this probably seemed like innocent fun and camaraderie. But messages were being sent. The Pacos were getting encouragement in the war against street gangs: whatever works can be used. Ends justify means. The end result for Paco was tolerance for questionable handling of the homeboys, and court testimony that twisted the concept of equal justice. For some gang units, it sometimes resulted in clear mistreatment of gang members, illegal detentions on trumped-up charges, misleading representations to the public and public officials, and—as in Rampart—plain old police corruption and unjustifiable shootings of gang members.

NOTES

1. What I will report of these units comes primarily from two sources. The first is the unique research carried out by Professor Katz. He started with a case study of a single gang unit in a large Midwestern city. This was followed by a comparison of four gang units in Las Vegas, Albuquerque, Phoenix, and Inglewood, California. Finally, he reported on a survey of gang units in seventy-seven departments across the country. The second source is research carried out with my colleagues over many years. This research included close study of the criminal investigations carried out on gang members and a study across a number of departments of the quality of gang investigations with and without gang unit involvement (those with gang unit involvement were clearly more effective). Many hours were spent with gang officers on the job (and off) and in interviews on gang unit values and experiences in over 250 departments across the nation. These were, in turn, followed by surveys about the gangs they processed.

2. Cited in Shelden, Tracy, and Brown, *Youth Gangs in American Society*.

⑰

RAMPART: THE SMOKING GUN

First homeboy in a cartoon: "I'm a member of the most feared gang in L.A." Second homeboy: "You're LAPD?"

—Cartoon by Rogers, 1999, *Pittsburgh-Gazette*

My last contacts with Paco have been in court—dueling testimonies—and over the phone. We are distant now, the original tentative mutual appreciation having clearly dissolved. Close to retirement, he's still out there on the street, battling the enemy. He's gotten worse; more passionate, less careful in the use of his expertise, and more alienated from all but his gang unit buddies. But he hasn't become a corrupt cop as that term is usually used: rogue maybe, but not corrupt. How far away is he from police corruption; how easily could it now happen? A look at the Rampart scandal holds one important answer to the questions. The whole thing took place in the gang unit.

Simply put, if you place a guy like Paco Domingo in a battle with groups like street gangs and if you locate him in a special, elite unit with minimal supervision and the "wink of approval," some very bad things can happen. And they *have* happened in Miami, New York, Chicago, Las Vegas, Houston, Los Angeles, and other, smaller jurisdictions. In Oakland, California, a group of four officers known as the "Riders" were accused of faking evidence, planting drugs, and beating up suspects. When their actions were revealed, eighty-two arrests were overturned and 350 cases in which they were involved were reviewed. The city settled the cases of 119 alleged victims at a cost of $10.9 million, as the city attorney characterized the officers as "Clint Eastwood-types, tough cops who didn't play by the rules. They were overzealous." In Louisville, it was two narcotics unit detectives who were arrested on hundreds of charges including forging judges' signatures on warrants to obtain evidence illegally. But the real proof of the danger of elite units was in the Rampart Division of the LAPD.

The Rampart scandal ripped the department apart, revealing serious deficiencies in officer selection and training, unit supervisors, and departmental administrators. It severely damaged numerous past prosecutions and convictions, jeopardized new ones, and again undermined public confidence in the police. It only takes a few Pacos in a unit to do the job, cowboys on the loose.

In 1996, fully three years before Officer Rafael Perez blew the lid off the Rampart gang unit, a city councilman reported to his colleagues in a closed-door meeting that a rogue group of officers existed in the Rampart Division. Also present at the meeting were the chief of police and high-ranking members of the city attorney's office. They were gathered to discuss the city's liability in a case involving a Rampart officer who had a long record of misconduct. They agreed to pay the damages, rather than have the officer pay, "in the best interests of the city." That decision was made, but no action concerning the reported rogue group is known to have been taken by the city council, the chief, or the city attorney's office. The rogue group was labeled the "Rampart Reapers" in that meeting. There seems little question now that the Rampart Reapers were in the gang unit, known formally as CRASH.[1]

Three years later, gang cop Rafael Perez was arrested for stealing six pounds of cocaine from the evidence room in Parker Center, LAPD's headquarters building. A year after that, he struck a plea bargain; he took a five-year sentence in return for reporting on various crimes committed by Rampart CRASH officers, including himself. Then all hell broke loose, as the list of assaults, evidence plantings, false evidence productions, drug deals, and perjuries became known.

LAPD circled the wagons and undertook an internal investigation. This yielded a truly remarkable document that chastised the department for a whole range of administrative failings that contributed to the opportunity for the CRASH unit to go bad.

Remarkably, the report was titled "Rampart Area Corruption Incident" (March 1, 2000), whereas in fact the "incident" was an unending list of minor and major misconducts and serious felonies over some years. As former police reporter Michael Connelly said in his book, *The Last Coyote*, "The one thing about the LAPD is that it is not into self-flagellation." Beyond the *mea culpas* of the report, two facts stood out. LAPD reforms that had been called for by the Christopher Commission following the Rodney King incident and riots had not taken place. And LAPD still did not understand that the fundamental problems lay even beyond lax administrative failures, but in the long-standing elitist culture of the department itself.

I will summarize three aspects of the Rampart CRASH experience, keeping in mind that it represents where *any* gang unit, and *any* Paco, could end up under certain conditions. First is the damage done, second is the criminal acts involved, and third is the combination of contributing factors. This last, the contributing factors, will by now sound familiar to the reader.

The damages were of many sorts. First and foremost was the harm to scores and perhaps hundreds of legal and illegal residents of Los Angeles, whose lives were harmed by the lies, the harassment, and assaults committed by the gang cops at Rampart. The insults ranged from unjustified street stops to planted narcotics evidence, to shootings. The worst and most famous of these was the shooting of an unarmed gang member, Javier Ovando, by Officers Rafael Perez and Nino Durden, who then planted a firearm on Ovando to claim self-defense. Ovando was paralyzed for life, and eventually released and awarded $15 million in compensation. Perez ended up with both local and federal convictions. Durden received a seven-year sentence plus a restitution fee of $281,000.

The Ovando case was Rafael Perez's first revelation, but before he was finished there was a defense attorney frenzy as case after case was pursued. Twenty-nine civil suits were combined to yield a recommended $10.9 million in damages. Nearly 150 cases have been overturned. Many others have been dismissed because the investigations were so delayed that the statute of limitations had expired. In all, an estimated 275 cases were expected to yield $125 million in damages, ranging in size from $25 thousand to Ovando's $15 million. More than 1,000 past cases were screened, and some reports suggested as many as 3,000 might have to be reviewed for possible officer misconduct. Rampart CRASH, at any given moment, had about twenty-five officers, but over time, more than seventy were investigated and forty were fired, relieved of duty, or disciplined. Ten resigned or quit. And even now, as I'm writing this, the investigations and trials are continuing, as are the revelations from other sources of new occurrences involving Rampart-trained officers. Rampart Officer Ruben Palomares, already convicted in a major drug trafficking case, also became the central figure of an investigation of his leadership of a robbery ring involving corrupt officers from his and other departments (*Los Angeles Times*, May 11, 2003).

Who was hurt by the Rampart scandal, beyond the direct victims and the citizens whose taxes must cover the costs? The LAPD, known as "the blue meanies" in the nearby Los Angeles Sheriff's Department, lost all kinds of credibility. The district attorney's office and the D.A. himself suffered a serious public relations blow, enough to cost the D.A. his reelection in the next campaign. The city attorney's office fared poorly, as the failure of county and city attorneys to spot the false police testimony was highlighted: anti-gang injunctions have been postponed or canceled because of possible officer perjury in establishing them. The U.S. Immigration and Naturalization Service and the FBI got caught in conspiracies to deport illegal aliens falsely arrested and falsely identified by the gang cops as gang members. In a small but poignant reminder of costs, the Short Stop Bar on Sunset Boulevard went out of business; it had been a favorite haunt of Rampart officers and shooting parties, and was celebrated in the police novels of Joseph Wambaugh. Now it was avoided by nervous cops and sympathetic customers alike.

Public relations and collaboration between agents of government took a hit. The D.A. accused the LAPD of being "a department out of control. . . . I am profoundly disappointed with the chief and the department." The chief responded by ordering detectives to withhold access to information from county prosecutors. The mayor's office couldn't seem to make up its mind where to come down, and the city council split on remedial measures. A *Los Angeles Times* reporter's survey of community residents revealed, "anger, frustration, lost faith, helplessness, and resentment . . . a breach of trust."

An investigation of the LAPD by the Civil Rights Division of the U.S. Department of Justice threatened a major federal suit unless the department and the city agreed to a consent decree outlining long-needed and long-ignored reforms. After much haggling, the consent decree was agreed to, and it is estimated the reforms will cost the city from $20 million to $50 million a year for years to come.

Yet here is the final irony. In two separate lawsuits, two federal judges have ruled that the LAPD can be taken to court as a "racketeering enterprise" under the RICO provisions. RICO permits triple damages to be assessed for federal civil rights violations by CRASH officers. RICO is the statute used by the federal government and various police departments such as LAPD to convict drug dealers for conspiracy. Now LAPD, thanks to its Rampart gang unit, can be considered a criminally conspiratorial organization.

What offenses were these gang cops accused of to bring all this about? Five categories cover the bulk of the cases. The LAPD "incident" report, in a model of understatement, noted about citizen complaints that the officers' "work was less than professional, at best." Elsewhere, investigators found in various CRASH units "remarkably similar language used to describe arrests and probable cause for arrest" (so-called "boilerplate report practices") "a general lack of clarity or articulation in reporting probable cause for detention and/or search," and cases where booking reports, arrest reports, and analyzed evidence reports in the same case listed different quantities of narcotics seized. This first category, then, contains numerous instances of unnecessary or illegal stops and arrests—the sort of thing of which Paco is capable—where the object is to exert gang cop control and get the homies off the street, whatever it takes.

The second category of offenses, not unrelated, is the presence of lies in arrest reports and the perjured testimony to cover them up. I think Paco came to lie in court, but a more generous interpretation would be that he overgeneralized and failed to qualify his testimony that had to do with the nature of gangs. I have no way of knowing if he perjured himself about evidence as the Rampart gang cops did. Rafael Perez said that it was common for officers to carry a "drop gun" with which to frame suspects, and he said: "I would say that 90 percent of the officers that work CRASH, and not just Rampart CRASH, falsify a lot of information. They put cases on people." In a most convincing revelation, DNA evidence in four cases proved that arresting officers lied when they claimed suspects spit cocaine rocks from their mouths. The cases have been dismissed.

The third related category of offenses is where officers can usually get away with phony evidence because it's their word against the word of documented gang members. Judge and jury will almost always take the word of the testifying officer. Protestations from the defense attorney will be seen as just a part of what he has to do, not as alternative reality. Perez said the gang officers were "in the loop," agreeing to plant evidence, beat suspects, and cover up unjustified shootings. Ovando's was just one of five cases of such shooting cover-ups, he reported. Unit supervisors, as well, were "in the loop," so who's to know?

The fourth category is quite different, and perhaps peculiar to the situation in the Southwest United States, where immigration from Mexico and Central America is such a prominent feature of the social landscape. The Rampart Division lies within a heavily Hispanic section of Los Angeles. The street gangs in Rampart are Hispanic, including the locally notorious 18th Street and Mara Salvatrucha gangs. Many members are second-generation Mexican American and Salvadoran youth—U.S. citizens—but many also are first-generation and illegal immigrants. For the CRASH unit, this offered an intriguing new strategy for getting undesirable targets off the street; get them deported south.

Although the LAPD, under Special Order 40, forbade its officers to engage in activities leading to deportation of illegals, collaboration between CRASH and the Immigration and Naturalization Service (INS) over the mid- and late 1990s led to the deportation of hundreds of illegal immigrants. Many of these reported to be gang members later turned out not to be; CRASH was sweeping the streets with a very wide broom, and doing so in defiance of its own departmental regulations. Equally intriguing was the report from some of the INS officers that the FBI had pressured them into these deportations. With these revelations from Rafael Perez and others, accumulated citizen complaints, which had gone unheeded over several years, suddenly took on an overdue look of truth, to the considerable embarrassment of both local and federal officials. With federal connivance, Rampart CRASH was in the foreign policy business. An anti-gang activist named Alex Sanchez came to epitomize this harassment when both he and his grassroots agency, Homies Unidos, became the targets for CRASH harassment. Sanchez, a defense witness who it was said could clear a teenager accused of murder, was then arrested by a Rampart officer and turned over to the INS. Another *cause célèbre* had been created.

The beatings, the fifth category of offenses, were, of course, the most sensational. Perez talked of gang cops who liked to "thump" people. Javier Ovando was shot and paralyzed. Another youth had his head rammed through a plaster wall. Another's bloodied face was falsely explained away as the result of leaping headfirst out of a third-story window. How many such events took place can never be fully known, but documents confirm routine punching, kicking, choking, and other beatings as a form of gang intimidation. Remember that most officers, unlike Paco, work in pairs. Many arrests involve more than one pair. Thus, many of the assaults and the cover-ups in written reports (often approved by the on-site supervisor) and the sworn testimonies in court require collusion and the "blue code of silence." These acts were, in combination, individual offenses and gang *unit* offenses.

This Rampart story is bad; it's horrible. Yet, to people knowledgeable about special units in policing, it was not all that surprising. As we look at factors contributing to this scandal, we will find many of the aspects of Paco's story, but taken to excess.

First, of course, is the departmental culture; much as the LAPD denies its nature, others highlight that the elitist, "new breed," hard-charging and white-knight culture of the department permits excesses and resists inquiry from outside. CRASH is LAPD's product, and a proud one. The top brass over decades has resisted the police commission, the reform report that followed the 1965 Watts riots, the recommendations of the post–Rodney King Christopher Commission, the requests of its own inspector general, and everyone's call for the implementation of community policing that, incidentally, discourages the formation of special, elite units. LAPD's motto, "To Protect and Serve," has not led well to protection and service for all and, as noted by an investigating committee director, it has garnered "no reservoir of good will among the public."

But I am not here to launch an attack on the LAPD. These comments are relevant because they help set the context for the Rampart aberration. In most modern departments, it probably could not have happened, or certainly not over such an extended time without notice and correction. Thus LAPD's internal report on the "incident" is quite correct in pointing to lax management and administration, and quite incorrect in not also detailing the "wink of approval" accorded CRASH units. In fact, that "wink" comes not only from the department's command staff, but often from the political leadership of the city. When that leadership became highly concerned about drugs and gangs, reported a high-ranking LAPD official in a public statement, "They say: 'I don't care how you fix it, just fix it.' When the city fathers tell us these things, we do them."

A second contributing factor was the heavily ganged-up neighborhoods within the Rampart Division. Here, the gangs engaged in widespread "renting the block," the practice of charging "rent" or "taxes" to engage in street vendor sales, drug sales, or prostitution by local residents. Just as Paco's career was shaped by the major increases in gang numbers and violence, so the gang pressures in the division led to increased police pressure—"we intimidate the intimidators" was the CRASH motto—relaxed standards of proper conduct, and quiet approval of the results. Extraordinary problems were said to justify extraordinary measures, legal and otherwise. It is important to note that violent gang crimes are particularly hard to solve using the normal investigative procedures because the assailants are often strangers to the victims and witnesses are reluctant to come forward. There's an old joke among officers:

> *Question:* What's the difference between the cops and everyone else standing around at a murder scene? Answer: The cops are the only ones who don't know who did it.

A third contributing factor is the culture of the CRASH operation generally—in all stations, not just at Rampart. Contrasting CRASH units to the gang units in the Los Angeles Sheriff's Department is instructive, as shown by *Los Angeles Times* reporter David Freed in 1986. Sheriff's gang cops wore civilian clothes, rode in plain (nonpatrol) cars, often remained in the same area for many years, and placed more emphasis on field investigation than on enforcement. CRASH officers were in uniform, in "black and whites" (patrol cars), often transferred after two or so years, and emphasized heavy surveillance and "selective enforcement" (harassment).

"We've found that being friendly with these gangs just doesn't work," said one Paco-like CRASH cop. The sheriff's people found just the opposite, and ended up with far better gang intelligence than did LAPD. Thus, the Rampart CRASH history was a shared one, reflecting its department's attitude. The license to be hard on gang members was given; the limits of that license were established by law, but not so much by explicit department policy. The exception, Order 40 covering illegal deportations, was easily surmounted as Rampart cops showed.

Two other points, one raised by the LAPD itself and the other by Professor Katz's work, round out this picture of contributing factors. The first is the failure of supervision. Just as Paco avoided supervision, so did the CRASH cops. Their own supervisors were shown in the investigation to be sometimes absent and sometimes "in the loop" with Rafael Perez and his comrades. Furthermore, supervision from outside the unit was shown to be inconsistent and also often absent. The "suits" were not paying enough attention, and the CRASH guys were able to get away with offenses and subterfuges of many kinds.

Not unconnected to these supervision issues was the "decoupling" discussed by Katz. In its later and worst days, Rampart CRASH was not at Rampart, but housed in a totally separate facility at some distance from the station. The Pacos of Rampart were on their own.

Thus developed what was called "the Rampart Way," the conduct code that went along with the Intimidators' motto, the Rampart Reapers reputation, the "beauty contest" by which CRASH members selected their own new officers, and what even LAPD's report acknowledged became "a feeling of cultural elitism." CRASH, the report noted, "routinely made up its own rules and, for all intents and purposes, was left to function with little or no oversight." One officer has testified specifically that he lied about the beatings out of fear of reprisals from his fellow officers: "I was covering my butt, and everyone else's that was there."

Let's be clear; my Paco was not at Rampart. But many Pacos were. What if he had been assigned to Rampart CRASH in the mid-1990s? Would he now be under indictment in the scandal? I'll be forever haunted by that question. Paco has been a stalwart fellow, but the culture of the unit can be terribly powerful.

Consider the testimony of Officer Nino Durden, who testified to federal authorities that he had never violated the law prior to joining CRASH unit but soon thereafter did so on a regular basis. "It was just gradual . . . it just snowballed into something else." A top cadet at the police academy, Durden was partnered with Rafael Perez in CRASH. "I was just happy to be in the unit . . . I thought it was really important to me in my career and I just didn't say anything."

Perez and the others harassed gang members on the street and lied in court. So did Paco. The CRASH cops beat suspects, shot unarmed suspects, and stole and sold narcotics. To my knowledge, Paco never did. He violated civil rights but never committed street felonies. Yet the parallels haunt me. For example, take the description of Rafael Perez, taken from one of the investigating deputy district attorneys and related by Peter Boyer in his 2001 *New Yorker* article, "Bad Boys": "Perez was something of a courtroom legend, a witness who could sway jurors with an air of utter credibility—even, as it turned out, in those cases when he was baldly lying."

Well, that's my Paco. So is the former CRASH gang cop who said "You go in there and rock n' roll. It's a groupthink. It's a kick-ass think." And highly reminiscent of my Sergeant Paco Domingo was this Rampart CRASH sergeant described in the LAPD scandal report:

> He was a no-nonsense, tactically oriented, military veteran, who had the unique ability to gain the unquestioned allegiance of peers, subordinates, and even superiors. . . . While he inspired esprit de corps and cohesiveness within the unit, he consistently undermined management and set an inappropriate tone for young officers. . . . He and several of his cohorts often challenged directives and policy . . . and would ostracize anyone who disagreed with or challenged their philosophy and approach to police work. . . . There was no evidence that this sergeant was aware of or would ever condone illegal activities. . . . Nevertheless, his influence and philosophy of strict loyalty to the unit and its members coupled with his vehement disdain for management certainly helped to establish a climate in which some officers felt safe bending or ignoring the rules.

So, was this the end of CRASH? Of course not. The department still feels the need for its elite units. The current units were disbanded and the officers dispersed. But new "anti-gang details" have been established under the broader rubric of "Special Enforcement Units." In a new public relations effort, the Los Angeles Police Protective League—the officers' union—has

started marketing a series of LAPD dolls. There's a patrol officer doll, ba-
ton in one hand and drawn gun in the other. A female officer doll is due
soon; also planned is a K-9 officer doll complete with dog, a motorcycle officer, an air-support officer with helicopter, a mounted officer with horse, a
bicycle cop with bicycle, a SWAT officer and a riot control officer, both with
full armored gear. It is unclear what the narcotics officer will carry. Will
there be a gang cop, and how will he appear? At $32 each, the LAPD dolls
will continue the culture of Rampart's department.

Meanwhile, what some have called the Rampart cover-up continues. The
"incident" remained an open wound, as the department failed to issue its
promised final investigative "after-action" report more than two years later
and the chief faced failure to have his contract renewed for a second term.
A new chief issued a request more than three years later for an independent, outside "blue ribbon" panel to review the Rampart investigation that
he described as "totally inadequate." And gang violence has escalated dra-
matically despite the new gang units.

Is Paco's retirement the end of Paco? Of course not. Other Pacos are out
there, and new ones will emerge. Some combination of individual character, street-gang pressure, and organizational character will support the present and encourage the new Pacos. Perhaps new gang researchers will
emerge as well, ready to do battle—data versus stereotypes.

NOTE

1. The initial acronym was TRASH, Total Resources Against Street Hoodlums,
but an LAPD command officer suggested that "TRASH" would not constitute good
public relations in minority communities.

EPILOGUE

Just as Paco Domingo became something less than my favorite gang cop over the years, another one did emerge as my favorite. He had a long, thirty-six-year career on the force, almost thirty of them in the gang world. He was a collaborator for researchers, a teacher for other gang cops, a creator of new gang intelligence technologies, and a careful describer of gang realities. I have been his admirer for many years. When it came time for his retirement, I was one of almost three hundred people who crowded the banquet hall and was honored to be one of the few asked to address some remarks to him and his comrades-in-arms. I started off by asking all the criminology professors to please stand up. Of course, no one did. I was alone in a sea of law enforcement. After all the speakers were through, with plenty of good-old-boy jokes and Marine Corps memories, my friend was presented with a gift. Asked what he most wanted for his retirement, he had specified just one item, and so it was delivered. What he most wanted, and accepted with great joy was a .38 caliber handgun. Once a cop, always a cop.

My portrait of Paco Domingo is, of course, a composite, a construction, but Paco is very real nonetheless. He is a gang cop taken from the lives, experiences, values, and perceptions of many gang cops. Every quote attributed to Paco in this book is a real quote; I've been collecting them over many years. His department, too, is a composite.

Furthermore, every incident reported in this book that involves Paco is a real incident. In most cases, I was there. Whether in the field, in a lecture, in court, or elsewhere, these events occurred. I met Paco exactly as described in Chapter 1. The ride-alongs, the crack house raids, the lecture incidents, the European events, the assaults, and more occurred, as described.

I have been as careful as memory and notes permit in recording the quotes and the incidents. There is no fiction in them, because I have wanted to build the credibility of the Paco Domingo story. Some of the personal background attributed to Paco is more fictional, yet even this is based on actual people. His Hispanic history, his military service, the retreat to "the river" and its description, and other personal items are features based on real people, mostly on police officers.

Paco is ubiquitous, but more common in some departments than in others. He is not a typical police officer, but he is not thereby uncommon. Especially in gang units and, I presume, other elite units as well, he is a familiar fellow. He needs to be recognized, understood, and, to some extent, neutralized. Referring back to the Rampart gang unit scandal, the district attorney's report on dismissed cases resulting from it told the *Los Angeles Times* (November 26, 2002): "Rampart showed us that there were some bad law enforcement officers who themselves became the gangsters they were supposed to be policing. Rampart also showed us that these bad law enforcement officers must be detected early on, investigated thoroughly, and prosecuted vigorously."

However, this book is not only about one kind of gang cop; it's about the nature of street gangs as well. Here, too, I've striven to be both instructive and credible. For the students and the lay reader impatient with textbook approaches, I've used Paco and his perspectives to present what is currently known about street gangs, known on the basis of sound, scholarly research. There is now a broad knowledge base about gang structures, cohesiveness, and norms; about the characteristics of gang members and "leaders"; about general gang member behavior and crime; about the contexts of neighborhood and community. And, finally, we have been learning more about the results of various kinds of programs designed to prevent or control the street gang problem.

The shame of Paco and many of the police departments in which he can be found, is that there is such a disjuncture between what Paco believes and what is known. Police work with gangs is driven primarily by selective personal experience, stereotypes, and ideology, and seldom by objectively gathered knowledge about their nature. So long as this remains true, police work with gangs will be ineffective. So long as this remains true, Paco's views may prevail.

RECOMMENDED READINGS

Because gang stereotypes are so pervasive, and because the general public depends on the media and the police for its picture of gangs, some readers may want to confirm the description I have offered. To that end, I list below a number of books that I believe can be handled by criminal justice students and the general public alike. The data on which my gang descriptions in this book are based can all be found in these recent books, each of which I take pleasure in recommending.

Covey, H. C., S. Menard, and R. J. Franzese, *Juvenile Gangs*, 2nd edition. Springfield, IL: Charles C. Thomas, 1997.

Decker, S., and B. Van Winkle, *Life in the Gang*. New York: Cambridge University Press, 1996.

Fleisher, M. S., *Dead End Kids: Gang Girls and the Boys They Know*. Madison: University of Wisconsin Press, 1998.

Huff, C. R. (ed.), *Gangs in America*, 1st, 2nd, and 3rd editions. Thousand Oaks, CA: Sage, 1990, 1996, 2001.

Klein, M. W. *The American Street Gang*. New York: Oxford University Press, 1995.

Klein, M. W., H-J. Kerner, C. L. Maxson, and E. G. M. Weitekamp (eds.), *The Eurogang Paradox: Street Gangs and Youth Groups in the U.S. and Europe*. Dordrecht/Boston: Kluwer Academic Publishers, 2001.

Miller, J., *One of the Guys: Girls, Gangs, and Gender*. New York: Oxford University Press, 2001.

Miller, J., C. L. Maxson, and M. W. Klein (eds.), *The Modern Gang Reader*. Los Angeles: Roxbury Press, 2001.

Spergel, I. A., *The Youth Gang Problem*. New York: Oxford University Press, 1995.

Thornberry, T. P., M. D. Krohn, A. J. Lizzotte, C. S. Smith, and K. Tobin, *Gangs and Delinquency in Developmental Perspective*. New York: Cambridge University Press, 2002.

ABOUT THE AUTHOR

Malcolm W. Klein has been studying street gangs and responses to them for over forty years. His methods of study have included street observation, gang member interviews, interviews with hundreds of police, probation and social service workers, and archival analyses of police and court records. He has struggled with the often wide gap between academic knowledge about gangs and the beliefs and perceptions of practitioners such as police, prosecutors, and gang workers. Although he has written seven prior books and scores of academic articles on gang issues, *Gang Cop* is designed to reach a wider audience in a more personal and informal format, using the character of Officer Domingo to frame important concerns about street gangs.

Called the "dean of gang researchers" and "America's leading authority" for his prior work on gangs, Klein has also done extensive research studies on police handling of juveniles, community treatment of juvenile offenders, crime measurement, evaluation of criminal justice programs, and comparative juvenile justice systems. At the University of Southern California, he served for thirteen years as department chair and initiated and led USC's Social Science Research Institute. He also served as visiting professor in Sweden and Spain and has been an invited lecturer in dozens of universities here and abroad He has received the McGee Award, the President's Award, the Tappan Award, and the Sutherland Award from various regional and national criminology associations. He has been elected a fellow in four national professional associations and served as consultant to scores of state and federal agencies and commissions.

In addition to his current writings, Klein continues as consultant to various gang programs, and is an expert witness and consultant in numerous criminal court cases. In 1997 he initiated the Eurogang Program, a consortium of over 100 U.S. and European gang researchers and policy makers involved in understanding the emerging street gang problems in Europe. This program continues to engage his time as six international conference and a half-dozen study proposals have moved the program forward.